THE
SHYNESS
BREAKTHROUGH

THE
SHYNESS
BREAKTHROUGH

A No-Stress Plan
to Help Your Shy Child
Warm Up, Open Up,
and Join the Fun

Bernardo J. Carducci, Ph.D.
Director, Shyness Research Institute,
Indiana University Southeast

with Lisa Kaiser

RODALE

Notice

This book is intended as a reference volume only, not as a medical manual. The information given here is designed to help you make informed decisions about your child's behavior and emotional health. It is not intended as a substitute for any treatment that may have been prescribed by your child's doctor or psychologist. If you suspect that your child has a medical or psychological problem, we urge you to seek competent medical help.

Mention of specific companies, organizations, or authorities in this book does not imply endorsement by the publisher, nor does mention of specific companies, organizations, or authorities imply that they endorse this book.

Printed in the United States of America
Rodale Inc. makes every effort to use acid-free ∞, recycled paper ♲.

Book design by Carol Angstadt

Library of Congress Cataloging-in-Publication Data

Carducci, Bernardo J.
    The shyness breakthrough : a no-stress plan to help your shy child warm up, open up, and join the fun / Bernardo J. Carducci.
       p.   cm.
    Includes bibliographical references and index.
    ISBN 1–57954–761–3 paperback
    1. Bashfulness in children.   2. Child rearing.   I. Title.
BF723.B3C37   2003
649'.1—dc21   2003011207

Distributed to the book trade by St. Martin's Press

2 4 6 8 10 9 7 5 3 1 paperback

This book is dedicated to
Edward Carducci, my father,
to the memory of Mary Carducci,
my mother, and Rozana Carducci,
my daughter. Their love and
support made all of my
breakthroughs possible,
shyness and otherwise.

CONTENTS

ACKNOWLEDGMENTS

Breakthroughs are never accomplished alone. Acknowledging this, I would like to recognize many individuals for helping me make *The Shyness Breakthrough* possible. First and foremost, I would like to thank the thousands of shy individuals, parents of shy children, and educators who have written and called me to share their stories of shyness and participated in my on-going research. Such individuals inspired the "collective voice" I am representing in *The Shyness Breakthrough*. This book is really their story, reflecting their passion, their concern, and their desire to help children to break through the painful barrier of shyness, be they their own, those of loved ones, or their students. I also received special support from a group of individuals whose intimate participation made *The Shyness Breakthrough* a reality. These "special contributors" are Barbara Augsburger, Sara and John Burke, Karen Chan, Jasmine Chung, Donna Eaves, Ariel Fuchs, Robert Greenan, Doris Jenkins, the Kaiser family, Laura Labott, Greg Mann, Suchi Reddy, Ray Santiago, Donna Smith, Eytan Tsioni, Jane and Sarah Velez,

Marilyn Wagner, Nancy Totten, Gabrielle Carr, Jacqueline Johnson, Marty Rosen, Melanie Hughes, Dennis Kreps, Gayle Sallee, Robert Caudill, Mervil Carmickle, and the "lunch bunch," Lesley Deal, Kathleen Norvell, and Brigette Colligan.

Amy Kovalski provided meaningful and constructive editorial help to sharpen the ideas presented in *The Shyness Breakthrough*. Finally, a special heartfelt expression of my gratitude goes to Lisa Kaiser, who helped clarify, solidify, and amplify the message I wanted to project in *The Shyness Breakthrough*. Lisa helped me to create a literary battering ram that will make it possible for parents and educators to empower children to break through their shyness barriers.

There are two other individuals who deserve special thanks. Jessica Faust, my agent, became the first person truly to believe in the message of *The Shyness Breakthrough* when it was just a proposal. I knew after speaking with Jessica for the first time that she—with a sense of excitement in her voice—shared my enthusiasm, commitment, and urgency to make the *Breakthrough* happen, as she said, " . . . as quickly as possible because this is really going to help lots of parents, teachers, and shy kids." Such support is an author's dream. Lou Cinquino, my editor at Rodale, became the rudder that kept this project on course. While Lou knew instinctively what was good about the *Breakthrough,* he provided the kind of editorial advice that made it even better. As my mother used to say, "You always want to be around people who will make you better." For me, Lou has been one of those people.

As I said, breakthroughs are never accomplished alone. So, to all of these special individuals who have, in their own unique way, become a meaningful part of my life, I say, "Thanks for helping me make my dream of *The Shyness Breakthrough* come true. I owe you one, each and every one of you."

—BJC

INTRODUCTION

I listen to their stories. I see their faces. I hear their secrets. While, almost by definition, few shy people openly talk about their experiences, as director of the Shyness Research Institute at Indiana University Southeast in New Albany, I've reached out to countless shy people to hear what's usually left unsaid. I hear what it's like to feel shy, to be left out, to be on the periphery of stressful social encounters. I hear about the struggles, the roots and causes of shy feelings, and what these emotions have prevented otherwise brilliant people from accomplishing. But I'm also lucky enough to hear what's helped them, how they've broken out of their limitations, and how many of these adults have risen to great achievement.

I've found that while shy children and adults often feel isolated in their silent fears, they're not alone. According to my research, almost 50 percent of adults believe that they are shy. And it is this self-definition that counts when speaking of shyness, because an individual's self-definition affects their thoughts, feelings, and behavior—in short, their entire world. Almost half of these shy individuals say that their shyness was caused by their childhood experiences. In addition, more than 90 percent of adults say that they've experienced shyness at some point in their lives.

It's clear that shyness must be a perfectly natural human response to a wide variety of social encounters. Yet shyness remains as an obstacle to success for many adults. For 3 to 13 percent of shy adults, shyness is a debilitating condition that causes extreme anxiety reactions that interfere with their lives. For the rest of us—the vast majority of us—shyness is much more moderate. Yet, when we don't confront it head-on, even moderate shyness can hold us back and keep us from achieving our goals.

Shy adults aren't the only ones who turn to me for help, however. Parents, teachers, and concerned loved ones contact me for advice regarding the shy, bashful children in their lives. Just as shy adults struggle with the same unspoken but common fears, parents of shy kids ask me the same questions and feel the same sense of responsibility and anxiety.

I can understand why parents and loved ones are so confused. After all, conventional wisdom is telling them that their shy kids will "grow out of it," while their intuition is telling them that their kids need more guidance and care. In addition, many of these parents are shy, too, and struggle with the same situations their children face.

As someone who has read scores of studies on childhood shyness, conducted my own research, observed shy kids in action, and listened to the quiet wisdom of shy people, I can tell you that shyness in childhood is complex, incredibly common, and—the reason I'm writing this book—something that can be managed successfully once it's understood for what it is—a dynamic process that just about every human experiences.

I've also discovered that when shyness is addressed in child-hood, rather than waiting until adolescence or adulthood, the ben-efits can be enormous. The life skills a child develops in managing shyness will also help him confront difficult people and situations later in life. By helping your child to manage his shyness early on, you are unlocking doors that might otherwise always remain closed to him. In this book, I'll explain how you—as a parent, teacher, or other concerned adult—can help the shy child in your life understand his feelings, move past his fears and inhibitions, and become what I call "successfully shy."

Fortunately, working through this process doesn't require stressful therapy, making over your child's personality, or de-priving him of your love and comfort. It merely requires the will-ingness to listen and learn, the ability to open your mind and heart, and the commitment to be an involved parent.

I understand your concerns because I've been there. I'm still there. I'm a dad, and I've tried hard to do what's best for my daughter, even when the answers aren't that clear. In fact, I feel like I'm still working on my parenting skills, even though she's an adult and leads an independent life.

I feel the same way about my own shyness, too. I work on it every day. Now, as an adult, I consider myself to be successfully shy, but when I was a teenager, I was extremely shy. Sure, I had plenty of neighborhood friends whom I'd known since I was five, and I had no problem expressing myself with them. But once ado-lescence kicked in, something changed. I just couldn't talk to girls. I suddenly became shy.

In college, I threw myself into my studies. I didn't date much, but I had plenty of friends and work that I loved. Then, one day in 1975, I came across an article by Philip G. Zimbardo, Ph.D., in *Psychology Today* that literally changed my life. In the article, Dr. Zimbardo discussed what shyness is and what shy people experience. It was like a thunderbolt. I vividly remember thinking, "That's me!" Finally there was a researcher who took shyness seriously and was interested in helping shy people cope with their everyday obstacles.

From then on, I incorporated this newly revived shyness research into my professional and personal life. I read more about shyness and developed my own shyness-related research projects while working toward my doctorate in psychology and, later, when I became a professor. I applied what I learned to my personal life and started breaking through my own shyness. Now, in midlife, I still feel shy at times, but it doesn't control how I feel about myself, what I do, whom I talk to, or anything else. When I feel it sneaking up on me, I know how to cope with it before it spirals out of control. My strategies are included in this book, so you can say that I've personally road tested my own advice.

Another "eureka" moment happened a few years ago. As part of my professional interest in shyness, I organized a panel of shyness researchers and wrote a *Psychology Today* article with Dr. Zimbardo that summarized all that we've learned since his 1975 article. Almost as an afterthought, I created a brief survey to include with the article. I didn't anticipate its reception: More than 1,000 people responded at that time, and more than 25,000 people have responded to variations of the survey when it was reprinted elsewhere. I believe that it's the largest shyness survey ever.

What surprised me is that many respondents added personal testimonials about their experiences—their pain, their triumphs, and their sincere hope that they'd be heard. I listened to them, and I was touched. I've included many of their comments in this book, since I believe that these individuals are shyness experts too.

In many ways, this book brings together my personal and professional interest in—and fascination with—shyness. While I was writing this book, I remembered the hopes and fears I had for my own daughter and how our relationship continues to unfold. I thought back to the days when I felt unbelievably shy and of the shy friends I had as a kid. And I drew upon all of the research that I've collected on shy people—those complex, fascinating, and wonderful people that we all know and love.

But one lone voice stood out amid all of the data, memories, and testimonials. I heard her when I spoke about shyness during a small, informal "brown bag" discussion at my university. This sweet, grandmotherly woman came up to me after my talk, and with tears in her eyes, said, "I wish I would have heard what you said when I was ten—not eighty! I missed out on so much!" Her simple statement reaffirmed my belief that shyness must be understood and managed early in life, when kids develop their beliefs in themselves and their first relationships with their family, friends, and schoolmates.

I hope that you remember her as you read on and as you apply what you've read to help your child break through shyness and take advantage of all the wonderful opportunities life has to offer.

Understanding Shyness and How It Affects Your Child

You're about to venture into a little-known world: the world of a shy child. This is a world of secret fears, hidden strengths, and remarkable individuals. It's the world of your child, and one that you'll participate in as you help your son or daughter break through shyness. You don't need to make over your child's personality to create a shyness breakthrough. You merely need to help your child become what I call "successfully shy"—in control of his shyness rather than controlled by it.

Throughout this book, I'll lead you through this secret world. First, in chapter 1, we'll look at its foundation, the complex and fascinating phenomenon that is childhood shyness, and why the traditional age-old wisdom about shyness is usually wrong. In chapter 2, you'll begin to view shyness not as a fated personality trait, but as a dynamic process that almost all of us feel at some point in our lives. You'll also learn which types of common social situations trigger shyness in children, whether it's being called on to answer a question in class or facing a playground full of unfamiliar kids.

Once I've laid the foundation for understanding what shyness is—and isn't—I'll explore how you can take action. In chapter 3, I'll discuss the life skills that are needed to break through shyness and how you can teach them to your child. Then you will create your child's shyness profile through a series of journal activities in chapter 4. This interactive feature is highly personal and highly effective. You'll assess your child's specific experience with shyness and pinpoint goals you want to achieve, whether it's helping your child become more comfortable with other children in day care or guiding your child through the social demands of middle childhood.

All together, these four chapters will lay out the core elements of The Shyness Breakthrough Plan. They are:

The Process. By understanding the three phases of the Shy Process, you will gain insight into what's holding your child back—and what you can do to ease him through each phase.

The Skills. There are simple yet effective skills you can teach your child to help him combat the shyness triggers in his life. I'll explain each one and offer guidance on how your child can develop and take advantage of them.

The Profile. Each person's experience with shyness is unique, and therefore the "solution" is unique for each person as well. This aspect of the Plan will help you to identify and understand the unique aspects—as well as consequences—of your own and your child's shyness profile.

The Strategies. In parts 2 and 3, I'll help you to apply what you've learned to your child's unique situation, whether she is starting her first day of kindergarten, attending her first school dance, or comtemplating her life after high school.

By picking up this book, you have already taken the first step toward creating a shyness breakthrough in your own home. Wtih each new insight and technique you discover along the way, you and your child will move, hand-in-hand, to a future bright with opportunity and achievement.

CHAPTER ONE

WHAT SHYNESS IS— AND ISN'T

As is often the case with behavioral research, the real story on shyness can sometimes get lost in statistics and emphasis on obscure laboratory experiments. So while I conduct large-scale surveys and observe shyness in different kinds of settings, I conduct my research where the action is—in real life. As director of the Shyness Research Institute at Indiana University Southeast in New Albany, I listen to and observe shy people, I analyze the thousands of survey responses I've received, and I read scores of e-mails describing shy people's situations. Yet even with this crush of data, sometimes it takes the vivid example of an individual to best communicate the voice of shyness.

ONE SHY VOICE

Recently I spoke with Sharon, an interior designer, who struggled with shyness as a child. We began with her memories about what it felt like to be a shy kid and what she thought caused her to feel shy during her childhood.

"Being shy as a kid, I felt left out of many things," Sharon told me. "I was unable to express myself freely, and teachers and classmates often misunderstood me and mistook my shyness as disinterest. So, in many social activities, I was not included as part of the crowd. Or maybe I was just overly sensitive and thought people treated me differently, because I felt different."

But Sharon was smart enough to see the benefits of being shy. "In some ways, being the shy and quiet one made me feel special," she explained. "Teachers were always kind to me and liked my quiet demeanor, but always commented on my report card that I should participate more in class. I wasn't a total outcast, of course. I did have friends who were similar to me—shy, soft-spoken, bookworm types. We clung together and gave each other support."

I asked her if school gave her difficulties, or if bullies had ever picked on her.

The bullies, she explained, picked on everyone, and not just her, so she retains only the usual amount of resentment toward them.

"But it was difficult for me to speak freely in class, mostly because I was afraid that what I had to say was not important enough," she said. "I do think my shyness has affected my academic development. Without my shyness, I could have sought out more help when I was having trouble, or participated in more academic or extracurricular activities."

I asked Sharon where she thought her shyness really came from, whether she was fated to be shy by a "shy gene," or whether she accumulated her shyness through her experiences.

"My mom always tells me she was a shy kid like me, and I would say that most of the grown-ups I grew up with are relatively shy people," she told me. "The men in the family are all very soft-spoken and introverted. The women—my grandmother, mother, and two aunts—are more outgoing, but they became less self-conscious gradually with age. So, maybe part of being shy is biolog-ical or inherited."

At this point, Sharon thought for a moment and reconsidered her last observation. "I think there are also environmental factors, too," she said. "I'm Chinese-American, and my family is a rather typical, traditional Chinese family. Asian children are not normally taught independence at an early age like many Western children are. In my family, having social skills as a kid was just not a pri-ority."

I asked her if she still considers herself to be shy, because with a successful interior design career, an active social life, and a side gig as a guitarist in a band, she seems to have come so far from her introverted childhood. On the surface at least, you'd never think that she'd struggled with her social self or sense of self-confidence.

"I often consider myself to be a shy adult, but not always," she said. "I have definitely grown out of a lot of my shyness. I see my-self becoming more outgoing and more confident with age. How-ever, in some social settings, I retreat into shyness—the times when I'm forced into certain social situations I don't want to be in and that don't feel natural to me. Most un-shy folks would probably pretend to be having a good time. But, somehow, I don't know how to do that and don't want to. Most people would probably see my reaction as shyness.

"In general, though, I can mostly go on with my days without feeling shy."

THE CAUSES OF CHILDHOOD SHYNESS

While Sharon's story reveals a smart, sensitive person who has quietly, but intelligently, coped with her withdrawing nature, her story also reveals the many possible causes of childhood shyness.

As Sharon noted, even she's not sure what causes her to with-

draw—nature or nurture, or some combination of the two influences. Since so many of her relatives are shy, did she somehow inherit a "shy gene"? Or was her shyness learned from those same
relatives, or from their shared culture, as she imitated their behavior during social encounters? Or was it picked up throughout
her childhood from the way she coped with social or academic demands?

I believe that it's most likely that all of these factors—and not
one single cause—contributed to her shyness. Because the factors
are so mysteriously intertwined, each person's experience with
shyness is unique—and fascinating. Throughout this book, I'll explore the many tangled roots of childhood shyness. And in chapter
5, I'll offer a detailed discussion of the biological basis of shyness—
specifically, to what extent that shyness is inherited.

THE UNIQUENESS AND UNIVERSALITY OF SHYNESS

While each shy individual has a unique voice and a unique story,
shy adults and children all share an incredibly common, universally
experienced personality trait. And shy people are in good company, because some of our most celebrated artists, politicians, and
scholars are shy. This illustrious list of shy people includes Eleanor
Roosevelt, Robert Frost, Jack Kerouac, Robert De Niro, Sting,
Prince Albert of Monaco, David Letterman, Michelle Pfeiffer, Barbara Walters, Sigourney Weaver, Steve Martin, and Mike Myers.
All of these remarkable people have either said that they are shy,
or someone close to them has described them as being shy.

Like the celebrities I've just mentioned, shy people are a diverse
group. Each of the thousands of shy people I've heard from has a
unique story. Each has her own history, relationships, family,
hopes, dreams, and, in short, her own personality. The cast of
characters is also unique. Our shy heroine is surrounded by people

who love and care for her, even if they don't know how to cope with her bashfulness and timidity. Some friends or relatives—especially her extroverted family members and peers—may not understand her, while some may reach out to her and help her feel more comfortable in her own skin.

What's more, this shy heroine lives in a specific place and time, both of which affect her opportunities, understanding of herself, and her resources. A shy person in a small town may feel comfortable in her safe social network made up of people she's known forever. She may not feel a pressing need to become more outgoing, but she may nonetheless feel limited by her shyness. A shy person who lives in the city may feel lost in the crowd—or she may revel in her anonymity. Getting help may be easier for urban shy people, while those in rural areas may lack professional resources to help them with their shyness.

The shy heroine also lives in a specific culture. Some cultures value shyness-related qualities, which can help her feel like she fits in. Other cultures—loud, fast-paced, aggressive, and individualistic—work against her shy nature and oftentimes create enormous personal pain. There's simply too much, too quick, too soon.

In addition to all of these factors, the way a shy person interprets and reacts to a typical event such as being embarrassed in class is unique, yet universal. She may decide to keep quiet for the rest of the year and hope that she isn't noticed. Or she may resolve to be as perfect as possible so that she's never caught off-guard again. She may try to deflect her embarrassment by becoming the class clown, the kid who both loves and loathes attention.

No matter which unique coping strategy she chooses, she, like all shy people, feels shy under the skin. I think of this invisible yet universal shy experience as the body, mind, and soul of shyness because it affects shy individuals' behavior, thoughts, and feelings, and, ultimately, their identity. It separates and isolates shy people in their silence and pain. This is the frustrating part of shyness, the part that's so tough to break through. Yet the good news is that breaking through shyness is *not* impossible, and each step in the right direction, no matter how small, is significant.

THE IMPORTANCE OF ADDRESSING SHYNESS EARLY IN LIFE

Our children sometimes seem so young and fragile, and they grow up so quickly. The world can be a scary place, so what's wrong, you might be wondering, with not wanting to engage it? Why not let your child try to "grow out of" shyness on his own?

The truth is that not addressing shyness early on, in childhood, can have negative implications for adult behavior. In fact, researchers have noted that shy children often become "off time" adults, meaning that they typically enter stable careers later, marry later, and become parents a little bit later than their more outgoing peers. While there's no indication that shy adults are less successful than more extroverted adults, it's easier to go through these rites of passage when we're "on time," when our friends are having the same experiences.

This off-time tendency can begin early in life during times of transition such as the beginning of the school year or the start of a new social encounter. Because shy people—kids and adults alike—tend to adjust to new people, places, and challenges slowly, they're often left behind others who "warm up" to new situations quickly. You can see this tendency begin in childhood. Think about a first grader who's too bashful to join a group of kids playing tag or a fifth grader who requires three months to acclimate to her new classroom and routine, and you're conjuring up images of an "off time" child. The kids who can jump into new situations quickly get a head start, while the slower, shy child holds back and waits until he feels more confident and secure.

This tendency snowballs and can affect how shy individuals approach bigger challenges and life transitions, such as going off to college or making a career choice. They try to delay going through these rites of passage, but end up hurting themselves through inaction and withdrawal.

I believe that coping with shyness during childhood—before it becomes a lifelong social strategy—is the easiest and most effective way of modifying shy behavior, thoughts, and feelings. By helping your child to understand and manage his shy feelings, you will be empowering him for the years ahead. When kids are able to work through their inhibitions regarding typical social encounters in childhood, such as being in day care or the school play, they're setting the stage for how they'll work through their inhibitions about their adult challenges, such as entering college or making a good impression on a first date. They'll gain a solid understanding of themselves and develop skills that are necessary for a well-rounded life. They'll learn how to meet challenges without giving up or shrinking away in fear. They'll feel secure in themselves and their abilities, because success builds on success, whether it involves a social challenge like joining a soccer team or an intellectual challenge such as earning good grades. Eventually, they'll gain their confidence and independence, and they'll be able to reach their goals with little assistance.

What's more, helping your child become successfully shy—still shy at times, but not limited by it—establishes a pattern of involvement and communication early in your child's life. While you don't want to be too overprotective, if your child is in the habit of discussing problems with you when she's young, she'll have an easier time confiding in you when things get more difficult and complicated during adolescence.

If you're a non-custodial parent, rest assured that you can still have these conversations with your children even though you don't live with them. I'm the divorced dad of a wonderful daughter, and although we lived in different states when she was growing up, I made a point of calling her at a set time every week. While some of our conversations were only a few minutes long, and the calls occasionally required a lot of effort and adjustment, we were able to establish a strong, open relationship despite the miles. So don't let distance or a divorce prevent you from maintaining strong contact with your kids. Over time, they'll realize that you truly care about them, and that's what is important.

FINDING A BALANCE: THE COMPLEXITIES OF HELPING A SHY CHILD

While I've come to appreciate not only the universality and uniqueness of shyness, I'm also fascinated by its complexity. As we've learned from Sharon, shyness isn't always the direct result of playground politics, biological fate, or unkind teachers. Children may be shy even when they're surrounded by well-meaning, affectionate people, like extended family members or friendly but unfamiliar classmates.

Because shyness often appears in these welcoming but inexplicably threatening situations, it's complex not only in cause but in "cure." After all, childhood is supposed to be filled with minor milestones and ever-expanding challenges—like attending day camp and rowdy birthday parties—yet these are the same challenges that provoke shyness.

Aren't parents supposed to expose their children to these situations, even when these challenges frighten their shy child? Absolutely. The key is to prepare the shy child for the stressful event and provide him with coping strategies. Unfortunately, parents of shy children often don't know how to do this. Yet my reason for pointing this out is not to place blame at the feet of parents. While my research indicates that about 20 percent of shy adults blame their parents for their shyness, I feel that parents deserve a little more understanding about their parenting strategies. Few parents have received good advice about raising a shy child, and many assume—or hope—that their child will magically "grow out of it" without any special effort.

Most parents' hearts and heads are at cross-purposes regarding the best way to guide their child out of shyness. Parents must create a balance between protecting their shy child and exposing him to necessary challenges. Finding that balance is difficult. For example, when a son or daughter wails at birthday parties, or hides behind the sofa when company's over, or won't leave Mom or Dad's side when out in public, it's natural as a loving parent to give in and let the child cling and calm down. The flip side, of course, is the tough-love approach that many parents believe they must take—forcing their child to take on all new challenges, no matter how squeamish, unprepared, or frightened the child feels inside.

In the following chapters, I'll explain just how you, as a parent, caregiver, or other concerned adult, can use my Shyness Breakthrough Plan to find a good balance and guide the shy children in your life through these necessary, but sometimes difficult, situations so that their shyness will subside. Instead of being limited by their fears, these children will gradually wear down the invisible barriers that have been holding them back and become successfully shy.

THE SUCCESSFULLY SHY CHILD

Although the causes and expression of childhood shyness are complex and sometimes perplexing, I've found that managing childhood shyness isn't terribly difficult once you understand the daily challenges your child faces and learn some practical strategies to help ease him through them. While shyness may be a lifelong and occasionally frustrating personality trait, it doesn't need to limit an individual's choices, success, or happiness. Shyness is merely a dynamic personality trait that appears in some common social situations. You and your child can better cope with shyness by understanding it as a process, controlling that process, and making appropriate choices.

Being in control of the "shy process" is the first step in my Shyness Breakthrough Plan, and it is a major part of becoming "successfully shy." The successfully shy child comes to understand that sometimes she'll feel a little scared by new people and new places, but eventually she'll feel more comfortable—and more outgoing. And, what's more, when she can stay in these intimidating situations and eventually become more comfortable, she's able to feel that she's accomplished something, and that helps to build her self-esteem and sense of mastery. So instead of shrinking away in fear, the successfully shy child will take a time-out until she feels a little stronger—strong enough to start playing with a new friend, or to venture onto Auntie Louise's lap at a family reunion, or to get caught up in the excitement of her classroom's trip to the children's museum.

As I'll explain throughout this book, children can—with the help of parents, teachers, caretakers, and other loved ones—become aware of and cope with their uncomfortable feelings created by stressful social encounters and environments. With enough practice and encouragement, these shy kids will shine.

A Word about Change

The "successfully shy" transformation requires the commitment to change, and change is never made without a little struggle or frustration. In fact, the rhythm of change requires this struggle, so as you help your child incorporate new behavior and thought processes, please remember that the newly acquired behavior always gets worse before it gets better.

For example, when an individual goes on a diet, the first day or two without desserts and snacks can be fairly easy, and the new dieter thinks she's got it under control. However, on the third or fourth day, the cravings will kick in. If she's not prepared for this inevitable downturn, she'll grab a doughnut and think that she'll never get used to her new diet. But if she's aware of the rhythm of change, she'll brace herself for the bad times that follow the initial good ones—and then hang on until she's put her old eating habits behind her.

Likewise, if you want to help your child to cope successfully with shyness, you may have to put up with some fussing and resistance as he learns how to handle himself differently during social encounters. What's more, going through this process may require that you change your behavior as well, because you must increase your communication with your child and expose him to a variety of social situations that might be new to both of you. But if you're committed to incorporating new social behavior, then I'll be there to help you and your child during the inevitable rough spots, which I promise won't be as troublesome as you may think.

The Two Main Misconceptions about Childhood Shyness

It's become clear to me that parents have to junk two misguided notions of conventional wisdom about shy kids before the family can make progress. These two main misconceptions—the notion that shy kids will just "grow out of it" without any extra guidance and the idea that labeling a child "shy" doesn't do any harm—should be discarded once and for all.

"He'll Grow Out of It"

The idea that children will outgrow their shyness—and that parents should therefore take a hands-off approach—is pervasive in our society. Even Sharon, the successfully shy interior designer, claimed that she just "grew out of" her childhood shyness.

But when I pressed her for exactly how she became less shy, she told me this:

"What helped me to be less shy was finding friends who appreciate me for who I am, people who recognize the good in me and what I have to offer as a friend and as a person. I also learned to be a more independent and confident person in college, where I explored my talents and built upon them. And I met many different kinds of people and didn't limit myself to any social cliques. It also helps to have a supportive family who believes in me."

So Sharon didn't just wake up one morning to discover she'd "grown out of" her shyness as if it were a pair of too-tight jeans. Rather, you could say that Sharon "grew with" her shyness. She took an active interest in building her social skills and social life, and she developed her self-image and self-confidence in the process. She reached out to supportive, encouraging people and wasn't afraid to meet new people, even if they probably did intimidate her a little at first. I applaud her efforts and recognize just how far she's come.

I encourage more people to take Sharon's approach and gradually increase the number of faces and places that become familiar and welcoming to them. Unfortunately, some people lack Sharon's ability to effectively manage this process entirely on their own. Throughout the pages of this book, I'll explain how parents, caretakers, teachers, and loved ones can help shy children to slowly expand the number of places and situations where they feel comfortable and to increase the circle of people with whom they feel at ease.

"She's Just Shy"

On the face of it, there doesn't seem to be anything terribly wrong with pointing out the obvious when a child shrinks from attention. In many cases, "She's just shy" merely means, "She's so cute."

But listen to what one saleswoman has to say about the shy label:

"When I was growing up, adults always thought that I was so 'cute and shy.' I hated that because I knew my lack of confidence was what this dumb shyness was all about. I couldn't understand why adults would think shyness was a positive attribute."

The shy label is so problematic and so powerful that I urge you to refrain from using it—today and forever. The label reduces to a single adjective the very complex way that your child relates to the world. Even worse, labeling a child as "shy" has the power to stigmatize him for years to come.

Consider how ridiculous it would be to comment on other facts about a child, such as "How cute—he's asthmatic!" or "Gosh, isn't he nearsighted?" Yet somehow it's okay to label a child "shy" when she's just doing what her body, thoughts, and emotions are telling her to do. And, like children with asthma or bad eyesight, shy children are able to do everything other kids can do, provided they make a few thoughtful adjustments.

In addition to the added stigma, a child's shyness is exacerbated by the unwanted attention inherent in a "shy" label—attention typically given by adults or authority figures, who may already seem intimidating to a shy child. As the saleswoman pointed out, while adults may think a timid, vulnerable child is adorable, inside, the shy child feels anything but cute. She feels bewildered, frustrated, and angry with herself for being so afraid. And, to make matters worse, the well-meaning adults are shining a spotlight on her fear and confusion, and then holding a microscope to it. And what they find is even more shyness.

If that isn't bad enough, the label then often becomes a self-fulfilling prophesy, because as the "shy child" shrinks away from new challenges, she's able to retreat to a safe and comfortable place—her mother's lap, for example, or a quiet place on the edge of a crowded playground. In effect, the child is rewarded for her timidity, because retreating to these safe havens makes her feel less anxious and reinforces her decision to flee from what's so stressful. But this social strategy also makes her world very small and terribly private.

The cycle doesn't stop there. Because she's stuck with the shy label, she's excused from facing new experiences, like fully participating in field trips with her class or becoming friends with a new neighbor in her apartment building. She ends up learning to be shy, identifying herself as a shy person, and being treated like a shy person for the rest of her life.

I don't want children to be labeled shy when they're young and then feel that they're stuck with that label for life. I want children to feel that they're in control of their shyness and not controlled by it. By making a conscious effort to avoid labeling your child, you'll help him to understand that shyness is something he experiences at certain times, not something he *is*.

Your Successfully Shy Journal

Throughout this book, I'll provide opportunities for you to analyze your child's unique shy situations and challenges. By exploring the details of your child's particular experience with shyness, you'll be able to personalize the general strategies I provide. The best way to begin this process is to write down your thoughts, ideas, and observations. So please locate or purchase a blank notebook—this will become your Successfully Shy Journal.

Journal writing is a truly interactive experience that will make the words on the pages of this book come alive. Instead of passively absorbing information, you'll uncover ways to apply this information directly to your child's life. What's more, research shows that journal writing benefits you on many levels and in many different ways. First, journal writing stretches your intellect. The very act of writing helps you clarify your perceptions, think about them systematically, link them to other areas of your life, and gain some perspective. All of these acts contribute to what psychologists call "depth of processing," which will serve to add a greater degree of understanding, meaningfulness, and commitment to your journal entries.

Journal writing is good for your soul, too, because according to research by James Pennebaker, Ph.D., professor of psychology at the University of Texas at Austin, journal writing decreases stress and helps you put your experiences in perspective. While you may feel that what you're writing in the pages of your journal is adding up to a lot of nothing, you're actually making a lot of progress that you're usually unable to see in the moment.

Journal writing also helps you prepare for future challenges. Whether it's developing a strategy for guiding your

(continued)

child through a stressful social encounter or rehearsing what you'll say during a heart-to-heart conversation with your shy child, your journal becomes your safe place in which you can experiment with new ideas.

Finally, remember that until you act on your ideas, you are merely acquiring information. This book is designed to enhance your relationship with your shy child, but merely reading it or writing in your journal is only the first step on a long journey. You must put your thoughts into action to help your shy child.

Ready to begin? On the first page of your journal, write the date and then answer the following questions:

- Are you shy? Why do you say that you are (or are not)?

- When do you most often feel shy?

- How do you feel about being shy?

- What do you do to alleviate your shyness?

No matter how you've answered these questions, you've answered correctly. What matters is the thought you've put into this exercise. Because you're addressing the issue of your own experience with shyness, you're preparing yourself to make a difference in your shy child's life. A caring, involved parent, even one who feels shy or makes mistakes at times, is what your child needs and craves. Be that parent for your child.

A Few More Words about Parenting

I have a terrific daughter, so I know firsthand about the ecstasy and agony of parenting. And I've sifted through a lot of advice, both for personal and professional reasons, regarding children and parenting. But the most valuable insight I've found is also the most simple: *Love your child for who he is, and not who you want him to be.* And to parents of shy children, I'd like to add: *Love your child for who he is, and not how outgoing you want him to be.*

It's very easy to feel that a shy child, like every child, is both a blessing and a disappointment. It's easy to feel quietly relieved that your child is shy, compliant, and too timid to break too many rules. And it's also very easy to get angry and frustrated with your shy child when he's feeling unsure of himself and unable to meet your expectations about his social behavior. But when you feel this way, please step back and examine your expectations and revise them if they're not appropriate. Your children will never fail you if you're tuned into who they are and what they're capable of.

Another bit of wisdom was the one I received from Linda, the mother of Stephen, a farm boy you'll meet in chapter 3, so I'll let her have the last word.

"Actually, being a parent is not that hard," she told me with a small laugh. "I say that it's not that hard because kids will let you know what they need. If you listen, they won't be shy. If they're comfortable, they will open up and tell you what they need and what you need to know, even if they don't have the words for it."

CHAPTER 2

A BREAKTHROUGH VIEW OF CHILDHOOD SHYNESS

C hildhood is tough for nearly everyone. It's a time when your world—and your role in it—widens. As such, it's full of missteps as well as new opportunities. So why do some children become shy as their world expands while others don't? Through my years of studying shy individuals, I've discovered that there are common threads, or themes, that run through each and every shy person's experience, both in childhood and adulthood.

In this chapter, I'll explore these common themes and explain how they have led me to a new, breakthrough view of shyness. I'll introduce you to the three interlocking steps that make up the shy process that every shy child—and shy adult—experiences. And best of all, I'll show how you can help the shy child in your life work through his unique shy experience when it's triggered. When your shy child works through it with fewer shy reactions, slowly and surely he'll become successfully shy.

TRANSITIONS: SHYNESS TRIGGERS

Listen to some shy adults and you'll hear them list the same familiar causes for their shyness, such as a move to a new town, combat with nasty classmates, or too much unwanted attention. I call these causes "shyness triggers."

Although at first glance these triggers may seem diverse, they're similar in that they involve a transition from a safe social situation to a novel, unpredictable, and evaluative one. When these factors are taken together, they can create anxious shy behavior, thoughts, and feelings.

Let's dissect the elements of shyness triggers.

Novelty. "One of the factors that contributed to my painful life as a shy person was a move from one neighborhood to another in my childhood," a bookkeeper named Julia told me. "I spent a year with no friends and no one to relate to on a personal level."

I agree that moving to a new neighborhood is a lot to throw at a kid. Julia had to deal with a new location, a sense of having her family uprooted, and the challenge of being surrounded by suddenly unfamiliar classmates and neighbors. As far as I'm concerned, it was perfectly natural for Julia to feel shy or timid when she had to make this transition.

Yet while Julia's reaction was natural, shyness was not the only appropriate response, nor must it affect Julia's behavior so many years later. Julia could have been helped by a little guidance from a caring parent, teacher, peer, or mentor.

For example, Julia's parents could have eased their daughter's transition by gradually but steadily increasing Julia's exposure to new people. Her parents could have invited new neighbors over to the house so that the entire family could have met them at the same time. They could have taken Julia to her new school before classes started so that she could learn in advance about her new teacher, requirements, and the layout of the school building. Her parents could also have found other students who live in the neighborhood and organized rides to and from school. And, as Julia and her parents worked through all of these encounters, the family could have had constant conversations about their fears, their progress, their new insights, and their commitment to turning their new house into their new home.

While this kind of parental involvement takes some time and effort, think of how it would have helped Julia adapt to her new neighborhood and school and develop more confidence in her social abilities. If Julia had gotten a little more encouragement and guidance from her parents at this critical moment in her development, I bet she'd have a much different view of her adult self and her childhood.

Unpredictability. In addition to being new, shyness-triggering situations are also terribly unpredictable, and shy kids interpret this unpredictability as being threatening.

Listen to what this botanist had to say about a typical childhood trauma:

"I feel my shyness started in grade school and that I let the losers make me feel like a loser. I projected to others my insecure feelings about myself."

Most kids know that they've got to deal with playground "losers" who can fill their lives with unwanted "surprises" and attention, but they deal with these unpredictable encounters in different ways. While some of the bolder kids may possibly fight back or band together to create a more secure social circle, shy kids tend to keep quiet to avoid this unwanted attention. In addition, shy kids also assume that they're threatened not just by the "losers," but also by every other kid, too. Shy kids' fears and perceived lack of confidence then affect their self-esteem, their social skills, and their ability to tell friend from foe.

Because these encounters are so fraught with tension, they produce a lot of anxiety and set shy kids on edge throughout the day. And as some scholars have noted, just anticipating what can happen often feels worse than the actual encounter. According to recent research by Mary W. Meagher, Ph.D., of Texas A&M University, we feel more uncomfortably aroused when we're merely anticipating doing something thought to be unpleasant, like going to a slumber party with kids who make us feel uncomfortable and unwelcome. However, once we're in that seemingly unpleasant situation, our arousal level drops and we don't feel so bad.

Talking to your shy child about his fears can help a lot. For example, if you notice that your child is tense, avoids certain kids in his class, and has frequent nightmares or stomachaches, and you can't pinpoint precisely what's causing these symptoms, it's time to intervene. Bring up these issues during a casual chat—perhaps while cooking dinner or driving to school—and let your child know that you're trying to help him and not add to his problems. Eventually, your child will be comfortable enough to speak to you about what's distressing him and both of you can work toward a solution.

Evaluation. Shyness triggers are also linked by their evaluative component, meaning that the individual's sense of self is on the line because he feels that other people are judging and criticizing him. But the judge is not someone else—it's the shy person. I've found that shy people tend to have very vocal, very negative internal critics. By listening to this harsh self-criticism, shy people become increasingly self-conscious. They withdraw to silence the critic.

Let's listen to nine-year-old Katie's story.

"My daughter isn't a joiner," Katie's mother explained to me.

"You know, things like team sports or dance lessons or piano lessons—she just doesn't want to do them. Now, she's really good one-on-one, and I don't think any of her teachers would consider her to be shy, just quiet. But she doesn't do well in group situations."

Katie's mom just revealed a lot about her daughter's main shyness trigger—being evaluated in a group. Being part of a dance class requires Katie to learn something new, with a new teacher, among a group of fellow dancers, and, let's not forget, in front of a row of mirrors in the dance studio. I'm sure she feels like she's being held under a microscope during these lessons. If she's unsure of her dancing talent, or if her teacher is unusually strict, Katie will naturally resist going to dance lessons. And because Katie probably feels the same way about playing T-ball with a team, or working with a stern piano teacher one afternoon per week, her mom thinks that she's not a "joiner."

However, I think Katie is capable of joining other kids when she feels comfortable and confident about her abilities and performance. Why? Because when Katie feels confident about her abilities, she'll anticipate a favorable evaluation and silence her internal critic.

The key here is finding an activity that Katie really enjoys, like painting, perhaps, and then allowing her to share that activity socially. For example, her parents, along with Katie, could throw a painting party with her friends and a few unfamiliar kids. Katie would then feel secure on her own turf, doing what she likes, and with at least a few kids she knows. In time, Katie could build on this social success and spend more time at the art museum or enroll in art classes. Her reputation as someone who isn't a "joiner" will be a thing of the past.

So, taken together, shyness is triggered during new, unpredictable, seemingly threatening and evaluative social situations. In addition to moving to a new neighborhood, being intimidated on the playground, or taking a dance class, the following childhood events also commonly trigger shyness. While this list is not intended to be comprehensive, it is interesting to note the new, unpredictable, and evaluative aspects of each.

- The first day of school
- Divorce and other family disruptions
- Going to camp or a slumber party
- Speaking in front of a group or classroom
- Encountering strangers and unfamiliar children
- Going through puberty, especially if it's early or late

Successfully Shy Journal

In your Successfully Shy Journal, write down up to four of the shyness triggers in your child's life. Then answer the following questions.

- What's new, unpredictable, and evaluative in these situations?
- What do you do to help out your child in each situation?
- How well have your endeavors succeeded?
- What are two new ways you could walk your child through each experience?

Finally, write down some "shyness triggers" in your own life and your typical coping strategy. Go ahead and reach back into your childhood for examples.

Take a look at your answers. Do your shyness triggers gen-

(continued)

erally overlap with your child's? If so, you may feel a lot of empathy for your child. If you're still struggling with responding to these triggers, you'll have to work on your own coping strategies as well as the strategies you'll need to help your child. Don't worry—that's what I'm here for. You'll discover dozens of new shyness-lessening tips as you read this book.

If your answers don't overlap with your child's, you may have an easier time guiding your child through my shyness strategies, but a more difficult time understanding her bashful nature. Once again, don't worry. You'll gain many insights into the hidden world of shy children as you read this book. Just be patient and keep an open mind as you continue reading.

THE SHY LIFE

Shy people aren't the only ones who experience shyness triggers—every individual has gone to school, met strangers, and struck up friendships. We don't live in a social vacuum, after all. And almost all of us experience shyness from time to time, although only about half of us consider ourselves to be shy. So why do some people allow these shyness triggers to affect not only their behavior in difficult social encounters, but their entire identity, too?

That's a difficult question, and one that I've studied for more than 20 years. The best answer I can come up with is that shyness has the power to affect a person's entire being—the body, mind, and self. And because shyness affects the individual on all levels, it has the power to affect the individual's identity. After all, shy individuals don't think they "feel" shyness or "have" shyness—they feel that they "are" shy. And when they identify themselves in this manner and allow shyness to permeate the majority of their decisions, thoughts, and activities, they live what I call a "shy life."

That's a huge statement, and a fairly controversial one, but I stand by it.

The Shy Body, Mind, and Self

To better understand how shyness can affect a child at certain basic levels, eventually taking over his identity, let's take a closer look at the shy body, mind, and self.

Body. The "shy body" describes the uncomfortable physical sensations that accompany shyness, such as blushing, sweating, low-level dread or anxiety, or having a dry mouth or trembling voice. While I'll delve into these sensations more deeply in chapter 5, I want to make it clear now that they do not indicate social failure, an inability to meet new people, or a fated response to spending time with unfamiliar people. They indicate that the individual is interested in and physically aroused by what's happening. Period.

Mind. The "shy mind" describes the typical thoughts of a shy person—thoughts that many people share but don't dwell on to the extent that a shy person does. The key point to remember about the shy mind is that when a shy person thinks about his social behavior or ability, his thoughts tend to be self-focused and negative. Eventually, these negative, self-focused thoughts apply to more than just the shy person's social behavior and creep into his ideas about who he is and how he behaves in a variety of situations. And, because these negative thoughts eventually become automatic, the shy individual becomes his own worst critic without getting reality checks from other people.

Self. Because the shy individual feels an uncomfortable physical arousal and has so many negative feelings about his actions and abilities, his discomfort begins to affect his sense of self and self-worth. Instead of thinking of himself as a person who experiences shyness in some situations, his shyness takes over his identity and he becomes a "shy person" who lives a "shy life."

THE SHY PROCESS

While the shy body, mind, and self have the power to affect the individual's entire identity, I believe that the right kind of guidance and the right kind of choices will help a "shy person" become someone who's free of the negative constraints of shyness, someone who's "successfully shy." After all, shyness is merely a normal, universally experienced process that is triggered in some common social situations, like being in a classroom full of unfamiliar kids or being called on in class. I believe that understanding shyness as a process or a chain reaction of events—not a condition—will allow a shy individual to detach from the negativity of shyness and cope with social demands in a less shy, more confident and pro-social manner.

Every person who feels shy feels the "shy process" that's made up of three orderly, interlocking steps: the approach/avoidance conflict, which leads to a slow-to-warm-up tendency, which leads to a narrow and rigid comfort zone. (I'll explore these steps in detail below.) This process is set into motion by "shyness triggers"— those new, unpredictable, and evaluative events I just discussed. Shy people interpret a high number of events as shyness triggers, and therefore encounter this process often. But even usually outgoing people work through this process when they occasionally feel shy.

What's critical is how people interpret and navigate this process. Shy people make decisions and act in a specific way that skews the process toward more avoidant, socially withdrawn behavior. They may interpret this behavior negatively, and allow it to affect their self-esteem and identity. This leads to a cycle of shyness and a "shy life." However, more outgoing people—or successfully shy people—make different decisions and engage in different behavior while they're experiencing the shy process. They break through the shy process because they understand it and can control it.

What's more, this shy process changes and fades in and out during the course of a person's life and with certain people. After all, most people are not shy in all situations—they're shy only in new social situations that contain shyness triggers. And, because most new situations become old situations over time, shyness, like a treasured photograph or your favorite blue jeans, will fade with time, exposure, and use.

Interestingly, this process applies to just about every situation where shyness appears in our lives, from the toddler years to the golden years. The shy process creates the same confusing emotions and the same anxious, withdrawing behavior, whether it's experienced on the first day of school, the first day on the job, or the first date as a divorced fortysomething.

If, however, you and your child can work through the process and alter it during his early years, your child will gain the upper hand over his shyness and learn how to control, rather than be controlled by, his shy reactions to events now and in the future. To learn more about how he can do this, let's look at each of the three phases of the process more deeply and critically. For each, you'll find specific strategies that will enable your child to more successfully manage that stage. These strategies are the first component of The Shyness Breakthrough Plan.

The Approach/Avoidance Conflict

Let me tell you a story about little Mario. Mario was excited about going to see a live version of his favorite TV cartoon show and talked about it constantly in the weeks leading up to the performance. But when he got to the auditorium on the big day with his mom Justine, he froze in his tracks and stared wide-eyed at the wild props, puppets, singers, and dancers.

He certainly was mesmerized by the show, but not in a good way. Mario was overwhelmed. While the wild colors and noises and gigantic puppets were interesting, and kind of familiar and kind of bizarre, Mario felt overloaded. He simply shut down. When other kids in the audience began dancing and cheering along with the singers and dancers, he screamed and clambered onto his mom's lap, where he sat for the rest of the show. While he shook with fear, Justine was bewildered as to what caused Mario to tremble during a performance that he had anticipated so eagerly.

Mario, like all shy people, was caught in the first step of the shy process, the approach/avoidance conflict. This conflict, which was written about in the early 1990s by Dr. Jens Asendorpf of the Max-Planck Institute for Psychological Research in Germany, is the battle of emotions, thoughts, and feelings that creates the social anxiety that's so difficult to contain and alleviate.

Mario shows all of the classic symptoms of this conflict:

- *An initial willingness to participate in a social activity.* Mario had wanted to go to the show and talked about it incessantly for weeks.

- *Anxiety as he realizes that he doesn't want to participate in the activity.* Mario froze in his tracks when he was blitzed by the chaos of the performance and audience.

- *Low-level panic as he second-guesses his role in the activity.* Mario screamed when the other kids cheered and wouldn't sing along with the songs.

- *An attempt to avoid and flee the situation and get to a safe haven.* Because Mario couldn't leave during the performance, he nestled safely on his mom's lap and did his best to block out what was happening.

While shy people like Mario get stuck in the approach/avoidance conflict, they must remember that there are two sides to this conflict—not just avoidance, but approach, too. After all, people who feel only avoidance shun others altogether and feel no anxiety. In fact, these avoidant people aren't even shy—depending on degree, they're either introverted or socially avoidant. Shy people, on the other hand, actively want to be with people—the "approach" part of the conflict—but they second-guess their desires and social ability and get hung up on their avoidant tendencies. And that conflict produces a lot of anxiety, blushing, stammering, sweating, and other symptoms of physical arousal.

I maintain that adults can help the shy child in their lives work through the approach/avoidance conflict without too much fuss. Actually, it may be fairly easy to do this, since kids are more willing to learn and change their behavior than adults. In fact, learning and modifying behavior is a child's life task, so please, be a good guide for your child.

Let's return to Mario and his terrifying trip to the theater and look at how Justine could have gotten Mario to become less anxious and avoidant. Now, Justine was well meaning and certainly didn't want to cause Mario any harm. She noticed that Mario was acting strangely, which is a good first step, but she misidentified the signals he was sending. Therefore, instead of encouraging Mario to participate in the performance, she strengthened Mario's avoidant tendency by giving him comfort on her lap.

Justine could have strengthened Mario's approach tendency in a number of ways, and, taken together, they would have boosted Mario's enjoyment of the show. Here's how it can be done:

Prepare your child. While Mario expressed a lot of interest about going to the show, he probably didn't realize what he was in for. Justine could have prepared him for the big puppets, the dancing, the noise, and the rowdy crowd. She could have explained what he'd encounter at the event, and they could have watched a video of a similar event or acted out some "let's pretend" situations in the guise of the characters.

Bring along a familiar friend or object. Justine could have invited one of Mario's playmates to help Mario feel more comfortable. Or she could have brought one of Mario's stuffed animals and explained that the character was now dancing on the stage.

Gradually ease into the transition from the new and uncomfortable phase to the more familiar and more comfortable phase. Once Justine saw that Mario was struggling, she could have suggested to him that they take a break in the lobby. In addition, if they had arrived early, they could have watched all of the other children arrive, rather than entering when the auditorium was already packed with a noisy crowd.

Acknowledge your child's feelings. When Mario looked wide-eyed and terrified, Justine could have asked him how he felt. Then she could have said, "I feel scared sometimes, too, especially when I'm in a crowd of noisy kids. Look at that little girl over there—she looks a little scared, but I bet she's kind of happy to be here, too."

Relabel your child's feelings. Justine could have said, "Wow, Mario—isn't it exciting to be here? I feel a little jittery and nervous because I'm so excited for the show to start."

Perform a social grace. You can prevent anxiety from spiraling out of control by shifting your focus of attention and thinking of others. Justine could have introduced Mario to the other kids seated around them and asked them if they wanted to play with Mario's stuffed animal.

Participate. If you want your child to participate, you must participate too. For example, Justine could have clapped and sang and pointed out to Mario all of the interesting things that were happening on stage. Eventually, Mario would have felt comfortable enough to join her—and the entire audience.

Successfully Shy Journal

Think back to an incident where you experienced the first stage of the shy process, the approach/avoidance conflict.

- What was the experience like? (List some details about time and place and who else was there.)

- How did you feel during the experience?

Now describe an incident where your child feels this conflict.

- What is his or her reaction to the experience?

- What strategies can you think of to help your child work through this conflict?

Finally, write a few sentences of dialogue that will help you strengthen your child's approach tendency instead of strengthening his avoidant tendency.

For example, if your child drags his heels in the morning before leaving for day care, you don't need to suffer with tears. The key is to reward him for approaching day care, and not for avoiding it. You can talk about all of the fun things he'll do once he's with his friends. You may want to see if his best friend

(continued)

would like to carpool with you, so your son will focus on that, instead of his long day without you. You can also create some rewards for every morning that goes without a hitch, even if it's just an extra hug when you say goodbye. Over time, your child will learn that going to day care is far better than fussing and resisting in the morning. What you don't want to do is punish him for feeling anxious or nervous, or excuse him from day care. These strategies send the message that his feelings are wrong or so out of control that he can't cope with daily challenges. Whichever lesson you teach him now, when he's young, he'll learn it well and use it throughout his life.

The Slow-to-Warm-Up Phase

We've all witnessed the following scene at every wedding reception: The band starts playing, one brave soul gets out on the dance floor, a few more join her, a few more on the edges of the dance floor are persuaded to get out there and dance, and, by the end of the evening, just about every guest has danced at least one dance, although a few guests remain on the edges of the dance floor. And the guests that remain on the perimeter are, for the most part, the shy guests.

This scenario illustrates the second step in the shy process: the warming-up period that everyone goes through when deciding how to break free of the approach/avoidance conflict. While everyone has a typical warming-up period, its length varies from person to person and from situation to situation. Some people require less time to approach others. They therefore have a short warming-up period and plunge into conversations, parties, and friendships. Others require a little more time before they feel comfortable approaching someone or accepting invitations to unfamiliar gatherings. They're held back by their desire to avoid these situations, even though at the same time they're making an effort to approach, too. They eventually strike up conversations and create friendships, but they take it slowly and require more patience and understanding before opening up.

These slow-to-warm-up people are shy people. Thanks to the research conducted by New York University Medical Center's Stella Chess, M.D., and Alexander Thomas, M.D., we know a lot about slow-to-warm-up people, especially slow-to-warm-up children. While I'll review Chess and Thomas's studies in more depth in chapter 5, here's an example of how a child experiences the slow-to-warm-up phase in a social situation:

Chelsea and her father Nick went to their hotel's swimming pool to cool off after a long day at a theme park. Since Chelsea loves to swim and always has a great time when she's splashing around in her grandma's swimming pool, Nick thought Chelsea would love to splash around in the larger pool in the hotel. And sure enough, when she stood on the steps while Nick jumped in, she brightened and laughed. But when Nick held her and swept her over to the shallow water, where a bunch of kids were playing with a beach ball, Chelsea's demeanor changed.

"Come on, Chelsea," Nick said. "Maybe you can toss the ball around with these nice kids."

Chelsea looked at the other kids, then stared at her dad, then hung on to him for dear life.

"Could you please throw the ball over here?" Nick asked the little boy with the ball. "My daughter and I would like to join you."

"Cool!" the boy said, and tossed the ball Nick's way.

Nick caught the ball, and then gave it to Chelsea so she could throw it to the other kids. She handed it back to her dad and looked over toward the door.

"I guess she doesn't want to play," the little boy said. "She's shy."

"She just needs a little more time to get to know you," Nick said while swimming toward the steps with Chelsea in tow. "But thanks anyway."

After bobbing up and down in another section of the pool, Nick asked Chelsea if she wanted to try to play ball with those kids again. "That one boy in the red suit seemed very nice," Nick said. "I think he was a little bit hurt that you didn't want to play with him. Maybe we can give it a try for just a little while to show him that you're not afraid to play with him."

Chelsea agreed and they swam back to the kids, and Chelsea caught and threw the ball not just once, or twice, but until the pool closed at the end of the evening.

As you can see, while Chelsea initially tried to avoid playing with the unfamiliar kids in the pool, she was able to join in once she had enough time to warm up to her new social encounter.

Unfortunately, many parents would merely label Chelsea as shy and attribute her behavior as more evidence. They would let her splash around by herself and that would be the end of the story. What they would mistakenly overlook is Chelsea's capacity to warm up and feel more comfortable as time wore on. And they would also miss a golden opportunity to teach Chelsea how to tolerate some frustration, a key life skill.

This slow-to-warm-up tendency isn't limited to discrete social encounters like playing with a beach ball in a swimming pool. It may also affect the way the child copes with many other new challenges, such as becoming toilet trained, speaking in class, or getting used to the new demands of junior high school.

Like Chelsea's dad Nick, you can help your child stick with these uncomfortable, frustrating experiences and work through the slow-to-warm-up phase. Here are a few tips:

Prepare your child. Explain what will happen and why you must stick with your decision to be socially involved. While getting ready to swim, Nick could have explained to Chelsea that other kids—nice ones, at that—would be swimming in the hotel pool.

Explain the benefits of what you're doing. Stress the positive aspects of friendship instead of focusing on your child's negative reactions to being a social creature, like blushing or feeling tongue-tied. For example, Nick could have told Chelsea that tossing the ball around is fun and something that she'd really enjoy.

Take a time-out. If your child is unnerved by the situation, take a breather and explain that it's okay to feel nervous, but feeling nervous is just a temporary feeling. Nick's brief time-out with Chelsea was handled well.

Talk about previous challenges that made her feel nervous at first. Drawing on past experiences helps a child put the current encounter into perspective. Nick could have reminded Chelsea that she likes playing with her friends at home, and now she has an opportunity to make new friends in the swimming pool.

Retrace your steps. Follow Nick's lead and put your child back in the situation. If she's still terrified, wait a few minutes and then take her out. But try another approach if you can.

Get involved and stick with your child. Nick didn't just tell Chelsea to play with the kids—Nick played with them and included Chelsea in what he was doing. Remember that even if your child holds your hand throughout the entire encounter, at least she's doing what she set out to do.

If it's just not working, give it a rest—but try it again some-time soon. One encounter may not provide enough warm-up time for your child. If Chelsea hadn't been able to play with those kids that first evening, Nick would have been smart to take her back to the pool the next night, when the warming-up period would continue.

Talk about the experience afterwards. Praise goes a long way, especially when it's earned. Later that night, Nick could have told Chelsea that she played with those unfamiliar kids so nicely, even if they did kind of scare her at first.

Prepare for the next challenge. Explain how today's success will turn into tomorrow's success. For example, Nick could tell Chelsea that because she warmed up to the new kids in the pool today, she'll probably also warm up to the kids standing in line at the amusement park tomorrow.

It's crucial to be sensitive to your child's unique warming-up period and not rush him through shyness-triggering situations, because kids like Chelsea deserve a second chance—and a third, and a fourth. They deserve as many chances as they need until they are able to warm up to a new social environment and feel strong enough to share themselves freely.

In addition, please remember that children who experience a long warming-up phase are quite able to handle all of their transitions and shouldn't be penalized for their innate need to take it a little bit slow. I understand that raising a slowly adapting child can be difficult at times, especially in our accelerated culture. In previous generations, acclimating slowly was normal, since just about everything unfolded at its own pace. Today, though, everything happens so quickly that the slow-to-warm-up child just doesn't get enough time to get used to new people or social events. There's absolutely nothing wrong with these kids, but perhaps we should re-think our capacity or willingness to process so much information and so many people and so many experiences in such short bursts of time. Perhaps these slow-to-warm-up kids are reminding us of how we used to live—and how we should live.

Successfully Shy Journal

In your Successfully Shy Journal, assess your own ability to warm up to people, as well as your actions during your warm-up period. Think back to your most recent stressful social encounter, and then answer the following questions.

- Did you feel anxious before the event?

- How long did it take you to warm up and feel comfortable once you were there? Ten minutes? Twenty minutes? Or did you still feel edgy and uncomfortable at the end of the encounter?

- What did you do to alleviate your discomfort?

- How effective were your strategies?

As you look through your answers, think about what it felt like in the moment. Did your 10-minute warm-up period feel like 110 minutes? Now consider what your child must feel like when she is warming up to new situations. She doesn't have the experience or intellectual capacity to draw on that you, an adult, have. The next time that you see her get stuck in a drawn-out warming-up period, you'll understand why you must provide her with strategies that will bring her relief, instead of allowing her to work through it alone and in crisis.

Finally, recount a few episodes when your child was able to warm up adequately and shine socially. Write down

(continued)

why your child was successful, and how that success can be repeated in the future. Remember that emphasizing your child's strengths will help her work through her perceived weaknesses. And, of course, remind her that she does have strengths even when she feels weak when she's warming up.

Expanding the Comfort Zone

The final step of the shy process, enlarging the comfort zone, follows naturally from the warming-up phase. This step is the final result of the thoughts, decisions, and behaviors created during the first two steps of the shy process. If positive, pro-social actions were taken during the approach/avoidance conflict and warm-up period, the comfort zone will be flexible and expand easily. If avoidant, withdrawing, and negative actions were taken during the shy process, the end result is a narrow, rigid comfort zone.

The comfort zone concept is pretty easy to understand. Every person has a comfort zone made up of familiar people, places, and activities. This comfort zone stretches and constricts as we add new people to our lives, lose touch with others, and accumulate more experience while closing ourselves off from other activities.

By and large, people who consider themselves shy have narrow comfort zones, and sometimes they get even narrower unless the person takes a few calculated risks now and then. Now, there's nothing wrong with being comfortable with a few old friends or close relatives, doing a few activities, and hanging out in the same settings. But I've come to realize that shy people very much want to enlarge their comfort zones. After all, if they didn't want to meet new people, or try a few new behaviors, or explore new places, they'd be perfectly content. And if you didn't want your child to become more comfortable in her ever-widening world, you wouldn't have picked up this book.

Because everyone's got a comfort zone, everyone's got to stretch it out now and then. In fact, when I feel like I'm in a rut or overwhelmed by a new challenge that's totally foreign to me, I know I need to expand my comfort zone, or that it's expanding too quickly for my personal warm-up period. When I feel this way, I assess my personal comfort zone and then move around its components, kind of like I'm playing chess or doing a jigsaw puzzle, only I'm analyzing a social problem and not one on a chessboard. It's not that difficult at all. Actually, I find it to be satisfying, because I get to be creative, use some life skills, and alleviate my anxiety.

To expand your child's comfort zone, identify which people, places, and activities are within his current comfort zone. Then, take two components of his current comfort zone and add one new component, and you've just figured out how to expand your child's world.

Let me explain. Say that 12-year-old Brandon is happiest when he's on his skateboard. Occasionally he skateboards with some kids at the park, but he usually skateboards alone in his driveway or on his street. Brandon's comfort zone is made up of three components: a few people (the kids in the park), in a few places (near home or at the park), doing one thing (skateboarding).

Brandon can gradually expand his comfort zone by expanding any of its three components:

- *Include new people.* Instead of skating only with the kids at the park, he can invite some of his school friends to skateboard with him.

- *Include new places.* Instead of hanging out in his driveway or the nearby park, Brandon can check out other places around town that cater to skateboarders.
- *Include new activities.* Instead of just skateboarding with some of his park buddies, he can invite them over for dinner or to a movie.

Making these changes may feel a little scary, but not overwhelmingly so. Because Brandon is gradually expanding his comfort zone—and not creating a totally new one—he's drawing on past safe experiences and building upon them. He should also remember—or be reminded—that he'll feel a little awkward at first and might need some extra warming-up time to let his anxiety subside naturally.

When your child's comfort zone expands gradually like Brandon's, he will feel more comfortable in a variety of situations and be successfully shy. In addition to shifting the people, places, and activities in your child's comfort zone, try these zone-stretching strategies:

Become more involved with your child's acquaintances and their parents. Your child will feel more supported and confident if you like his or her friends. If your daughter and another child share a common interest, make sure they share that interest together or sign up both of them for a class, and then spend that time with the friend's parents.

Develop your child's talents and sense of mastery. Success builds on success. If your daughter shows an interest in gymnastics, encourage her. And then ask her if she'd like to try a similar activity, like karate.

Develop your child's sense of social interest by helping her find ways to share her talents. Your backyard gardener would probably love to spend more time at the botanical garden, and your budding vet would learn a lot at dog-training classes.

Expose your child to new experiences. Curious about that new café that just opened up? Take your daughter there for juice and bagels. Saw an ad for your local rep company's production of a big Broadway show? Buy tickets for you and your son, and then inquire about becoming an usher at the theater. If your child is old enough, volunteer your time together or become more involved in community activities.

Prepare your child for her new challenges, but remind her of what's still in her comfort zone. Remember, your child may feel nervous about going to the mall with someone she knows only from her school bus ride. Explain to her that if she and her new friend have a good time on the bus, they'll have a good time at the mall.

Get feedback. If your child had a great time doing something new or being with a group of new people, congratulate him and suggest that he try it again. If your child is miserable afterwards, sort out what happened and make some changes before trying it again.

Add to your own social circle. If you want your child to widen her social circle, widen your own, and make sure that your child understands what you're doing and why.

In addition, you may want to talk through the process of expanding the components of the comfort zone with your son or daughter so that solving social problems becomes second nature and something to be enjoyed. Eventually, an ever-widening comfort zone will become a part of your child's actual comfort zone.

Successfully Shy Journal

In your Successfully Shy Journal, draw three large boxes.

- In the first box, list all of the people who are part of your child's current comfort zone.

- In the second box, write down all of the places where your child feels comfortable.

- In the final box, list the activities that are part of your child's comfort zone.

Now, follow the same steps that I provided for Brandon and modify each of the components. For example, combine a friend from your child's current comfort zone with a place where he feels at ease. Then, for the activity, choose something that is currently not part of your child's comfort zone but that you think he and his friend would enjoy with some time and experience. Continue exploring how to expand your child's comfort zone by choosing new people and places as well.

Next, write down your own comfort zone components and start moving them around, too. (Hint: When they overlap with your child's components, you've just identified activities that the two of you can share.)

Finally, put a checkmark by the components you listed that are the newest additions to your comfort zone, whether they're people, places, or activities. When did you last make these changes? Perhaps it's time to expand your own comfort zone.

A FEW FINAL THOUGHTS

We've just covered a lot of material, and I've given you a lot to think about—not only your child's behavior and identity, but perhaps your own as well. And while this "new view" of childhood shyness may seem a little unusual to you right now, I hope you'll be able to incorporate this message into your relationship with your child.

Throughout the following chapters, I'll explain how these ideas apply to the trials and tribulations of a shy childhood and how the two of you can successfully cope with school challenges, friendships, puberty, and questions of identity. We'll also explore whether or not your child was born shy. But first, I'll share some basic coping skills that will enable you to start helping your child today.

CHAPTER 3

LIFE SKILLS
TO BREAK OUT
OF SHYNESS

The more you understand about your child's shyness, the better you can adapt my Shyness Breakthrough Plan to your child's situation and needs. But I'm sure you're eager to start, to begin helping your child *today*. Happily, you can learn more by doing than just by reading about it. With that in mind, here's the second part of the Shyness Breakthrough Plan that you can start teaching your child today. When combined with the first component of the Plan—understanding and controlling the three phases of the shy process—these powerful skills will have an immediate and significant positive impact.

THE SUCCESSFULLY SHY ESSENTIAL LIFE SKILLS

Becoming a successfully shy child isn't achieved through magic, but it can have magical results. When parents work with their shy children and encourage them to explore their ever-widening world, they're giving their children more than much-needed social skills—they're giving their kids life skills that are essential to building a robust, well-rounded life. Like hammers, nails, and drills, life skills are basic tools—tools that enable people to develop healthy strategies that apply to a variety of knotty issues.

Throughout this book I'll return to these life skills because they're so important—and not just to the shy child, but to all children and the adults in their lives. Learning these lessons early helps unlock each person's potential so obstacles don't seem so daunting.

Problem Solving: The Four I's

Problem solving is a primary life skill. It isn't some dry, dusty mathematical application—it's a skill that's as vital as breathing, and it has enormous benefits for shy kids, who often lack the ability to work out problems on their own. Dr. Jens Asendorpf of the Max-Planck Institute for Psychological Research in Germany summarized some research linking children's problem-solving skills and their popularity. This research found that popular, socially savvy kids are good problem solvers, while shy kids are less adept at finding solutions to problems. The researchers found that when shy kids were asked to solve a problem, they generally attempted the same solution over and over and over again without success and then gave up. Socially confident kids, on the other hand, were able to think creatively, try a variety of solutions, and complete their task.

Fortunately, problem-solving skills can be taught, and boosting shy kids' problem-solving skills is a good first step toward helping them become more comfortable in tough situations, whether they're social or academic. Problem solving can be broken down into four steps, which I call the "four I's"—Identification, Information, Incorporation, and Implementation. Let's take a typical shy problem and put the four I's to work.

Let's say that Randy, a shy fourth grader, is baffled by his teacher's explanation of long division. Now, it's the end of a very long day, and his classmates are staring at the chalkboard and Mr. Gardner's long lists of numbers and it seems like everyone—everyone except Randy—understands. And because Randy's looking at the chalkboard, and looking at his own notes, and looking at everyone else following along in silence, Randy's too nervous, confused, and embarrassed to raise his hand and ask a question.

Later that night, when Randy is working on his homework and his dad, Sean, is reading his E-mails on his laptop, Randy throws his pencil down on the floor.

"What's the problem?" Sean asks.

"I can't do my homework!" Randy wails. "I must be dumb or something!"

"You're not dumb, Randy," Sean says calmly. "Let me help you out, okay?"

Fortunately, Sean knows how the four I's can get Randy out of this jam:

Identification. Identifying the problem may seem like a no-brainer, but it isn't always so easy. While Randy thought he was dumb, Sean knew better. After walking Randy through a math problem, he realized that Randy wasn't aware of how to carry the remainder over to the next column. When Sean asked Randy if Mr. Gardner explained that step in class, Randy shrugged his shoulders. He then asked if Randy raised his hand to get more information, and Randy said that he'd wanted to do so, but was afraid of looking dumb or acting nervous and blushing in front of his classmates. After this discussion, Randy and Sean both understood the real problem. It wasn't Randy's math ability, but that his anxiety got in the way of his ability to learn.

Information. Once the problem is identified, it's imperative to get more information about its cause and potential resolution. Now that Randy identified the true problem, he was able to concentrate on his father's explanation of long division. In addition, Sean explained that it's hard to think about math while you're worrying about those uncomfortable, but normal, feelings that come from speaking in front of a class full of kids.

Incorporation. Information is only meaningless data if it isn't incorporated into a potential solution. After Sean explained the basics of long division, Randy worked on another math problem, and he was able to do it with just a little help from his dad. Soon, he was able to incorporate what he had learned, and he finished the last 10 math problems on his own. Randy realized that he isn't dumb or bad at math or penalized for being shy—he was distracted by his shyness-related anxiety.

Implementation. This final step is both tricky and incredibly easy. It's tricky because people who don't implement all of their problem-solving skills are just engaging in self-defeating behavior that gets them stuck in a rut. However, implementation can be very, very easy, because once individuals get to this stage, they can be confident that they've done all that they need to do to create a successful solution. So Randy, armed with the knowledge of long division and his ability to keep up with Mr. Gardner's lessons, won't be so intimidated by future academic challenges. "Actually, Randy," Sean said as they cleaned up their books and notes, "I get a little nervous before I talk in a staff meeting. But I go ahead and talk anyway, and those feelings disappear when I'm concentrating on my words and not my nerves." Maybe, just maybe, Randy will remember his dad's advice and feel a little more confident about raising his hand in class.

Building Frustration Tolerance

Poor Courtney. When she visited Santa at the mall, she wailed. When she went to the local arcade, she turned into stone. And when she went to the petting zoo, she had a total meltdown.

Poor Courtney? Poor Courtney's parents! Because immediately after each of these crises, Courtney's parents had to rescue their sweet, shy daughter and put her fears to rest. "It's okay, Courtney," they told her. "We're here and you don't have to sit on Santa's lap and we don't have to shop for more presents now. We can go home now and play with your Barbies." So the family dutifully left the mall, the parents spent and frazzled, Courtney relieved, and their plans for the day shot.

Many parents of shy children are like Courtney's, and rush in to prevent their child from crying or fussing during upsetting encounters. I can understand that impulse, because tantrums in public are embarrassing and painful, and watching your child suffer is even worse. But each time a parent intervenes and protects their child from what's so upsetting, the child learns a lesson: *If I'm scared, I'm powerless. If I'm scared, I'm excused from facing my fears. If it doesn't feel good, I can scream and Mom and Dad will make everything better.*

While it may be hard to watch your child get frustrated and frightened in new, seemingly difficult situations, I do encourage you to watch and listen and learn. I promise that with each minute spent in that scary environment, both you and your shy child are developing a life skill—frustration tolerance.

Like problem solving, frustration tolerance is an essential skill children need to add to their life-skills toolbox. According to Columbia University's Walter Mischel, Ph.D., and his colleagues, kids who are able to control their impulses and delay gratification—the ones who can tolerate a lot of frustration—do well academically, can handle stress, and are rated favorably by their peers. Children who aren't able to tolerate the frustration that comes from waiting to have their needs met tend to be the shyer ones, the ones who are a bit stubborn, resentful, mistrustful, and stressed out. And, generally, these kids have lower self-esteem than the ones who can delay gratification.

Now, I'm not encouraging you to turn a blind eye to your shy child's discomfort just so she can learn an important life lesson. That would be abusive. Instead, I'd like you to explore ways you can guide your child through stressful social encounters instead of immediately removing her, because your child's fears will subside with each passing moment.

For example, Courtney's parents could have handled her visit to Santa differently by preparing her for what would happen and then coaching her through her entire visit. They could have talked to her about Santa, his loud, booming voice, what she would have to say to him, and who else would attend his arrival at the mall. They could have taken a few walks around the mall to check out Santa's surroundings before standing in line so Courtney could become more comfortable in the busy environment. And while standing in line, they could have pointed out all of the other children who were sitting on Santa's lap and telling him what they hoped he'd bring at Christmastime, and how the elves were helping all of the other kids. Lastly, they could have practiced running through the list of items on Courtney's list.

Undoubtedly, all of this preparation would have helped Courtney get ready for her time in the spotlight. And, once she got to approach Santa, her parents could have cheered her on and prompted her with all of the items on her Christmas list.

But the encounter with Santa doesn't end there. In fact, one of the most important shyness-relieving steps occurs after the social interaction—recapping the encounter and pointing out what the child did well and how she can improve the next time around. Many parents skip this step because they're relieved that the experience is behind them, but shy kids need this gentle reinforcement because they dwell so intensely on their fears and supposed failings. Articulating the child's successful behavior helps strengthen her self-confidence in social situations.

After the visit with Santa, Courtney's parents could have talked through the experience and reminded Courtney of what she did correctly. For example, perhaps Courtney said "thank you" to all of the elves who helped her out. Her parents could have pointed to that behavior and said, "See, Courtney, since you got along well with the elves, then I'm sure you'd get along with Santa if you spent more time with him. Maybe you'll have a longer visit with Santa next year. And we're so proud of you for waiting in line so patiently even though visiting Santa was kind of scary."

If Courtney's parents had walked her through all of these steps, her encounter with Santa would have been very, very different. While her parents thought that excusing her from visiting Santa was their best strategy, sticking with it would have been more valuable.

Throughout this book, I'll delve into more ways to help you build frustration tolerance in your child, but for now, it's a good idea to watch out for these situations and observe your reaction to them. While your first impulse as a caring, loving parent may be to rescue your child in an instant, you may want to think twice and let your child learn how to fuss and cry and wail—and eventually stop doing all of these things and relax and open up. Like Courtney, your child can learn how to stick with a scary situation until it turns into a comfortable—even pleasurable—experience.

Developing Social Interest

One of the greatest gifts we can give a child is an ever-expanding interest in their world. Children are naturally curious, but we often lose this capacity for wonder and astonishment as we get older. Just watch a child get excited about running through the sprinkler on a hot day, or opening a specially wrapped gift, and you'll know what I mean.

We're not just curious about our world, however. We're also curious about the people who fill it. Being curious about other people—having what's called "social interest"—is only natural, but a shy individual has a hard time showing it. He may feel that striking up a conversation with someone would be perceived as being too nosy or rude, and he certainly doesn't want to bother someone else and face rejection. Sometimes, just thinking about approaching someone can make a shy person too anxious to speak.

But having social interest is not being rude or bothersome. It's how we acknowledge that we live in a fascinating social world and that each person affects another. It's the first step toward participating in a larger community, giving to others, and receiving support from other people.

Social interest gives shy people permission to break through the invisible barriers that separate and isolate them. But once they've given themselves permission to make contact with strangers, they must act.

I've found that the best way to act on social interest is to perform social graces. This can be taught to children, not just through words, but also with deeds. If parents encourage their shy children to act on their budding social interest when appropriate, their shy children will become more comfortable with people from all walks of life.

Being kind and gracious is incredibly easy. Here are a few examples of how you can work social graces into your child's day:

Teach your child manners and use them constantly. If he knows when to say "please," "thank you," "excuse me," and "you're welcome," he'll go a long way in life. It also gives him a ready "script" so he doesn't feel like he doesn't know what to say in certain situations.

Do nice things for others, make sure your child is a part of the action, and explain to your child what you're doing and why. For example, if a neighbor isn't feeling well, take a dinner over to the neighbor's house, and take your son along, too. Then explain why being sensitive to someone else's plight is so important. (Hint: It's the Golden Rule.)

Make contact with others while you're out in public. When you go to the grocery store, hold open the door for another shopper, compliment the cashier on her helpfulness, and strike up a conversation with another person in line. Your child will notice your actions and copy them. During your next shopping excursion, ask your child to help you hold the door for someone else. Even if your child only taps his hand on the glass, he's making progress and deserves your praise.

Turn a talent into a social activity that allows you to participate in your community. For example, if you love to garden, sign up for the Earth Day clean-up or develop a community garden in your neighborhood. And, of course, invite your child along, too, and explain what you're doing and why you enjoy it.

Include your children in your social activities as often as possible. This is important because modeling socially active behavior—in addition to discussing what to do—is the most effective way to teach this valuable lesson. While these activities can include more formal functions such as attending the company picnic, they can also include the little things, like running errands or inviting a friend over for coffee.

These small steps are significant ways to help develop your child's willingness to act on his inherent social interest and increase his comfort level in a variety of social situations and interactions.

Enhancing Self-Awareness

Whenever I discuss shyness, someone always asks me, "Does shyness equal low self-esteem?" And my answer, inevitably and emphatically, is always "no."

Shyness and self-esteem are intertwined, because shyness seems to be so integral to a person's sense of self—an individual "is" shy, instead of "experiencing" shyness or "having" shyness—and because shyness has a value attached to it. And that value, as we all know, is negative. Although I think this is unfair, few shy people love being shy, and no one tries to develop shyness in the hope of having a better life. Therefore, many people believe that shyness automatically equals low self-esteem or a lack of confidence.

But it doesn't. Extroverts don't have a monopoly on high self-esteem, and shy people don't have a run on low self-esteem. You can be shy with high self-esteem, shy with a moderate, healthy level of self-esteem, or shy with low self-esteem. And you can be outgoing and have all of those levels of self-esteem as well.

Frankly, though, I'm not that interested in self-esteem, although I do encourage people to develop healthy attitudes toward themselves and their abilities. And while I know that parents are concerned about raising children with high self-esteem, empty praise ("You're so special!") and affirmations ("You are a star!") won't get a child anywhere. Like adults, children must earn their self-worth.

(But more on that later.) While I'm not overly concerned with self-esteem, I am concerned with self-awareness, the ability to see oneself objectively and appreciate all of the complicated, fascinating, and wonderful facets of one's personality. I've found that shy people often lack this kind of self-awareness, because instead of seeing shyness as merely one facet of their personality, they allow shyness to permeate all of their sense of self—and to do so with a negative spin.

Let's take, for example, Lindsey's first day of third grade. Now, the first day of school is usually difficult for everyone, not just for shy children like Lindsey. Teachers understand this and overlook most signs of nervousness—having sweaty palms, a shaky voice, or a stomachache—everything that Lindsey was experiencing. While Lindsey got stuck on these symptoms and then felt that her entire year will be spent feeling this way, and that her teacher doesn't like her as much as her peers, a more self-aware child will understand that these symptoms are fleeting, and happen quite a lot, actually, and never do any lasting harm.

What I would suggest to Lindsey's parents is that they have a few casual conversations with Lindsey about her fears. They should let her know that it's okay to feel a little nervous in new situations, and that all of her classmates probably felt a little unsure of themselves, too. They should also remind Lindsey that she was nervous about entering second grade, too, and got over that feeling quickly. And her parents should also tell Lindsey stories about when they feel scared, or shy, or uneasy—on the first day of a new job, or when they're at a party and don't know many fellow guests. Finally, they could also let her know that they always had a hard time getting through the first day of school, too.

All of these discussions will increase Lindsey's self-awareness, and will help her understand why she feels the way that she does, and what she can do to make herself feel better. In addition, Lindsey and her parents are establishing a pattern of mutual involvement and communication that will stand the test of time. So when Lindsey becomes a bit unnerved by challenges in adolescence, she'll be able to ask her parents for support and advice, and her parents will be able to reach out to her with love and respect.

BRINGING IT ALL TOGETHER

I had an encounter recently that illustrated just how all of these life skills come together to create a healthy, happy, confident kid. While having dinner at my friends' home on their dairy farm, I was struck by the situation in which 11-year-old Stephen found himself.

Like many farm kids, Stephen is involved in 4-H, as it brings him together with other kids with similar interests and enables him to learn more about plants and animals, knowledge that he'll need in the future. Stephen's already the owner of a prize-winning calf and the veteran of a handful of local competitions. Apparently, these competitions are no problem for him, because he works really hard at raising his calves properly and practices showing off his animals before getting in the ring.

But Stephen was now facing an altogether new hurdle—delivering a speech about calves in front of a panel of judges. Plus, he'd have to travel to the state capital for this competition, something he'd never done before.

His mom, Linda, admitted that Stephen was hitting a rough patch with the speech, but she and her husband thought that the experience would be good for their son and came up with a strategy to get him through it. First, they reminded Stephen that if he wanted to compete, he'd have to do the prep work himself, just as he does when he shows off a calf. Instead of doing the work for him and producing a hollow victory, they gave Stephen a notebook for his research and writing and told him to dig up as many facts as he could.

Stephen started researching and writing, and writing and rehearsing, and revising and rehearsing endlessly. "He isn't nervous about rehearsing it in front of us," Linda told me, "but he does have some anxiety about doing it for the judges."

I thought that Stephen could take it to the next level by giving his speech for me, so I suggested that Stephen give his speech for us after dessert. While he resisted at first, he couldn't resist altogether and he grabbed his notebook. He was a little shaky at first, but got stronger as he went through his speech. The cheers afterwards didn't hurt, either, and he had to admit that some of our suggestions were helpful, too.

As the competition neared, Linda and her husband picked up on Stephen's anxiety. Although he was confident about giving his speech, he felt that making the trip and encountering all of those other 4-H members was a little bit scary. Linda decided that Stephen needed just a little help with his attitude toward competing.

"We talked to him about it, and what I hope came across is that it's nice to win, but it's more important to do a good project and to have the experience of competing. We told him that we just want him to have this experience," she said. "He doesn't have to be perfect. We've told him that it's okay to get up there and not say anything—that's okay too."

Armed with his parents' encouragement and his confidence in his well-prepared speech, Stephen went to the competition. While he didn't get a blue ribbon, he did get kudos for being one of the youngest ones to show up and do a great job. Afterwards, he told his dad that he wanted to go to 4-H summer camp so he could become better friends with the kids he just met. What's more, Stephen earned a sense of accomplishment, because just a few months ago the mere idea of giving the speech seemed overwhelming.

I like this story not just because Stephen is a nice kid with a nice family. I like how Stephen used life skills to act responsibly and face his challenge with courage and tenacity. With his parents' help, he solved his problem of figuring out how he was going to give the speech, tolerated a lot of frustration when he was sick of rehearsing and revising his speech, developed social interest by sharing his talents with his peers, and became more self-aware by expanding his self-image from a kid who was good at showing his calves to one who could speak eloquently about them, too.

And, through it all, Stephen's parents gently but effectively guided him through his endeavor. I admire Stephen's parents for having constant but appropriate involvement and communication with their children. They found the right level of involvement, a level that all parents should find—somewhere between "sink or swim" and finishing all of your child's sentences. In addition, Linda and her husband listened to Stephen and created an atmosphere in which it was acceptable to make mistakes. By doing so, they sent out the right signals about Stephen's place in his world and his ability to meet ever more difficult challenges. Stephen, thanks to his parents, knows that he has a lot to offer others, can reach out to people who'll support and encourage him, and won't let some nerves hold him back from any goal he sets for himself. And these are the lessons that I hope you will teach your shy child.

CHAPTER 4

UNDERSTANDING YOUR FAMILY'S SHYNESS PROFILE

fter 20-plus years of studying shy people, I'm still fascinated by each individual's experience. Although many
experiences are common—such as the feeling that
strikes before attending an intimidating party, or getting stuck in
a negative mental loop after a disappointing social encounter—
each shy person, no matter how young or old, is unique.

You are unique, both as an individual and as a parent. Your
child is unique as well, and so is your family. The third component
of my Shyness Breakthrough Plan is to identify and comprehend
your own Shyness Profile and that of your child. Once you complete this exercise, you will be well on your way to solving your
child's unique shyness-related difficulties.

By now, you have written a number of entries in your Successfully Shy Journal. I hope that they have helped you to start thinking
about your child's shyness in a new way—and that you've already
started brainstorming ways you can help your child become suc-

cessfully shy. You're now ready to move on to the next step: Exploring your child's unique experiences, personality, and reactions so that you can best personalize your approach to helping him confront his shyness. In this chapter, I'll pose a series of questions that will guide you through these discoveries and help you uncover your own and your child's distinct Shyness Profiles.

As you work through the following questions, I'd like you to write your responses in your Successfully Shy Journal. I want you to write out your answers completely, even if you feel that you're not a great writer, because it's important that you process and clarify your thoughts deeply and fully. If you aren't able to complete all of the points in one sitting, please make sure to complete them before moving on to the next chapter. If you have difficulty answering some of them, make a mental note that you should get more information either by discussing that particular topic with your child or by observing your child more closely.

Begin by getting out your Successfully Shy Journal and writing down today's date at the top of a fresh page. Please do your best to be completely honest; after all, there are no wrong or right answers—just *your* answers. Your answers should express how you feel right now. But please note that your responses may change as you learn more about childhood shyness and your role in your child's life. In fact, you may want to refer back to these pages as you read later chapters in this book to gauge and evaluate your progress and insights.

These questions aren't merely an internal inventory of your thoughts and feelings right now. Rather, I've designed them as a tool to help you develop your relationship with your shy child. Once you've thought through your answers, you'll be better able to discuss them with your child and keep working on developing that pattern of communication and involvement that's so critical to being a good parent and raising a successfully shy child. In addition, you may want to ask your son or daughter these questions, too.

YOUR SHYNESS PROFILE

Before exploring your child's experience with shyness, it's helpful to explore your own unique experience with shyness, whether you consider yourself shy or not. As you help your child break through his shyness, you'll draw on all of your own experiences, memories, beliefs, hopes, and fears. Remembering how you felt when you were a child will help you to view the world from your child's perspective. This increases your empathy, which has been identified as a critical factor for those who help others. After all, if you can't visualize what your child is experiencing, how can you help?

Please write down your responses to these personal points:

- Do you consider yourself shy now? If so, what triggers your shyness?

- How do you feel before, during, and after stressful social encounters? How do these encounters affect your body, mind, and sense of self?

- If you are shy now, or have been shy in the past, what do you think caused your shyness? How do you work through it? What has not worked? How has your shyness changed through the years? Which aspects of your life do you feel are most and least affected by your shyness?

- If you consider yourself shy, please write down three words to describe your shyness. Then write down three negative and three positive aspects of your shyness. If you are not shy, please write down three negative and three positive aspects of shyness in general.

- If you're not shy now, have you ever been shy? If so, what changed? What did you learn about yourself? What did you do to break out of your shyness?

- What are the signs of shyness in other people? What are other possible explanations for their behavior? Can you empathize with them? Now that you know more about shyness, are you better able to identify some people as being shy?

If you consider yourself to be shy, you may have a lot of empathy for your child. In fact, this should make you exceptionally sensitive to your child's pain. However, as a shy parent, you may not be providing your child with the social skills and opportunities he needs to expand his comfort zone. But don't let that worry you. As you start using my shyness strategies, you'll begin breaking through your own shyness as you help your child break through his. Remember the discussion of the shy process in chapter 2 and keep this process in mind as you observe your child's shy behavior. If you don't consider yourself to be shy, you may have a harder time understanding your child's feelings and behaviors. You may feel frustrated or that you're doing something to stunt your child's social growth. Again, don't worry. Your child is a unique individual. Although the two of you don't share the common trait of shyness, you still have a lot in common, and by reading this book, you'll come to understand and appreciate your child's special qualities even more.

Your Personal History

Now that you've explored your current personal experiences, please reach back into your childhood and explore your personal history with shyness.

- Were you a shy child? If you were, write down a few of your shy experiences from your childhood.

- If you were a shy child, what were the typical triggers? How did your parents react? How did you cope with your shyness? Which coping skills have you carried into adulthood?

- Were you ever labeled shy? If so, how did that affect you? Did you talk to anyone about your feelings? Did anyone help you? Did anyone make your shyness worse? How?

- Think back to the people you knew as a child. Which of your friends, siblings, or classmates were shy? Why do you say that they were shy? How do you feel that shyness affected their ability to make friends and cope with academic challenges?

- Which of your relatives are shy? Do you think their shyness is inherited, or do you think that personal experience or environment plays a role? Did your family encourage the development of social skills?

If you were a shy child, you can probably pinpoint the exact moment when you started feeling shy. You may see similarities between you and your child. I know that you want to shelter your child from the pain that you felt as a shy child, but the best thing that you can do for your shy child is to expose her to smart, calculated risks that expand her comfort zone. You may want to focus on a critical skill in childhood—making friends. In chapter 7, I'll discuss the steps that kids can take to make a new friend. You'll even be able to use some of these tips when making friends as an adult, too!

If you were not a shy child, you certainly knew some shy children when you were growing up. In fact, almost half of your classmates were shy, even if you didn't pick up on it at the time. Recall Sharon's story in chapter 1 about the difficulties she faced everyday because of her shyness. With this in mind, you can discuss with your child how she feels when she's feeling shy. You may be surprised by what she tells you.

Your Social Comfort Zone

As I explained in chapter 2, everyone, shy or not, has a comfort zone that's made up of familiar people, places, and activities. Let's explore the social aspect of your personal comfort zone through the following points.

- List all of the people with whom you come into contact on a typical day and the nature of each interaction. Is this list longer or shorter than you anticipated?

- Draw an X next to each person on your list with whom you feel comfortable. Draw a checkmark next to the people with whom you feel uncomfortable. Which traits define these two types of people?

- Draw a star next to all of the people with whom you could nurture a closer relationship. How could you change your interactions? How could you create this opportunity? What is preventing you from doing so?

- Which social graces did you perform today? What response did you get? How did you feel afterwards?

- Which social activities do you enjoy? How often do you do them? Which activities would you like to try? Who would be interested in sharing these activities with you?

- List the people in your life you consider to be shy. Have you discussed their shyness? What do you do to help them with their shyness? How does their behavior change when they're in socially stressful settings? What do you appreciate most and like least about your friends' shyness?

If your social comfort zone is smaller or more rigid than you'd like it to be, you'll find that as you expand your child's comfort zone, yours will expand as well. As you bring new people, places, and experiences into your child's life, you'll face these new elements, too. You may want to return to the discussion in chapter 2 on how to slowly but smartly expand your comfort zone. This strategy works for adults, too.

If your comfort zone is large and expands easily, you've got a head start. But note that while you may stretch your comfort zone easily, and perhaps without effort or thought, you'll have to make this process explicit for your child. When you're helping your child warm up to new social situations, slow down, explain what you're doing, and remind your child of all of the familiar elements that are in your environment. (The discussion of the comfort zone in chapter 2 provided strategies for doing just that.)

Your Child's Shyness Profile

You picked up this book because at least one child in your life is shy, but how well do you know your shy child and what he or she encounters on a daily basis? While these points apply to all children, regardless of age, I've included points specific to adolescents in a later section. If you are concerned about more than one shy child, please answer each set of questions for each child.

- Explain what your child does to make you feel that he or she is shy. When did you notice that your child was shy? How did you respond? Do you label your child shy?

- What triggers your child's shyness? How does your child typically react? When is he or she more outgoing? Is your child becoming more or less shy with age?

- With whom is your child comfortable? Why do you think this is so? With whom is your child uncomfortable? Why do you think this is so?

- How does your child's personality resemble your own? What are your differences? How does his or her personality resemble that of other members of your family?

- Which activities does your child love to do? Which activities does your child resist or refuse to do altogether? What do you think is the reason for these refusals? How do you react to such preferences?

No matter how old your child is, you're right to want to help her with her shyness. It's much easier to change shy thoughts and behavior in a child before these patterns become habitual and almost hard wired. If your child is a toddler with strong reactions to new situations, chapter 5 will help you understand his response. If your child is struggling with approaching other children and making friends, take special note of chapter 7. If your child is struggling with the first few days and weeks of school, chapter 8 will help you out. And if your child is having a hard time while at school, turn to chapter 9 for a full discussion of the shy student.

Your Child's World

Many parents are surprised to find that the son or daughter who is chatty and outgoing at home becomes more withdrawn and reticent around unfamiliar children at school or in day care. The following points will help you understand your child's social world and how you can play a positive role in it.

- Who are your child's friends? What do they do when they're together?

- How do you prepare your child for stressful social encounters? How do you help your child during these encounters? Do you ever use shyness as a reason to excuse your child from challenging social activities?

- Have you discussed your child's shyness with his or her teacher, coach, or caregiver? What was recommended? Did your child's behavior change when you tried these strategies?

- How much emphasis is placed on learning social skills or life skills in your child's classroom? How much time is allowed for group and independent play?

- How has your child's shyness changed through the school year or since joining day care? How does your child struggle in school? How does he or she shine? Does your child come to you for advice on handling problems at school? What is your child's reputation at school?

- How much structured free time (for example, in after-school lessons or sports) does your child have? How much unstructured free time does your child have? How much time does your child spend doing solitary activities?

If you had a hard time answering these questions, you'll need to learn more about your child and his world before you can help him with his shyness. You'll need to develop ways to talk to your child and build a sense of trust and companionship. These questions are a good place to start, so go ahead and ask him about his friends, his activities, and his feelings. In addition, take steps to include your child in more of your everyday routine—running errands, making dinner, and going to social events. Likewise, get more involved in *your child's* everyday routine. He'll be more excited about joining a soccer team, for example, if he knows that you'll go to his games and ask him about his practices and coach.

If you had an easy time answering these questions, you seem to know a lot about your child. You probably have a clear idea of which shyness-related problems you want to resolve. But don't let it end there. Since you already have a close relationship with your child, involve him in more challenging conversations about his shyness. This will help him dispel his fears about certain social situations. (The discussion between Randy and Sean in the problem-solving portion of chapter 3 is an example of how you can talk about some tough issues presented by shyness.)

Your Shy Adolescent

It's natural to feel awkward and tongue-tied during adolescence, which is why so many teens go through a withdrawn "shy phase" during these years that feels incredibly intense. Despite its prevalence, adolescent shyness isn't always obvious on the surface, though. Answering these questions can help you, as a parent, become more aware of your teen's experiences.

- Why do you say that your teen is shy? Has your teen always been shy, or is his or her shyness a recent phenomenon? When is your teen most shy? When is he or she most outgoing?

- Have you discussed these issues with your teen? How often do the two of you have one-on-one conversations about anything? What do you and your son or daughter enjoy doing together?

- What are your teen's talents? What does he or she struggle with or refuse to do? What does your teen enjoy?

- Who are your teen's friends? Is your son or daughter's social circle becoming wider or narrower? Do you like your teen's friends, or are they a source of conflict between you and your child?

- How much time does your teen spend socializing? How much time is spent online or watching TV? How much time is spent alone? When is he or she able to communicate freely?

- How are you fostering your child's growing independence? How have his or her responsibilities and expectations changed?

Adolescence is a particularly difficult time for shy individuals. In fact, I think of adolescence as one big shyness-trigger life phase. In chapter 11, I'll discuss the shy teen's world and how he typically copes. What's critical at this age is that you involve your teen in each shyness strategy. This will help build independence, confidence, and trust. You may want to have your child read the first three chapters of this book and then discuss his thoughts on being shy. If you don't get a great response at first, keep trying. Your teen needs to take his time warming up, especially if it involves changing his behavior. Bring up these subjects again, and let your teen know that you're willing to help and chat whenever he feels like it. He'll come around when he's ready.

YOUR RELATIONSHIP PROFILE

Raising a shy child is no more or less difficult than raising an outgoing child. However, many parents convey hidden but potent emotional messages that affect their relationship with their child and their expectations for their child.

- Why are you reading this book? How would you like your child's thoughts, feelings, or behavior to change as a result of your increased understanding of shyness?

- Do you think that it's easy or difficult to be a shy child? Do you think it's easier to raise a shy child or an outgoing child? What are the easiest and most difficult aspects of parenting a shy child?

- Have you discussed your shy child's feelings with him or her? If so, what did you say, and what was your child's reaction? Have your efforts benefited your child?

- Have you sought out advice from friends and family, read books or articles about shyness, or considered medicating your child for social anxiety? What was helpful?

- When was the last time you praised your child for a job well done? What did you say, and how did your child react? When was the last time you criticized your child, and what kind of reaction did you get?

- How do you teach social skills to your child? What do you tell your child about dealing with strangers? Do you explain the importance of manners and friendship to your child? How do you model socially sensitive behavior?

These questions are meant to help you understand your influence on your child—your skills and strengths as a parent, as well as your attitude, involvement, and opinions. In chapter 6, I'll discuss the family's influence on a shy child, which is a powerful thing. In fact, about 40 percent of shy adults I've surveyed said that their family environment was the most important factor in their development of childhood shyness. Use this influence to help your child become self-accepting, confident, and socially involved.

REFLECTING ON THE SHYNESS PROFILE

I hope that working through this shyness profile has given you a greater appreciation for your child and your role in helping your child become more confident and successfully shy. I also hope that these points spark conversation between you and your child, and among your friends and relatives, because understanding your unique thoughts and your child's unique experiences is key to helping him or her become happier and successfully shy.

But these questions and answers do more than just develop your understanding of your child. In fact, you've just worked through the first step in the problem-solving process—identification. If you go back through your shyness profile, you'll find that certain themes come through loud and clear and repeat and reappear. These answers point to how you can help your child become successfully shy. Use them to set specific goals, and use this book as a road map to get you there.

No two readers will have the same goals, because no two readers—or their shy children—are alike. But some goals will be common. For example, you may have just realized that you know very little about the specifics of your child's life, and you've never discussed your child's shyness. In fact, it may not have occurred to you to talk to your child about shyness because nobody ever asked you about your shyness when you were a kid. If so, you may want to set a goal of becoming more involved in your child's life, and helping your child to discuss his feelings about himself and his shyness. This is a great target to shoot for, and your child will be grateful for your efforts and understanding.

Now that you've become keenly aware of your and your child's unique personal profile of shyness, you're ready to explore the strategies presented in Part Two of this book. First, we'll take a look at the many possible causes of shyness. Then, we'll discuss the most common obstacles for shy children as they're growing up, and I'll give you plenty of practical advice you can use to help your child successfully navigate through them.

Strategies
to Warm Up, Open Up, and Join the Fun

Now that you have a new view of your child's shyness, you'll learn how you can implement the fourth step of The Shyness Breakthrough Plan—the strategies. In the following chapters, you'll discover how to apply the new ideas and insights you gained in Part One to whatever unique challenges your child is currently facing. Instead of backing off and hoping that your child will magically "grow out of" his shyness, you'll learn how to help your child "grow with" it and become successfully shy. To do so, you'll need to understand how the shy process interacts with your child's intellectual, physical, emotional, and social development. With the right kind of coaching and encouragement, your child will never again feel limited by his shyness.

Part Two provides a timeline of a child's development, from birth to pre-adolescence, and explains how shyness is experienced during this time. In chapter 5, I'll explore one of the most common questions about shyness: Are some people born shy? I'll discuss the physical aspects of shyness, which even show up in infants, and what you can do to make your child more comfortable in difficult social environments. In chapter 6, I'll explore the family's influence on a shy child—the factors that can increase or reduce shyness—and how family relationships influence a child's social orientation. In chapter 7, I'll turn to how a child extends his social skills with people outside of the family via the vital skill of knowing how to approach another child and make a friend. This skill is essential, and it's one that can be reinforced throughout the years. Then, in chapter 8, I'll tackle the school jitters experienced by so many kids at the start of the school year. In chapter 9, I'll discuss how shyness affects students within the classroom as they attempt to master their tasks and achieve their academic goals. Finally, in chapter 10, we'll take a tour of the social lives of kids in middle childhood, and how shy kids fit in.

Throughout these chapters, I'll continue presenting exercises for your Successfully Shy Journal and ask you to put your words into action by helping your child take steps to reduce his shyness. You won't need to do anything drastic or dramatic—just smartly and systematically extend your child's comfort zone to create a shyness breakthrough.

CHAPTER 5

ARE WE
BORN SHY?

When I tell people that I'm a shyness researcher, the same questions inevitably pop up: Are some people born shy? Is there a shy gene that runs through families? Must my bashful child become a shy adult? And what causes shyness, anyway?

After more than 20 years investigating these questions, I've found that shyness is a dynamic phenomenon. It changes according to the situation, the phase of life, and the person's desire to understand it. It becomes more intense at times of stress and less bothersome in relaxed, caring relationships.

Because shyness is so dynamic, and because each individual's experience with it is unique, I believe that there's no one cause for shyness, such as a shy gene or a particular triggering event. I agree with most experts that shyness is rooted in the body's natural functioning, and that this general physical tendency may perhaps be passed down the family tree. But shyness is not solely a physical trait, like eye color or height. It encompasses so much more than physical responses. What can begin as a general tendency to get irritated and aroused by social stimulation can lead to emotional and social stress and difficulty with self-acceptance and interpersonal relationships. On the other hand, this physical tendency can also be controlled or lessened, leading to a life that's free of the constraints of shyness and full of self-awareness and fulfilling relationships.

In this chapter, I'll explore the evidence on the "shy gene" and the "shy body," as well as how the physical symptoms of shyness can be diminished with time, guidance, and smart choices.

JOY'S STORY

Recently I spoke with Joy, a counselor who was intensely shy as a child. "I was shy to the point that when the teacher listed a bunch of adjectives on the board, and one of them was 'shy,' everyone pointed to me and said 'Joy.' Kids would tease me to try to make me talk, and that would make me even more shy. They would say, 'You don't know how to talk' and things like that. They were so mean it was almost abusive."

I asked Joy why she thought she was so shy then. "We moved when I was a kid and that bothered me a lot. This is back when kids knew each other through all of their school years, beginning in kindergarten, and I didn't know any of them. I was also clumsy, and I didn't think I was pretty or athletic, and I think that gave me low self-esteem.

"But I wouldn't doubt that there's also a genetic component," she added. "I have five children, and I would say that only one of them is outgoing. I'm adopted, but I met my biological mother, and she's shy. She has a daughter who's so shy she wouldn't go to school when she was in high school. My adopted dad was an introvert, too. He didn't socialize at all, other than the usual church-related Sunday activities. He was a helpful guy—he volunteered a lot, and he taught Sunday school too. But he said that he was uncomfortable socially, that it was just too much for him."

As you can see from Joy's example, the many threads that weave together to produce childhood shyness can come from many sources—biology, the influence of parents, childhood relationships, and the child's feelings about herself. Each story is unique, and I thank Joy for sharing hers with me.

Successfully Shy Journal

This chapter may challenge your beliefs about whether shyness is inherited or acquired through experience. Before looking through the evidence on shyness, I'd like you to challenge your assumptions about other personality characteristics. In your Successfully Shy Journal, please write down the following characteristics and then note whether you think each is inherited, acquired, or a combination of the two. The characteristics are:

- Sense of humor

- Intelligence

- Musical ability

- Social skills

- Athletic ability

- Depression

- Academic success

- Allergies

- Alcoholism

(continued)

- Weight

- Self-confidence

- Hair color

- Near-sightedness

- Happiness

- Anxiousness

- Impulsiveness

- Stubbornness

- Aggression

When you're finished, count up the number of characteristics you determined are caused by a combination of both genetics and life experience. This number is likely greater than you would have imagined. While some characteristics may seem to be inherited, upon closer examination you probably realized that many can be modified through life experience. For example, a body type or shape may seem to be inherited, but it can be modified through diet, exercise, and other lifestyle choices. Likewise, self-confidence could be the result of support from friends, learning from failures, intelligence, optimism, the ability to develop strategies and solve problems, and the accumulation of successful experiences.

Keep these thoughts in mind as you read this chapter. You'll find that while shyness has a strong physical component, that doesn't necessarily mean that it's inherited—or part of an individual's destiny.

Nature versus Nurture: What Shy People Say

During my research into the causes of shyness, I've found that most people fall into two camps: Those who believe that shyness is innate, and those who believe that shyness is acquired through experience. These people may not know it, but they're taking sides in the age-old nature versus nurture debate.

To gain more insight, I surveyed shy people about the sources of their shyness. I found that about 9 percent of the shy adults I questioned feel that they were born shy and inherited a shy gene that they share with many of their relatives. This hairdresser is one of them: "I definitely believe I was genetically inclined to feel shy," she wrote. "As far back as I can remember, I've always been shy, and many of my relatives are shy, too."

In contrast, almost 40 percent of the shy people I surveyed are on the nurture side of the debate. These people believe that they acquired their shyness from their experiences—specifically, their childhood experiences—and how they coped with those experiences. This nurse's observations about her childhood are illuminating: "I was raised in an environment in which there was not much social interaction," she explained. "My parents were basically homebodies and didn't have any friends themselves. There wasn't much communication or discussion between parents and children, because children were to be seen and not heard. Overall, I wasn't raised in a warm, friendly, loving, touching family."

So, according to the experts—shy people themselves—nature does not trump nurture. Still, I can understand why some shy people feel they were "born shy." After all, the physical signs of shyness—the tension, blushing, clammy hands, and anxiety that's produced by the "shy body"—feel so terrible, like there's something different or abnormal going on. These "born shy" people can't remember a time when they didn't feel this way during stressful encounters, so they assume that this tendency to get intensely physically aroused must have been hard-wired at birth.

Yet, based on my research, I believe that these physical signs are completely normal, and, in fact, are a positive sign. What's more, later in this chapter I'll show you how to better understand the "shy body" and how its processes can be used to produce more sociable behavior.

THE SHY GENE

As part of my investigation into whether or not shyness is inherited, I studied the research concerning the so-called "shy gene," the gene that's supposedly passed through the generations to create a long line of shy people. Thanks to some advanced studies, we have a clearer view of the genetic component of shyness.

Many shyness researchers have investigated the family trees of shy people to determine the "shy links" among relatives. When a number of these studies were analyzed, a genetic link in some infant twins was in fact found. But this doesn't necessarily mean that there's a shy gene that creates shyness. These studies were conducted on very young children—less than 3 years of age. At this young age, their behavior is based on their physical impulses because they haven't yet acquired much life experience or developed the many thought processes and skills that are involved in shyness.

In another study, researchers at Harvard University looked at the heritage of children who showed a very high degree of inhibited behavior, since these intensely inhibited kids are assumed to be the most likely to become shy when they're older. The researchers found that these intensely inhibited kids tended to have other family members with the same reactions, while children with mild reactions had less of a family link. This seems to support the theory that there is a genetic thread that runs through families with intensely inhibited reactions. But there seems to be less of a link among those in the majority—people with a moderate amount of inhibited behavior.

So, as you can see, there is some evidence to support the belief that inhibited behavior can be passed on through the generations. But what, exactly, is being passed on, and why? And is this destiny?

SHYNESS AND TEMPERAMENT

Taking the investigation one step further, a group of researchers at Harvard University headed by Jerome Kagan, Ph.D., is looking at how a child's physiological makeup reacts to and interacts with his environment. When there's a group of related characteristics, that cluster is known as a temperament, or a general physiological tendency to act or react in a certain manner.

Everyone is born with a temperament type, which is most obvious during infancy and early childhood, before life experience and the intellect become factors. Some children adapt to new people and things easily. Some children fall in the middle and react according to the situation. But some infants and children do not adapt easily, and they resist new people and things. In infancy, they kick, cry, and fuss when they're faced with physical stimulation. When they grow up a little, they react to new things by becoming anxious, aroused, withdrawn, and uncomfortable. These infants and children are thought to have an "inhibited temperament."

Notice that some of these reactions are not what we normally think of as being "shy." Instead, some reactions are expressive and out of control. When babies feel uncomfortable due to stimulation created by new people, places, or experiences, they cry out, because they are only capable of expressing themselves physically. They can't talk about their feelings or develop strategies to resolve their discomfort. But as they get older, their actions become more sophisticated. When inhibited children feel uncomfortably aroused in the presence of something new, they stop and become watchful and silent before deciding whether to approach what's new or avoid it. This slow-to-warm-up strategy looks like shyness and is often labeled as such. When adults feel this high level of physical arousal, we don't show our apprehension and anxiety. Instead, we try to hide our tension, stress, and discomfort, and we clam up and shut down to stifle our instinctive reactions. This is often labeled shy behavior, too. Although these infants, children, and adults feel the same way internally, or physically, their external appearances are quite different.

When discussing her physical reactions to challenging social situations, Joy commented, "Although I don't think of myself as being shy today, I do notice that the physical signs of shyness still appear even now that I'm an adult. In some situations, I'll perspire or get a stress headache. I work very hard to cover it up so other people don't see it, but I still feel it inside."

I find two investigations into the inhibited temperament type to be especially compelling. One focuses on an infant's precise physical responses to stimulation such as noise or an awful smell. The other investigation describes the general behavior of children that we would typically label "shy." Both views help us understand how young, inhibited children react when they're confronted with new situations. They also show how these reactions can be overcome.

The Highly Reactive Temperament

As a participant in a study, baby Jeremy kicked and fussed when a cotton swab was waved under his nose. He became irritable when a colorful mobile was placed too close to him, and he became more agitated when a tape of disjointed sounds was played and a balloon was popped behind his head. When the researchers examined him, he had a pounding heart, dilated pupils, and a lot of stress hormones racing through his veins. He also kicked and fussed throughout the test.

According to Dr. Kagan, little Jeremy is a typical example of an infant who has a highly reactive temperament and responds to new and unfamiliar situations with extreme physical reactions. Dr. Kagan has studied these children for decades and has found that these highly reactive kids are quite common. About 20 percent of the children in his study have this temperament.

These temperamental reactions seem to be hard-wired into the child's system at birth. But when Dr. Kagan conducted follow-up exams with the children through the years, he discovered that temperament in infancy does not always predict behavior as the kids grow up. Dr. Kagan found that some highly reactive infants like Jeremy didn't become shy adolescents. Some of the infants with moderate reactions became shy teens. And some infants who were calm during the tests became more agitated by stimulation when they were older.

Looking at these changes, it appears that while physiology or temperament seems to affect behavior during infancy, its influence on behavior later in life isn't so clear. Many other factors come into play as a child grows. Her family relationships, her education, parental guidance, intelligence, and self-awareness are all factors that influence how a child expresses her seemingly instinctive reactions.

The Slow-to-Warm-Up Temperament

Two researchers at New York University Medical Center, Stella Chess, M.D., and Alexander Thomas, M.D., have another view of this inhibited temperament. Instead of following Dr. Kagan's strategy and identifying the precise physical reactions of inhibited infants, Dr. Chess and Dr. Thomas are interested in how older children acclimate to new situations like meeting new children, playing with new toys, and coping with new life challenges such as toilet training and becoming accustomed to new clothes.

Based on their many years of study, Dr. Chess and Dr. Thomas identified a "slow-to-warm-up" temperament in about 15 percent of the children they studied, while other children either rejected new situations or adapted easily. These slow-to-warm-up children take their time when confronted with new situations, including social situations, and are often labeled shy.

Like Dr. Kagan, however, Dr. Chess and Dr. Thomas don't believe that temperament is destiny, and they explain how temperament can be managed. They advise parents to aim for a "goodness of fit" between their child and her environment, no matter what her temperament. Goodness of fit can be achieved by selecting appropriate challenges and surroundings for the child. This includes finding a day care provider who is sensitive to the child's needs, the right time and method to introduce new foods, the right amount of stimulation at home and elsewhere, and appropriate social activities. We'll discuss more on goodness of fit in chapter 8.

Besides instructing parents on how to achieve goodness of fit, Dr. Chess and Dr. Thomas also warn parents to consider their own temperamental makeup and its influence on their relationship with their child. For example, quickly adapting, outgoing parents will need to be more patient with their slow-to-warm-up child. On the other hand, slow-to-warm-up parents will need to make adjustments for their quickly adapting child. A parent whose temperament matches their child's should be careful to teach their child to be more tolerant with others. Overall, though, they stress the importance of understanding the effect of temperament on all aspects of a child's life—not just social interaction.

Successfully Shy Journal

Although I do warn against labeling children unfairly, it is important to be aware of your child's general temperamental reactions to her world and to become more sensitive to the possible influence of the inhibited temperament on your child's behavior. To help you decide if your child has this temperament, I've developed a checklist of traits shared by these children. In your Successfully Shy Journal, please note which of the following traits your child exhibits. You may also want to identify which of your child's reactions have changed over time or if they apply only in specific situations. Then write down when these reactions usually appear.

- Becomes agitated in noisy environments
- Withdraws from new toys or new environments
- Is initially quiet with new people
- Is a picky eater
- Toilet trained late
- Is reluctant to stray far from parents or caretakers
- Prefers to wear old, comfortable clothes
- Has unusual fears or frequent anxious dreams
- Has sensitive skin or allergies
- Is relaxed around people he sees frequently
- Is overly sensitive to criticism
- Resists changes in routine
- Stands on the sidelines of play areas
- Shows interest in other children but is reluctant to join them

(continued)

If your child shows most of these behaviors, he's probably one of the 15 percent of children who have the inhibited temperament. If your child shows only a few of these behaviors, or only mildly, he's probably in the majority of people who feel inhibited at some times, but not always.

Once you've analyzed your child's behavior, consider your own temperamental reactions. Go through the list again and write down which responses you typically show now or showed when you were a child. Then compare your responses to your child's. Do you see a link?

SHYNESS UNDER THE SKIN

Although there is mixed evidence that the physical aspects of shyness are innate or inherited, any shy person will tell you there is solid evidence that there's a strong physiological factor in shyness. Whether people were born shy or not, any shy person can list a catalog of physical symptoms—blushing, trembling, tension, nervousness, sweating, panic. Under the skin, they're all highly aroused.

As with all physiological processes, we've got to ask why this arousal exists. The body is an extraordinarily efficient machine, and each part or process exists for a reason. If something serves no purpose, it's weeded out via evolution.

When the physical aspects of shyness are viewed through this evolutionary lens, their purpose becomes clear: The arousal alerts us to threats and forces us to become keenly aware of our surroundings. On a primitive level, this is known as the fight-or-flight instinct, and it protects us physically during times of stress. During our modern times, it's known as social anxiety or the physical component of shyness. The "flight" side of the equation can be thought of as inhibition or shyness, because it's an attempt to flee, hide, or avoid what's so threatening.

I recently spoke to a mother of a two-year-old boy, Adam, whose son seems to instinctively try to hide from threatening strangers. "Adam and I were visiting my husband at his office, and Adam jumped on a chair all by himself and was kind of squirming around," she told me. "Some people were walking past and stopped to talk near Adam. The people weren't engaging him at all; they were just standing near him. I could see Adam drop his head and get really still. He just kind of shut down. I said to my husband, 'He wants to be invisible.' And then when they left, I think he waited until he felt that it was all clear, and then he ran back to us. Sometimes when he is playing and has forgotten about other people, he'll suddenly notice them, get very still and very quiet, and then wait to see when it's safe and he can come back to us."

Adam's response is smart and highly instinctive. It's easy to imagine him in the jungle watching a group of lions wander nearby. He's alert to them and observes their actions intently. Because he's small and vulnerable, attacking them is probably not a great strategy. But standing still and not calling attention to himself is smart, safe, and allows the situation to pass without provoking these potential predators.

The Body's Response to Threats

The fight-or-flight instinct kicks in when we sense that something's amiss. It could be triggered by a physical threat as obvious as the roar of a lion in the jungle, or as subtle as a change in the vibration in the ground. Once a person is alert to the threat, his brain will send warning messages to nearly every part of his body, affecting everything from hormone levels to brain functioning. The body reacts efficiently and economically, sending energy to the parts that need it (our legs, say, if we need to run) and diverting it from the parts that don't require it (such as our salivary glands, which shut down and create a dry mouth when we're nervous). As you can see, the stress reactions that are produced vary from automatic responses, such as dilated pupils, to less automatic responses, such as deciding whether to flee or fight.

Some typical stress reactions include:

- Clammy hands
- Blushing
- Trembling
- A tight jaw
- A high-pitched voice
- Dilated pupils
- Butterflies in the stomach
- Dry mouth
- Pounding heart
- Shallow but rapid breathing
- Awkward movements
- Jumpiness

These reactions may feel terrible, but they're lifesavers. They boost our arousal in the short term so we're literally on our toes and can act in response to the danger in our midst. And the two ways we can act are to fight, or approach and attack the dangerous element, or to flee, or avoid and run from what's so threatening.

The Brain's Role in the Fight-or-Flight Instinct

Although the entire body is activated when we detect a threat, three parts of the brain stand out as being particularly crucial to the creation of the fight-or-flight instinct, stress reactions, and the "shy body." A simple anatomy lesson will reveal what's going on in these three areas—the hippocampus, amygdala, and the higher brain—and whether shy people are wired differently at birth.

Just above the brain stem in the nape of the neck is the midbrain, where the limbic system is located. This group of structures governs somewhat reflexive or automatic processes, and it's involved in the fight-or-flight instinct because it picks up on threats in the environment, releases hormones, and adds and retrieves memories and emotions.

While all parts of the limbic system are involved in the creation of stress reactions and shyness, two parts, the hippocampus and the amygdala, play critical roles.

The hippocampus is the brain's database; it retrieves, stores, and adds memories. Whenever we do something in the present moment, the hippocampus matches our current experiences with our past experiences and provides a sense of continuity and familiarity. Whenever you reach for an apple, for example, you do so because the hippocampus has memories of you eating apples when you were hungry. But the current and stored experiences don't have to match perfectly—the hippocampus will link specific information with contextual information, like how you felt while eating apples in the past or how this particular apple differs from other apples you've eaten. If you've eaten bad, sour, or rotten apples in the past, this will affect how you feel about eating the apple in the present.

The hippocampus also adds current experiences to its databank, so memories and experiences are constantly growing and reinforcing each other. Thanks to the hippocampus, the past is linked to the present and both are used in the future. If the hippocampus isn't working properly, this link won't occur, and experiences will seem new, even if they've been performed before.

SHYNESS TRIGGERS

COPING WITH COMPANY

Many parents tell me that they're embarrassed by their child's bashful behavior when company comes over. The child, usually a toddler, runs and hides, clings to Mom or Dad, refuses to look at the visitor, or starts crying if the visitor rushes in too close, too soon. Oftentimes, the visitor has children too, and the crowd only compounds the shy toddler's discomfort.

You don't need to suffer with your child's tears or your own embarrassment. Your child is merely highly reactive (and tearful) or slow to warm up (and withdrawn). Both are natural reactions to new people. Here's what you can do to help your child gradually come to enjoy those times when company comes to visit:

- Let the child react. This is her initial response and a natural response.

- Don't draw attention to her. This only makes her more uncomfortable.

To explore how the hippocampus operates, let's go back to Adam's experience in his dad's office. Since he's young, he doesn't have many events or social experiences stored in his hippocampus, so he may not be linking the present visit to the past because he doesn't have much of a past. Therefore his situation is new and can be perceived as being threatening. In addition, he could have had a bad time with either of these specific people, or people much like them, and he's making that negative connection. Or, lastly, he could have a specially configured hippocampus that doesn't retrieve many memories, even in familiar situations, and makes Adam feel that every experience is new. While this is still speculation, it's something to consider.

- Don't rush. Give her time to see that you're safe and she's safe.

- Demonstrate that all is well. Talk to your visitor and play with the children.

- Invite your child into the action. This may simply be to wave goodbye, but let her know she can come out of hiding when she wants.

- Talk about it later. Give her an extra hug and tell her you were proud of her.

- Try it again. Invite company over often and your child will get used to having new people in your home.

If your child doesn't come out of hiding during the visit, don't give up. Talk about how nice your visitors were and prepare her for further visits. Perhaps you can read a book about a similar situation or act out one when you're playing. Eventually, she will get used to sharing her space with company and even enjoy herself, too.

In addition to the hippocampus, its neighbor in the limbic system, the amygdala, plays an important role in the creation of inhibited behavior. I think of the amygdala as being the switchboard in the brain because it picks up on information and makes the decision that's so critical to shyness—the decision to fight (or approach) or to flee (or withdraw). It does so by taking the information about the past from the hippocampus and then deciding if this information poses a current threat. If the information is threatening, then the amygdala sends a signal so that stress reactions can begin. It also sends another signal that tells the body to flee from the threat or fight its way through it.

While we don't have a totally clear picture of how the amygdala operates in shy humans, we do know much about how it operates in inhibited animals. According to the University of Newfoundland's Robert Adamec, Ph.D., the amygdalas in inhibited cats send more signals to crouch or cower and fewer signals that create aggressive, attacking behavior. If this is true for inhibited humans as well, the amygdala will send more signals to withdraw from or avoid threatening social situations than to approach and confront them.

Dr. Kagan analyzed the size of the amygdala in a variety of animals and found that the portion involved in withdrawing behavior is more pronounced in highly evolved animals than it is in more primitive animals such as rats. This is only logical, because highly evolved animals—humans included—cannot blindly strike out when they're threatened. Like Adam at his dad's office, holding back and observing the action is a more sophisticated, enlightened route to take, even if it does seem anti-social.

In addition to the hippocampus and the amygdala in the limbic system, the higher brain is also intimately involved in creating the physical roots of shyness. This area of the brain is the most sophisticated, complex part of the brain, the part that makes us human. And, therefore, only humans can do what the higher brain governs—things like speaking, thinking, analyzing, interpreting, and planning.

Studies that focus on this portion of the brain have found no differences between the higher brains of extroverted people and shy people. While some differences may be found in the more primitive, more instinctual portions such as the limbic system, the most sophisticated parts of the brain are not "shy." Therefore, all of the higher brain's functions—including speaking, thinking, analyzing, interpreting, and planning—can be performed without the influence of shyness. And, what's more, this part of the brain can be used to make decisions that will lessen the negative effects of shyness, providing the path out of shyness and inhibition.

Now, young children are just developing the complex processes that the higher brain performs. Young kids can't analyze behavior and plan new strategies, because they haven't developed those functions yet. But young children can use their higher brain to interpret their physical arousal to mean "There's something wrong with me" or "I feel bad so I must not belong here."

In contrast, a parent can use her higher brain to make better decisions, interpretations, and strategies. And it's up to parents, teachers, and other concerned adults to help young children understand their physical sensations and act properly in social settings. In doing so, you're acting as their higher brain for a while. In the rest of the chapter, I'll explain how this can be done.

Successfully Shy Journal

Turn back to the list of stress reactions I provided on page 94.

- Which of these reactions does your child typically experience?

- For each one, what are some strategies you could take to lessen the discomfort created by the reaction? For example, if your child has a dry mouth during difficult social encounters, you could plan to keep a bottle of water handy so that she can take a few sips when she needs to.

By creating these strategies, you're using your fully developed, adult higher brain to resolve your child's instinctive reactions to

(continued)

stress. If your shy child is young, you'll have to intervene and lessen her arousal. If your shy child is older, explain to her how she can use these strategies on her own. Eventually, your child will be less bothered by her reactions, and more likely to make smart decisions and feel comfortable when she's connecting with other people.

Our Modern Instincts

The fight-or-flight instinct seems appropriate for our dangerous encounters in the pre-historic jungle. Yet even though we've evolved into more sophisticated modern beings, this instinct is still operating now, in less physically threatening encounters. Accordingly, it's set in motion during modern, subtle, psychological threats—threats to self-esteem, threats to our place in the social universe.

The modern "shyness instinct" is much like the ancient fight-or-flight instinct, but it is set into motion by a psychological process known as "evaluation apprehension," which is the arousal that's produced when we feel that we're being judged. This potential evaluation is threatening, so the body produces more arousal—more stress reactions—so that we're a little sharper and can perform at our peak. It also produces more intense self-consciousness, so we mostly focus on our selves and our discomfort. Think of the jitters you get before making a presentation at work, and you're thinking of evaluation apprehension. While it feels uncomfortable, it just shows that you care about impressing people with your performance.

Just as the shyness instinct is triggered by a modern-day threat, coping with it has evolved beyond fighting or fleeing. You can't lunge at a stranger to stop the evaluation, nor can you run and hide in the bushes, either. Instead, you must find socially acceptable ways to handle the threat. You can do so by approaching the threat and using social skills until you've been accepted by the stranger. Or you can fall back on the modern-day equivalent to fleeing— clamming up and withdrawing. You aren't being rude, but you aren't impressing anyone, either.

THE DOMINANT RESPONSE OF SHY PEOPLE

The fight or flight instinct has two responses: approaching or avoiding. When one response is used over and over again, it becomes easy—so easy that it seems almost instinctive or impulsive and doesn't require thought. But the response isn't instinctive; it's merely a dominant response, the easiest response at hand.

Some people's dominant response to social threats is to approach them. These people are thought to be assertive, sociable, outgoing, or even aggressive. Other people have a different dominant response to threats and avoid them over and over again. These people are thought to be introverted or passive and take no interest in other people.

Still other people want to approach because they're interested in reaching out and making connections. But because of their intense stress reactions, they feel physically uncomfortable and try to avoid the threat at the same time. This sets up a conflict between the head and the heart, curiosity and fear.

When a person's dominant response to a threat is to become embroiled in a tough internal conflict about whether to approach or avoid it, the person is shy. As we've already discussed in chapter 2, I believe this approach/avoidance conflict is the first step in the shy process. It then leads to a slower warming-up period during stressful social situations and a narrower comfort zone made up of non-threatening people, places, and activities.

The next time your shy child seems stuck between approach and avoidance, use his warm-up time to help him assess the pros and cons of each response. For example, perhaps you and your child are at the playground, and he is having a difficult time deciding whether or not to join a bunch of kids who are playing on the jungle gym, screaming, sliding down the slide, and swinging amid the bars and hoops.

Use the situation to help your child express some of his fears about approaching the new kids. Perhaps he's afraid they might be too rough and rowdy, or he might get hurt or rejected. Then help him see what the benefits might be of joining in. For example, you could point out that the playground equipment is more fun when you're playing with other children, and that he could consider the experience an adventure. When your child seems ready, start moving closer to the action ("Would you like to get in line for the slide?"). In this way, you're helping your child change his dominant response—a topic I'll delve into in greater detail in the next section.

Changing the Dominant Response

As we discussed, all people get aroused during stressful evaluative social situations. Further, shy people are not the ones who want to constantly avoid social situations—they're interested in new people and places, but they get stuck in their internal conflict and can't act on their interest. This conflict is at the heart of the pain that shy people tell me about. They want something but always feel that it's out of reach.

But I've found that what ails shy people also cures them. Shy people need to strengthen their instinct to approach. In time, this will turn into their dominant response, and they'll be free of their conflict and their distressing stress reactions.

There's no one right way to change the dominant response. What's needed is a number of small, incremental, gradual changes that give a child the opportunity to get used to new social situations. Doing this when your child is young is so much easier than trying to change an adult's behavior, which seems to be almost hard wired from years of experience.

With each social success, the dominant response shifts at a very deep level. The hippocampus stores positive memories that will be retrieved in the future. The amygdala's approach signal gets stronger from frequent use. And your child's rapidly developing higher brain decides to give people a chance instead of feeling intimidated and evaluated. Eventually, your child's tearful, inhibited behavior will become a dim memory, not a barrier to friendships and healthy self-acceptance.

Your role as a parent is to help your child approach other people, before her inhibited behavior snowballs and becomes full-blown adult shyness. Each step in this direction is meaningful and sends a message to your child that the company of other people is to be enjoyed, not feared.

To do so, you must analyze your own dominant response to your child's inhibited behavior. Do you rush in and rescue your child when he looks uncomfortable? Do you reward him with extra hugs and kisses when he sticks close to your side? Do you excuse your child from awkward encounters? If so, your dominant response may be to protect your child from discomfort and frustration. While this may be an effective short-term solution—your child feels better immediately, after all—this strategy will work against you and your child in the long run. Unless, of course, you plan on sticking by your child's side throughout his entire life.

A common strategy to try to ease a child's inhibition is to give him medication that will reduce his arousal. For about 10 percent of people who are intensely shy, this may be the answer. Many anti-anxiety medications, some of which are prescribed for children, try to soothe the amygdala by modifying the chemicals responsible for producing the experience of unpleasantness. The amygdala then picks up on less discomfort and perceives fewer threats in the environment. Because there are fewer threats, the individual feels more comfortable and less anxious and is able to be relaxed in social settings. In addition, the current pleasant experiences become stored in the hippocampus as pleasant memories, which are then retrieved during future social encounters.

But anti-anxiety medication is not the only way to reduce anxiety, and it can interfere with an individual's sense of control and feelings of success. While the medication may make current encounters easier because the individual is less aroused, that person's body may begin to tolerate the current dosage of medication and may need ever-increasing doses to feel the same. What's more, the individual may attribute his social success to the drugs and will be in danger of overlooking his role in creating positive social encounters.

I believe that positive social experiences can be created without medication, and parents have a duty to guide and teach their children to conquer their discomfort, even if that discomfort seems hard-wired or pre-destined. Parents must guide their children through difficult encounters by helping them to tolerate discomfort and frustration, develop strategies to solve problems, and recall past successes in similar situations. Without these lessons, no child will become successfully shy, even on medication.

Bringing It All Together Again

Recently I was told a story about how one temperamentally inhibited girl learned to tame her physical discomfort, and it's a great illustration of how a parent's intervention early in life can prevent the same struggles later in life.

Three-year-old Kayla shows many of the signs of being a temperamentally inhibited child. Kayla is a warm, loving, expressive child when she's with her parents, but oftentimes when she's in a group of people, she clams up and sticks close to her parents. She prefers to eat the same foods everyday and wear the same clothes over and over again. When she started going to day care, she held back a bit and didn't join in the games. But after about two weeks, she was able to participate in all of the activities and make a few friends, some of whom she plays with on weekends. Kayla's behavior reminded her mom, Nancy, of herself when she was a child.

While Kayla eventually incorporated her day care arrangement into her comfort zone, occasionally she'd get thrown off when a new, unfamiliar element was added. Recently, her group went to visit the antique carousel across town. Since it sounded like a fun day, Nancy went along with the group.

Nancy noticed that Kayla was a bit apprehensive on the drive to the carousel, so Nancy did what she usually does when her daughter stiffens up. She explained where they were going and what they could expect there—lots of noise, gaudy mechanical horses, a larger group of children, and a few more adults. Kayla listened but stayed silent.

When they arrived, Kayla stuck close to her mom and interacted with only a few of the children from her group. When they approached the carousel, Kayla's eyes got big and round and she stopped dead in her tracks. Nancy reminded Kayla about what they talked about in the car. When Kayla didn't look any more re-laxed, Nancy suggested they ride the carousel together. Kayla agreed, and the two hopped on. The loud music clanked and the carousel went around and around, and Nancy pointed out all of the sights and sounds. Kayla held on tightly but took a keen interest in everything that was going on. While her classmates were disap-pointed when the ride ended, Kayla seemed relieved. She relaxed a bit during the ride home, and by the time she ate dinner, she was back to her chatty self again. She even told her father about her ad-venture, and Nancy agreed that Kayla was very brave to get up on that big mechanical horse.

Knowing that Kayla takes her time when warming up to new activities and people, Nancy told Kayla that they would go back to the carousel, but this time, just the three of them. Kayla said she'd go and talked about what she'd do when she got to the park.

Kayla made good on her promises, because the second trip went much more smoothly. Nancy pointed out all of the familiar things at the park, like the cotton candy stand and the various ticket-takers, and Kayla remembered everything and gave her ticket to the attendant. She took her first trip on the carousel with her dad, but on her second trip, she rode by herself and smiled for the photos that Nancy took. After they left, Kayla couldn't stop talking about the carousel, and now constantly begs her parents to take her back.

Nancy's Smart Strategies

I'm always pleased to hear stories like Kayla's, because although Kayla requires a little more patience and guidance, she's able to conquer her fears and tame her physical arousal with the help of her mother. Here's how Nancy and Kayla worked together:

- Nancy was aware of Kayla's temperamental requirements in new environments. Just as she did when she was getting used to day care, Kayla needed additional time to warm up and acclimate.

- Nancy noticed when Kayla seemed stressed out. She eased Kayla into the new situation so Kayla wasn't forced to combat her body and the social environment at the same time.

- Nancy prepared Kayla for the new event. The talk in the car helped Kayla anticipate what she'd encounter at the park.

- Nancy didn't judge Kayla. Her daughter was merely acting naturally, so there was no need to punish or berate her for feeling a bit bashful and inhibited.

- Nancy stuck with Kayla and didn't excuse her from the activity. Kayla's positive experience helped her build up her capacity to tolerate frustration.

- Nancy praised Kayla for her bravery. This positive reinforcement created positive memories of approaching, not avoiding.

- Nancy encouraged Kayla to give the new event another try. Since repetition makes the unfamiliar familiar, Kayla's second trip to the carousel went more smoothly.

- Nancy gradually increased the challenge. Because Kayla seemed interested in the carousel, Nancy asked her to ride on it by herself, and she did.

Nancy was encouraged by Kayla's progress, and I'm encouraged by Nancy's ability to widen Kayla's comfort zone and create positive experiences in a sometimes-scary world. And because Nancy and Kayla began working out these temperamental glitches early in life, Kayla is likely to not feel any significant restrictions because of her physiological makeup. Because she was able to conquer day care, new foods, and bold new activities like riding a carousel at age three, she'll almost certainly feel that she's a successfully shy child.

What's more, Nancy and Kayla are establishing a relationship that's built on unconditional love. Nancy accepts Kayla for who she is, so Kayla can be honest about her fears and concerns. Nancy's supportive but indirect parenting style gives Kayla just enough responsibility so that she can feel that she's earned her successes. And this foundation will most likely remain solid and steady as Kayla's world expands and becomes more complicated.

What You Can Do

In addition to the tips illustrated in Nancy and Kayla's example, here are a few more suggestions for alleviating your inhibited child's physical discomfort:

Relabel emotions. While butterflies in the stomach can indicate fear, they can also indicate excitement.

Make new activities fun. Instead of schlepping your child around town, make your day out an adventure by finding interesting and unique aspects that will capture your child's imagination.

Relax your child. Rough-and-tumble play such as playing "horsey" or making noise may relax him physically so that he can shake off his stress reactions.

Remember that your child's dominant response is not her only response. Although your temperamentally inhibited child may typically withdraw from new things, your child is also capable of approaching them as well.

Notice background noise and the potential for overstimulation. If your child can't relax because of too many environmental distractions, turn down the volume or move to a calmer setting.

Start now, no matter what your child's age. The sooner you begin building positive experiences and memories, the better.

Respect your child's warming-up period. If you are a quickly adapting adult, or if you have other children who adapt quickly, remember that the warming-up period can vary. You may be rushing your child when he needs to slow down.

Continue introducing your child to new people and activities. Each experience adds to a well-rounded child and a higher, more robust quality of life. Every child will get used to new challenges if they continue coming.

Be proud of your child. Your child can only disappoint you if you set the bar too high. Notice your child's strengths and he'll overcome his weaknesses.

Now that you have a better understanding of how your child generally feels under the skin, and how the "shy process" affects his encounters during difficult situations, we'll move on to apply these basic ideas to the situations that shy people have identified as being the most critical to their childhood happiness. These situations range from coping with family relationships to creating friendships to participating in classroom discussions. After analyzing these situations, I'll provide you with lots of strategies to help you help your child break through his bashfulness and become successfully shy.

CHAPTER 6

THE FAMILY
INFLUENCE

W hile the inherited or physiological influence on shy children is fascinating—and perhaps will never be fully understood—I've found that most shy adults don't believe that it was the most critical factor in creating their childhood shyness. In fact, according to original research I've conducted, more shy adults (who, by the way, are the real experts on their condition) think that their early environment had a more profound effect on their inhibitions and lack of sociability than did any genetic influence. These shyness experts cite influences such as how their parents cared for them; their relationships with their siblings and other relatives; their contact with friends and extended family members; and general, almost hidden messages their parents sent about their expectations—messages about the child's worth and abilities, messages about the value of friendships, and messages about the wide world that exists outside of the home.

What my research says to me is that there's hope for children struggling with shyness: If the family environment plays a part in nurturing shyness, it can also play a part in nurturing a shyness breakthrough.

Consider the following comments from just a few of the thousands of shy adults who have contacted me:

"I'm a middle child and often felt like my parents didn't listen to me and were too busy worrying about my brother and sister," said a Web designer. "If they didn't listen to me, I felt nobody else would want to, either. Following my older sister through school also contributed to my shyness. She was an exceptional student, while I'm merely an above-average student."

In another letter, a current high school student confessed that she feels lonely without the support of siblings. "I think that being an only child has contributed to my shyness. Since I am the only child, my mother tends to be a little overprotective. She probably didn't force me to speak up for myself that much when I was younger."

It's true that close siblings can sometimes help a shy child come out of her shell, which was the case with a veterinary student who wrote to me. "I was very shy as a kid—shy and extremely neurotic," the student explained. "Every situation scared me if it required my interacting with others. Luckily, I had my twin sister with me a lot of the time and we fed off each other in order to make it through any interaction."

In this chapter, we'll hear numerous reflections from other shy adults and look at the many fascinating and complicated family issues that can contribute to—or, more important, lessen—a child's shyness. In addition, we'll examine one of the most common observations of parents of shy children—that their withdrawing, timid child in public is an outgoing, rambunctious child at home. The explanation for this behavior is far more simple than you may believe.

USE YOUR POWER WISELY

Although many shy adults blame their parents or sisters and brothers for "creating" their own shyness, I don't think that parents should place the full burden on themselves for their child's shyness. After all, parenting is the most difficult and complicated job there is, and I'm sure that you're doing the best you can. But I want you to understand that you have all of the power and all of the resources you need to develop a close, loving relationship with your child that's free of guilt, blame, and miscommunication. If you use your parental power wisely, you will be able to help your child become more confident socially and enhance his general well-being.

To help you understand your parental power, you'll need to think of your family as a "living social laboratory" that's full of elements that include your parenting skills, your hopes and fears for your children, your shy child's current and potential social skills, and your relationship with your child. These elements combine to create a constantly evolving family unit as well as constantly evolving family members.

In the living laboratory of your home, you and your children can experiment with new behaviors and take a few risks that you wouldn't normally take outside of this safe environment. Then, when you're ready, you can transfer what you've learned to the outside world and help your child become successfully shy. Feel free to mix, measure, and adjust according to your shy child's unique needs.

Successfully Shy Journal

In chapter 4, you began to explore your personal experiences with shyness both as an adult and a child. Now it's time to take an even more in-depth look at your childhood experiences, current parental expectations, parenting skills, and family environment. Once you've taken this grand tour of your family's social universe, you'll have a better understanding of how your family influences your child's shyness as well as how you can be a better parent to your shy son or daughter by creating a safe, compassionate home environment.

In your Successfully Shy Journal, reflect on your own childhood. It doesn't matter if you were a shy child or not because your current parenting skills will benefit from hindsight and analysis. Please answer the following questions:

- Was your home life as a child unpredictable and full of conflict, or was it orderly and predictable?

- Did you get as much attention as your siblings?

- Did you feel you could talk to your parents and actually be heard?

- Were your parents aware of your troubles as well as your triumphs? Did you feel safe and loved?

- How did your parents show that they cared about you?

- Did you socialize with other families or relatives?

Whether you were a shy child or not, you can benefit from looking at the past, because the past is the best predictor of the present and future. Many adults who were shy in their early years tell me that they had difficulty feeling that they were loved, heard, and properly nurtured by their parents. Many feel

(continued)

they had been emotionally abandoned, left to fend for themselves in a world that seemed harsh and cruel. They also feel that they lacked opportunities to become socially active, creating a closed loop of interactions among family members. Now, as adults, they vow to nurture their children differently. I wish them well, but I hope that they don't try so hard to raise outgoing children that they overlook the many wonderful qualities possessed by a shy child. Throughout this chapter, I'll show how you can strike a balance between encouragement and protection.

If you were not a shy child, you may not understand the powerful role you play in your child's life. You may not realize that many of your actions—some of which have nothing to do with social skills and communication—affect your shy child. I don't say this to blame you; rather, my goal is to make you more aware of the influence you have on your child. As you read this chapter, you'll learn more about your power and how you can use it wisely.

Your Family Is Your Child's First Comfort Zone

It's easy to see how a shy individual can point to their family as the main cause of their shyness. Children learn their social skills within the family as their parents, siblings, aunts, uncles, cousins, grandmas, and grandpas are their first friends and make up their first social universe. The family teaches each child—shy or not—social skills and life skills that will affect his general self-esteem and his self-regard as a social creature.

Naomi, a stay-at-home mom of two-year-old Maxwell, explained that, like most shy kids, Maxwell changes when he's in unfamiliar terrain. "When Maxwell is with me or my husband, he's just fine. But when we're with adults, or people he's not familiar with, he's uncomfortable. He'll get really close to me, or grab my leg, or bury his head in my shoulder.

"He's never the kid who will approach other kids. He needs to be drawn out. This happens even when he's with family members he has known since he was born, but who he doesn't see very often."

Naomi claims that she could tell that Maxwell would be shy at a very early age. "I first noticed that he may be shy when he was about 6 to 9 months, when he was at the age when he could tell who was holding him. When he knew that it wasn't my husband or me, Maxwell got really uncomfortable. This became more pronounced as he got older. When he was with people he didn't know well he got thrown off."

Although little Maxwell was born into a large, loving extended family, he has spent much of his brief life alone, with his mom. "We were a one-car family for a long time, so when my husband was at work, I couldn't go out much during the day. My son and I spent a lot of time alone, together, especially during the long winter months here in Minneapolis. We didn't have him in a play group, and he didn't get to spend much time with many other kids."

When Naomi and Maxwell go out, she tends to gauge his feelings so as not to overwhelm her slow-to-warm-up child. "If he wants me to hold him, I will, but I'll try to carry on with my business and not make him the focus of attention," she told me. "I'll let him feel his way out, and when he's more comfortable, he'll stop clinging. I don't force him to separate from me or focus on him. I know from being a shy child myself that calling more attention to his behavior just makes it worse. It's painful enough without everyone commenting on it."

I asked her if she thinks that Maxwell inherited his shyness from her. "I do think that we take on characteristics of our parents, so it wouldn't surprise me if he picked up on my cues," she said. "I'm not a loud person and I don't like a lot of commotion, so he's not exposed to that. But my husband is a drummer, and he's definitely not shy. And when we're at home, Maxwell is very gregarious and happy. He's just a normal little kid when it's just the three of us."

EVALUATING YOUR CHILD'S COMFORT ZONE

Naomi's observations of and experiences with Maxwell are common. Many children are outspoken at home and then completely change their ways in public by clinging to their parent and preferring to stay close to whom and what are safe and familiar.

Common, too, is Naomi's interpretation of the infant Maxwell's crankiness when someone other than her or her husband held him. While Naomi believes that this irritability foreshadowed Maxwell's shyness, I think that it was more likely due to a normal process of psychological development. Stranger anxiety, which occurs at about 7 to 10 months, happens when an unfamiliar person is around the child while the parent is present. Separation anxiety, which can occur between 6 to 18 months, rears up when the child is separated from his or her parent and is left alone with an unfamiliar person.

While Maxwell's behavior seems to look like shyness, it shouldn't automatically be labeled as such. Rather, it should be interpreted as a normal reaction to what's out of his current comfort zone. Being in his comfort zone allows Maxwell to be able to predict what's going to happen, and therefore feel safe and comfortable. Stretching—or abruptly breaking through—the comfort zone, without preparation or support, can make any child feel vulnerable and shy.

For a typical young child, the comfort zone includes:

- Familiar people, such as Mom, Dad, siblings, perhaps some extended family members (but not always), and other caretakers or friends

- Familiar places, such as the home, the car, and frequently visited areas such as the grocery store, the park, the day care center, and friends' homes

- Familiar activities, such as playing with her toys at home, playing at the playground, eating preferred food, and watching her favorite videos

When a child is abruptly taken out of her comfort zone, such as on the first day of kindergarten, her first reaction, like Maxwell's, may be to cling tightly and withdraw until the situation feels safer. When your child reacts in this way, it's a sign that her comfort zone is being stretched too quickly, and you'll need to give your child some time to allow her to warm up at her own pace.

Naomi related an interesting story about Maxwell's comfort zone. "Sometimes it feels like we have our own little world together, but sometimes when that world is invaded, he becomes shy," she explained. "Like when we're at the grocery store, he'll indicate to me that he wants to give the cashier my debit card. But when we get to that point, he won't give up the card. He can't bear to give that up. But I also noticed that in the past 6 to 8 weeks, he has started to come out of his shell a little. When he's with other kids he seems to be okay, but adults still seem to be a problem."

Taking the understanding of the comfort zone we discussed in chapter 2, let's separate Maxwell's "little world" into its three components:

- Familiar people: Naomi and her husband, other familiar children

- Familiar activities: Talking to and playing with Naomi and her husband, shopping for groceries

- Familiar places: Home, the grocery store

Notice that Maxwell's current comfort zone does not include handing the debit card to the cashier and being his normal endearing self around unfamiliar adults. However, Naomi can encourage Maxwell's growing independence by repeating his budding overtures to the cashier and making sure that he's exposed to friendly adults, like his grandparents or a neighbor.

Let's look at Maxwell's desire to hand Naomi's debit card to the grocery cashier. He told his mom that he wanted to do it, but when it came time to deliver, he withdrew. Naomi doesn't need to worry about his suddenly bashful actions. She needs to encourage his social interest and explain, step by step, what he should do.

She already has a head start because Maxwell wants to hand over the card. The next time she goes to the grocery store, she can ask him if he wants to give the card to the cashier. They can practice in the safety of the car. When they get into the store, she can ask him to hold the debit card so that he'll feel that it's his, that it's part of his comfort zone.

Before they get to the register, she should ask him to hand her the card, just like he'll hand the cashier the card. Then, she should praise him if he does well, or give him tips if he gets stuck. When it comes time to deliver, she should encourage him and support him if he needs it. Then, if he does well, she should praise him for a job well done. If he still resists, she should hold his hand while handing over the card, so that he doesn't have to do it alone but is still expanding his comfort zone. Later, she should talk over what happened and continue repeating his social gestures.

EXPECTATIONS WITHIN THE COMFORT ZONE

Part of what makes the comfort zone so comforting is its aura of familiarity and predictability. Each day, Maxwell pretty much knows what to expect and how to handle every challenge he encounters. In Maxwell's cozy world, he can count on lots of playtime with his mom and dad that depends on his preferences and mood. He can also count on scheduled meals and a bedtime routine, sympathy when he's hurt or scared, and lots of laughter during the good times. If he feels a bit bewildered by a new experience, he knows he can rely on his mom or dad to walk him through it.

It's easy to see why Maxwell, or any child for that matter, would be reluctant to break out of this familiar terrain and explore new territory. However, exploration is a normal, necessary part of childhood, and with it comes some tolerance of risk and frustration. What's more, as Maxwell gets older, his parents, friends, and society will expect him to continue stretching his comfort zone and become confident in a variety of new situations.

Even within the predictable comfort zone of home and family, however, parents like you and Naomi can do much to foster a child's social confidence. You can do this by encouraging a feeling of what's known in psychological circles as "expectation of reci-

SIBLING DYNAMICS

There are many theories about siblings and shy kids, but I believe the topic is too complex and varied to talk about with any degree of certainty. Shy kids can be the first-born or the baby of the family, the inseparable twin or the family loner. One thing I can say with certainty is that siblings are kids' first friends, and how they interact can have a profound impact on their other relationships. The following tips can help you foster friendship between your shy child and your other children:

- Don't compare them. If your shy child hears that he must be more like his extroverted brother, he'll feel less loved by you.

- Don't overprotect your shy child. If you do, your child will learn to use shyness as an excuse to get out of what's difficult.

procity," which is just some jargon for a twist on the Golden Rule: *If you treat others well, they will treat you well.*

Following this line of logic, expectation of reciprocity—or trust—suggests that when a child is polite and respectful, strangers will be polite and respectful; if strangers are polite and respectful, the child will have social successes and will build social confidence, develop a sense of control, and feel that there's some continuity and predictability in his social life.

On the other hand, if he anticipates that others will treat him unkindly or think poorly of him, he will not be confident of his ability to handle intimidating people and social situations. In time, he may withdraw into shyness as his social skills atrophy

- Don't rescue, but do intervene in disputes. Teach your kids how to negotiate, share, make good on promises, and treat each other nicely.

- Don't overlook your shy child. Shy kids are often the forgotten "good kids" in a family focused on a child with special behavioral or health issues. Reserve time for the shy one, and notice his good behavior.

- Be mindful of outside friendships. Do your kids' friends treat your family members well, or do they cause more problems? Notice who's in the house and how they behave.

Lastly, teach your children how to play well together and value each other as friends. They may not appreciate each other now, but in time, they'll stick together through thick and thin and weather every crisis. That's the best friend a shy kid can have—a true one.

and shrink. Therefore, I believe that children who know how to be kind will expect to be treated kindly and can become successfully shy.

Strategies for Building Expectation of Reciprocity

Children are less likely to become shy if they have a healthy level of "expectation of reciprocity" and feel that they can predict and have some control over what will happen to them in social settings. The best way that you as a parent can encourage this feeling is by building a safe, predictable home environment your child can use as his base before venturing out into the world. Here are a few basic strategies for building a stable family structure:

Have a routine. Children do best when they have a routine, especially in the morning and at bedtime. Be flexible when necessary, but make sure your child has structured time and regular activities.

Create a network of supportive people. Even if you don't have a large extended family to watch out for your child, many neighbors and friends will want to be involved in your child's life. Be sure to give them that opportunity.

Live out your expectations. If you talk to your child and treat her with respect, you'll develop a more honest, intimate relationship.

Match your words with your actions. Many shy adults claim that, as children, they couldn't predict which behavior would be rewarded and which would be punished by their parents. If you promise to do something, deliver on it.

Set a standard for behavior. As your child grows, so should her ability to master new behaviors. Continue teaching your child new skills and praise her when she does well.

Lessen the chaos in your home. Does the phone interrupt dinner nearly every night? Are you constantly arguing with your spouse? Clear the environmental clutter so your child feels safe and secure.

Start now. If your child can turn to you now, he'll be more likely to turn to you when he's older—and when his troubles become more serious.

Be kind. Your child loves you unconditionally, so be gentle with his feelings. Your loving example, even when you've had a bad day, will serve him well.

Stay involved. I can't say it enough: Your child needs your attention. After all, if you aren't involved, your child will fill that vacuum with someone you may not approve of.

Successfully Shy Journal

Now that you have more insight into how your general family environment affects your child's social behavior, take a moment to think about a typical week in your home. Then, in your Successfully Shy Journal, answer the following questions:

- What is predictable in your home? Think specifically about the people, routines, and activities that are a normal part of life in your home.

- What is unpredictable or inconsistent in your home?

- What strategies could you use to turn the unpredictable elements into more predictable ones?

- Finally, write down at least two instances where your expectations of reciprocity failed you. How may these instances have contributed to your own shyness?

Your answers should indicate what your child can rely on and what isn't so reliable, but could or should be. These factors, when stable, can help your child feel that life is predictable and follows some sort of order. This feeling will help him feel secure within his comfort zone—secure enough to stretch it with other people.

For example, perhaps you've set up a schedule for doing his homework together, but you don't always adhere to it. What this teaches him—rightly or wrongly—is that you aren't always around when he needs help, and he can't predict when you will be available. In the future, he may refrain from asking you for advice because your pattern of communication isn't stable. But, if you demonstrate that you can be trusted, he'll learn to trust you in the future with his secrets and vulnerabilities, and that's a wonderful gift you can give your shy child.

Your Expectations for Your Child

Just as your child should expect people to be friendly and kind, you have expectations about your child. Although it may be difficult to admit it, you have had hopes and dreams for your child since the day he was born. Some of these expectations are lighthearted—"I hope my daughter has my looks and my wife's brains" or "I hope he doesn't inherit my dancing skills!"—but some parental expectations are more subtle and unstated, such as "I hope my daughter will stand up for herself" or "I hope my son isn't a wimp" or "I hope my children have lots of friends."

Many of these expectations are tied to a parent's temperament or personality type. For example, outgoing parents naturally lean toward participating in more social activities, and therefore may feel most in synch with their extroverted children. Quieter parents, who prefer a less stimulating lifestyle, may be baffled and challenged by these same outgoing kids.

But parents don't always hope their children will share their temperament type. For example, some outgoing parents would be delighted to have more timid, quiet kids who don't demand so much energy. And some shy parents, remembering the difficulties of their own shy childhoods, would be relieved to have children who don't stumble through social activities that once tripped them up. Some parents may also want their children to be quiet and obedient at home and outgoing and entertaining in public so that others see them at their "best."

As common and natural as it is to have expectations for your child, I do have some words of caution. First, realize that expectations equal conditional love. If you have unfair expectations about your child's social behavior, your child will get the message that you will love her only if she is outgoing, if she is brave, if she doesn't cling to your leg when you're out in public. And although you may prefer that she becomes more socially confident, don't dole out your praise, affection, or attention based on these preferences. This inconsistent love will work against your child's healthy development.

Expectations also place children into a role. Various roles may be the responsible one, the clown, the peacemaker, the good one, the bad one, the quiet one, or the troublemaker. These family roles often have long-lasting effects. Consider what one woman, a homemaker, told me:

"I was an obedient and quiet child. I was expected to be good, do the right thing, and do well in school. Praise was reserved for extraordinary or exceptional situations. Anger and sadness were discouraged. Fear and crying were signs of weakness and were not tolerated. I hid these emotions and wouldn't let anyone know how bad I really felt."

All too often, shy children like this homemaker are the "good ones" who never give their parents a bit of trouble. This is often in contrast to, and possibly in reaction to, a sibling who demands a lot of attention for their bad behavior. But your shy child's quiet demeanor doesn't mean that he's content. His silence may be hiding a lot of unhappiness, frustration, and loneliness. And if you do not expect your quiet child to be troubled, then you may not recognize those troubles until it is too late, when your child cannot confide in you about being bullied or teased, or cannot approach a teacher about not understanding a homework assignment.

Lastly, expectations often lead to frustration, and when you are frustrated with your child's shy behavior, you will force your child into sink-or-swim, do-it-yourself situations. This tough-love approach isn't healthy in the long run. It merely encourages your child to hide his fears instead of understanding them. It's much better to work with your child throughout difficult social situations so that he understands how to navigate them successfully.

Successfully Shy Journal

In your Successfully Shy Journal, write down what you may not care to admit—your expectations for your child. Now answer the following questions.

- Have your expectations for your child changed over time?
- Are your expectations for your child's behavior the same as your expectations for your own behavior?
- Did your parents have expectations for you? How did they communicate them? Did you play a certain role in your family, such as "the quiet one" or "the troublemaker"?
- How do you communicate and reinforce your expectations for your child?

It's natural to have expectations for your child, so I'd like you to work with and challenge them. Do you think your expectations are fair? Do they reflect what you truly want? For example, if you expect your child to be socially involved during her free time, are you willing to play a role in this shift? Will you happily shuttle her to her games, groups, friends' homes, and so on? Or do you assume that she can do this on her own? Are you more interested in impressing other parents with your child's thriving social life than encouraging your child to enjoy herself?

If you find that your expectations are valid and appropriate for your child, you can begin to develop strategies to help your child meet them, such as providing support for her budding social life. But if you find that your expectations are unfair—or more about you than your child—revise them before developing your plan.

WHAT YOU CAN DO TO HELP
YOUR CHILD BUILD SOCIAL SKILLS

In an ideal world, every child would be well prepared for every encounter in the world at large. Every child would have a healthy level of self-esteem and show a healthy level of interest in and curiosity about the people in their lives. But as we all know, we don't live in an ideal world, and each parent is challenged to raise healthy, happy, well-adjusted children who handle growing demands with ease and confidence.

Fortunately, you can increase your odds of raising a successfully shy child by expanding your parenting skills repertoire and exposing your child to a wide variety of social situations, communication styles, and behavioral standards. By doing so, you'll get your child comfortable with a variety of interactions within the safety of the family's natural comfort zone. Eventually, your child can transfer this knowledge to areas that are outside of his comfort zone—school, play dates with unfamiliar kids, or family reunions.

In the following section, I'll explain some specific parenting skills that will help you increase your child's social skills. While this isn't terribly tricky, and I don't encourage you to make radical personality changes, I will expect you to be constantly involved and persistent. Your child is picking up important signals from you, and if you send inconsistent messages, she'll become confused and second-guess her instincts. She won't know what to expect from you and, therefore, won't know what to expect from people she doesn't know as well. Remember that the expectation of reciprocity is powerful.

Prepare and Practice

The first and probably most important parenting skill is to prepare your child for new encounters, explain how to manage them, and practice them at home before heading out into public. After all, you know the ropes and can navigate a variety of social experiences, so you can show your child how it's done. And when you do so in a safe environment, your child will eventually be able to apply these skills to more difficult encounters. He can expect to succeed in public because he's succeeded in private.

For example, a barber explained how his parents' lack of social experience affected him. "Growing up, I had a shy and introverted role model: my father. He was an only child whose father was an alcoholic. I did feel I was overprotected by an overbearing, dysfunctional, codependent mother. I believe that I learned some grossly inappropriate defense mechanisms from both my mother and my father, who was emotionally unavailable, showing only anger."

Before you participate in an activity you feel may trip up your child, talk through what she can expect to happen—who you'll encounter, what you'll do, and why you're doing it. If you're going to a large family gathering or party with friends and neighbors, for instance, pull out some photos and tell stories about the people who will be there. You may also want to brush up on basic etiquette by saying, "Let's practice your handshake" or "What do you say when you meet someone new?"

Delay Gratification

You may feel like you're being mean when you don't immediately respond to your child's wishes and demands, but he will eventually thank you for teaching him this important process. When you delay gratification, you teach your child to work toward and wait for a reward, and it's how frustration tolerance, a life skill we've already discussed, can be developed. When your child learns how to delay gratification, he will, eventually, be able to work his way through difficult times on his own, without being rescued by a caring parent or friend.

You can begin to build this skill very early in life, and it can have profound implications. Some interesting research shows that infants who are allowed to fuss a bit before being picked up and soothed tend to show less fearful behavior than babies who are comforted immediately. While conducting research at Harvard, developmental psychologist Doreen Arcus, Ph.D., and her team visited parents in their homes and observed their interactions with their children. They found that when mothers rushed to rescue their fussy babies, the babies were more likely to demonstrate inhibited behavior in subsequent tests. It seems that immediately soothing a highly reactive infant produces an unintended effect—more fearful behavior. Following this line of thought, we can assume that if the child doesn't know how to comfort himself on his own, he won't be able to soothe his discomfort in social situations when he's older.

Now, it's easy to give in and take over when your child is frustrated and crying out to be rescued, and you'll have to practice some frustration tolerance of your own by being persistent and patient as your child becomes more independent. You can delay gratification by adopting a "can do it" attitude as your child acquires new skills. You can do this anywhere, and in any situation. For example, you can discourage your child from clinging to you in public, but then reward him with a big hug once you're in the car, alone. Before entertaining guests, you can explain to your child that you, the host, are traditionally served food and drink last, and then model this behavior. When you're in a store or on the playground, wait your turn instead of cutting in front of shoppers or other children. Develop a set schedule for TV watching or computer use and stick to it. And when your child gets into a disagreement with other kids, allow your child to fight his own battles even if you are offering a bit of indirect advice on how to do so.

Avoid "Hot-Housing"

It's natural to want to protect your child from seemingly harsh, cruel situations, like bullying or suffering with a nasty teacher. Because your child is vulnerable, and you're a strong adult, you instinctively want to rescue your child and remove her from these fairly painful situations. But before you do, take a step back and consider all of the effects on your child. While you may be removing an immediate threat from your child's universe—the bully, the mean teacher—you may lose out in the long term by overprotecting or "hot-housing" your child.

Now, I admit there's a fine line between being your child's protector and being an overprotective parent. Being your child's protector means being a supporter as your child expands his world. Being an overprotective parent means that you *are* your child's entire world.

This most often comes up in issues surrounding school or day care. When a child encounters difficulties there, such as bullying, many parents instinctively try to rectify the situation themselves by complaining to the teacher or the parent of the bully (or even the bully himself) or allowing the child to take a sick day or two to recover from a difficult encounter. Some parents will even go one step further and pull their child from the school or day care facility and either transfer their child or home-school him.

Now, every situation is unique, and sometimes parents are doing the right thing by addressing the issue themselves. But this isn't the only solution, nor is it the best solution in many cases. My main objection is that if you use this strategy consistently, it sends the message to the child that you will solve his problems now and that you always will. This only reinforces dependency and not confidence and independence. It signals to the child that nasty, intimidating people are to be avoided and that the child is helpless. You, the parent, and, for example, the bully have all of the power.

When you're considering removing your child from a difficult situation, please consider all of your alternatives first. When you notice your child shrinking from social activities, help her put herself out there. Try to involve your child in the solution by rehearsing what she should say or introducing her to nicer children. Get her involved in regular social activities that are far removed from the stressor and highlight your child's skills and talents. Encourage your child with pep talks and share your own experiences with tough teachers or classmates. Overall, let your child know that while you empathize with his difficulties, you cannot take charge and take over.

Show Affection

This seems like a given, but showing affection doesn't always come naturally to some parents. If a parent hadn't been treated with loving kindness as a child, or is preoccupied with other worries and responsibilities, showing affection isn't always instinctive or a priority. In addition, if you are shy, or were raised by a shy parent, your comfort level with self-expression isn't always what it could be.

Showing affection begins with praise. Now, praise doesn't always come naturally, either, but praising a child properly can bring enormous rewards. Praise is simply positive feedback on a job well done with a description of what your child did—"You did a great job washing my car today," or "It was nice of you to thank grandma for baking cookies for you." This isn't empty praise, such as "You're the best little girl in the world" or "You're Mommy's favorite," which sends the wrong signals and leads the child to expect to be rewarded simply for "showing up" in life. She needs to feel that she's earned the praise and positive attention.

After you've pointed out the positive behavior, provide an internal reward such as saying, "Didn't it make you feel good to make grandma feel loved and appreciated?" If you want to show affection physically, with a hug or a literal pat on the back, you're absolutely right to do so.

Your child will get a great boost from this type of praise. All too often, shy children feel that they aren't as successful as their peers, or often are overlooked simply because they don't cause many overt problems. Noticing their good behavior and rewarding them for it allows them to build confidence in their abilities and feel that they have all of the resources they need to be successful.

Discipline Properly

The flip side to showing affection and praising your child is disciplining your child in a proper manner. This is vitally important, so important that in one study by researchers Mark Eastburg and W. Brad Johnson at the Fuller Theological Seminary Graduate School of Psychology, many shy adults stated that inconsistent or improper discipline was a factor in their developing shyness. It seems that when these people could not discern clear boundaries or rules, they didn't know how to act and therefore lost confidence in their ability to develop successful strategies and cope with difficult encounters. After all, if they jump on the furniture and get a laugh once, they should expect to always get a laugh, right? Not always, in their homes, and these mixed messages led to confusion and increased inhibition.

Another study indicated that shy children feel the sting of criticism in a different manner than do their more outgoing peers. Temperamentally inhibited children are more likely to internalize criticism and take it to heart, so watch your words and deeds.

Taken together, we can say that disciplining a shy child should be done fairly and consistently. To do so, try these simple tips:

Correct the behavior and not the child. Try to be constructive and sensitive. Saying "Remember to say 'thank you' the next time the waiter fills your glass" is more constructive than "You're so rude!"

Set consistent standards for behavior. When you do so, your child knows what to expect and therefore how to behave. He'll trust his instincts and decisions if he can anticipate rules and consequences.

Make sure that you and your spouse have the same set of rules. If you each have different rules, your child can play one parent off of the other, and you will get locked in the role of either disciplinarian or nurturer. This can be a particular problem when parents are divorced and have two households that may have different sets of rules. Discuss limits and boundaries with your spouse—or ex—before behavior spirals out of control.

Do not withhold affection because your child is acting up. Although it's difficult at times, don't reject your child when you've had enough.

Do not use words like "bad girl" or "bad boy," "dummy," "crybaby," or other terrible names. Your shy child will take it to heart and feel both unloved and unlovable.

Follow your own rules. Sure, you can stay up longer than your child, but if you want your child to have table manners or be polite to strangers, then you must follow your rules as well.

Shake It Up

All too often, we assume that shy children need nurturing, patient parents who like to maintain a quiet, soothing environment at home. Well, actually, they don't—at least not always. In fact, I believe that shy children benefit from participating in occasional "rough and tumble" play that gets their blood pumping and forces them to come out of their shell.

This type of play style is often associated with fathers' preferred style of play—throwing the child in the air, giving piggyback rides, scaring them, and, in general, just being loud. Even Maxwell, Naomi's young son, plays this way with his dad: "We can get very rough sometimes when we play," she explained. "He drums a lot with his dad, and he jumps around, and runs around, and crawls, and chases the cats."

Eventually, the child will realize that being a little out of control and overstimulated is an okay thing. The world won't fall apart if she is breathing heavily or screaming or struggling to maintain her composure. In fact, she may find that this feeling feels just fine, and that her parent can be trusted to make it stop—sometime after the child cries "uncle." And, in time, the child can allow herself to feel this way with people who are outside of her comfort zone. Although, according to Naomi, little Maxwell isn't there just yet: "He has an uncle who's called the 'fun uncle' and all of the nieces and nephews love to play rough with him, and tackle him and stuff. And I can see my son watching from the sidelines and he'd love to be a part of it, but there's something that just won't let him jump in."

I'm willing to bet that with Naomi's guidance, Maxwell will eventually join in and have a thoroughly wonderful time. When the "fun uncle" gets the kids going, Naomi can mirror his actions by throwing Maxwell up in the air or tickling him. She can then do the same with the other children and let Maxwell watch. And then she and the uncle can take turns playing with Maxwell and include the other children as well. As Maxwell gradually gets caught up in the excitement, he'll slowly work his way out of his fears and inhibitions.

Successfully Shy Journal

As we've seen in this chapter, your actions as a parent can have a significant impact on your child's shyness. In this Successfully Shy Journal entry, spend some time evaluating the parenting skills you currently have in your repertoire. To do this, read through the following checklist of traits that help you manage or change your child's behavior. Then write down the skills you think you demonstrate on a regular basis.

- You have a consistent message. Kids need predictability, a routine, and clearly drawn lines between right and wrong behavior. A consistent message helps. For example, if you want your children to be polite, you make sure that they always say "please" and "thank you" when they make requests.

- You behave consistently with your message. You don't have one set of rules for you and one for your child, nor do you slack off when you're tired or not in the mood. For example, because you want to set a good example for your child, you are polite with others, whether they're your spouse, your child, or a stranger.

- You have a consistent response. If your child breaks a longstanding rule, he must know that he has done so, and there will be predictable consequences. If your child doesn't share a plate of cookies with his friends, for example, you don't ignore it just because you know he really loves cookies and wants to keep them for himself.

- You provide alternatives and options. Some children act out because they don't know that they have alternatives. For example, if you don't want your child to spend all of

(continued)

her time playing video games in her bedroom, get her involved in other activities.

- You encourage and reinforce the desired behavior. You notice his strengths, not just his weaknesses, and you let him know that. For example, if he handled himself well when you took him out to dinner, you tell him you noticed his courtesy.

- You select social reinforcers or rewards. You don't buy your child's love, but you reward your child in other ways that boost his self-esteem and social interest. For example, you talk about how being polite makes other people happier and nicer, too.

Now that you've assessed some of your parenting skills, note where you feel you could improve. Then write down two ways you could make those improvements. By modifying your behavior even slightly, you may spark a significant change in your child's behavior. For example, if you aren't polite to strangers, yet you want your child to be, you're sending mixed messages that are too tangled to be sorted out by a child. Clear up one or two skills and you'll see a definite improvement in your child's behavior.

FAMILY TRANSITIONS

While you can control much of what goes on in your home and how you react to it, there are certain factors that affect your family that are beyond your control—you lose your job, suffer a death or serious illness in the family, move to a new town, change your child's school, get divorced, get remarried, or survive a national tragedy. Oftentimes these changes force the entire family, not just the shy child, to make a transition and adapt to the new circumstances.

Sometimes a transition means that the family itself changes, such as when a new baby is born. Some studies have found that the addition of a new baby into the family can trigger shyness in some children, as the older child must get used to sharing—and at times competing for—her parents' time and attention, otherwise known as good old sibling rivalry. What seems to be critical here is the age of the older child. It seems that if the child is at least 2 years old, she'll be more likely to cope with a new baby brother or sister without too much difficulty. If you have children who are less than 2 years apart, be aware that your older child may demand more of your time and attention. Pay attention to her behavior, try spending more time with her one-on-one, and have her help you out with the baby, perhaps by watching you feed and clothe the infant. She'll see the baby as her sibling, not her rival for your affection.

Whatever the cause, these transitions often trigger shyness or social withdrawal not only in children, but in parents as well. Ideally, once you've got your footing and establish a new comfort zone, these withdrawing feelings will dissipate and ultimately disappear. But, of course, we do not live in an ideal world and at times these feelings will hang around longer than we'd like.

The most important thing to remember is that regressing, acting out, or withdrawing are common and normal reactions. We often retreat during adversity or when we're confused by our new surroundings and circumstances. What's critical, however, is what we do during our time in the shadows. Do we get depressed or feel that we'll never get a handle on our new situation? Do we reward ourselves for closing ranks, or do we send feelers out into the world? Do we seek out advice or support, or do we shut ourselves off from those who can provide a helping hand?

When your child becomes more withdrawn after a family transition, do your best to help her establish her new comfort zone. Here's how:

DEALING WITH DIVORCE

When parents separate or divorce, each member of the family must work to create a new comfort zone. If you have a shy child, your new family situation can make him more withdrawing and sensitive, and increase his desire for routine. But even outgoing kids can become more shy and self-conscious, too, as they cope with the many changes in their lives. What you, as a parent, must remember is that withdrawal is a normal reaction to change. Fortunately, there are strategies you can use to help your child deal with this life transition.

- Acknowledge the changes. Your kids have to adjust to a different family arrangement and possibly a new house, school, classmates, and identity. Don't ignore their feelings.

- Stay involved. They need you and want to know that your relationship with them hasn't changed. Even if you aren't the custodial parent, you can call, e-mail, or visit on a regular basis.

- Keep familiar faces in the picture. This is especially important for kids who have to move. They need to know that

Remind your child of what's familiar. This might include his toys, his talents, and his ability to make new friends.

Provide a good example by incorporating your child into your own expanding comfort zone. For instance, if you've decided to purchase a new home, include your child in your house-hunting adventures, explore your new neighborhood together, and take him with you when you meet your new neighbors. Also, be sure to share how you're feeling with your child.

Include your children in your decision-making process. If you're looking for a new home, take your kids along for the open they're surrounded by loving, supportive people, whether they're relatives, family friends, or pals from school or the old neighborhood.

- Talk about it. Explain that you understand how they feel and that you're going to do everything you can to help them make this transition smoothly.

- Don't reward withdrawal. While your child may want to retreat for a while, encourage his desire to meet new friends and have fun with his old ones.

- Let her adjust at her own pace. Your child may be slow to warm up to new situations, so don't rush her natural tendency to hesitate before moving forward.

Lastly, remember that even after the major initial period of adjustment following a separation, your child will need to make a number of smaller but important transitions, such as adjusting to long visits, decompressing after a visit, and getting used to the new people in your, and your ex's, lives. Watch for signs of exaggerated withdrawal, and answer all questions and concerns as honestly and patiently as you can.

houses. If you're ill, take your child to the doctor's office with you.

Go to your child's strengths. If your child loves to draw, for example, get him involved in an art class or take him to the museum. This will be a good boost at a time when he's struggling.

Reward socially interested behavior. If your child talks about some of his new classmates, invite them over for a play date or get to know their parents.

Be patient. Your slow-to-warm-up child is just responding to her body's signals. Don't rush, don't push, and don't expect your child to adjust as quickly as you are adjusting.

Successfully Shy Journal

Now that you've learned more about the power of your family's influence on your child's behavior, you're ready to put this information into action. In your Journal, answer the following questions:

- What are three ways you feel your family contributes to your child's shyness?

- Choose one of the factors you identified. What are a few strategies you can use to change this influence on your child?

In this chapter, we've covered many ways the family can contribute to a child's shyness. Perhaps you identified one of the following common factors: overprotecting your shy child, giving in to shy or fearful behavior, providing inconsistent discipline, not having the right kind of involvement during a family transition, or not showing enough love and affection.

You probably discovered that there are numerous ways you can change this influence for the better. For example, if you overprotect your shy child, you can wait before rushing in and saving her when she's feeling fearful, insist that she accepts all of her invitations, and refuse to fight her battles with her friends and siblings.

Now I'm going to give you some homework—literally. During the next week, put the strategies you identified into action. It's only for a week, so even if you're feeling like you're being mean or throwing your child a curveball, do your best to stick with it. Then, in a week's time, evaluate what happened. Did you notice any progress? I hope so—and I hope you stick with your new strategies, because what your child experiences at home has a definite influence on how he develops friendships, which is the topic of our next chapter.

CHAPTER 7

MAKING
FRIENDS

Like many mothers of shy, slow-to-warm-up kids, Diana is concerned about how her daughter, Jamie, interacts with other children. According to Diana, Jamie has difficulty getting to know other kids.

"In any unfamiliar environment, Jamie's reluctant to engage directly in what's going on," Diana explained. "It could be the first day of school, or a big picnic, or a family gathering. She's reluctant to get involved, but she isn't unwilling, and she does indicate to me that she wants to get closer to the action. But it takes her a while—sometimes it takes her about an hour to become more open and friendly. Or she'll want me to do the activity with her, like swimming or playing on the playground. She'll tug me and pull me and beg me to do it with her, and sometimes it's difficult for me.

"When Jamie's with someone she's not familiar with, she's hesitant to talk. She will do an activity near them, or do the same thing but not necessarily with them, like going down the slide at the playground, but not talking directly with the other kids at the slide.

Eventually, about an hour later, she'll become more sociable and engaged."

According to Diana, Jamie sometimes puts up a fuss when it's time to go on an outing. She particularly resisted going to gymnastics class. "She had a lot of anxiety before going," Diana confessed. "She would tell me, 'I don't want to go today,' or ask 'Do I have to?' and whine a lot. And then when she was in the class, she would actually have a lot of fun."

Diana has tried to make Jamie feel more relaxed in social situations and has gently encouraged her to approach other kids, but that hasn't made much of a difference. She's tried a more tough-love approach, too, by forcing an unwilling Jamie to participate in activities she doesn't like, but that approach resulted in even more anxiety and embarrassing scenes in public. It seems that Jamie's slowly warming tendency always wins out over Diana's reasoning and support. Despite her mother's efforts, Jamie seems to simply need extra time to get used to new faces and places.

"So, what do I do during that first half-hour or hour?" Diana asked. "What could I do to make that time less stressful?"

Every parent of a shy child can relate to Diana's experiences and has asked Diana's pointed questions. Parents of shy children don't want their kids to miss out on social opportunities while they wait on the sidelines, but they've tried everything they can think of—encouraging, pushing, nudging, or giving in—and nothing seems to change their child's withdrawing behavior.

It's easy to understand why parents aren't getting the results they want. Their shy, slow-to-warm-up sons and daughters are merely listening to their instincts when they're faced with the anxiety of meeting and interacting with someone new. Pushed out of the safety of their family's familiar comfort zone, these children are simply doing what comes naturally to them—watching, waiting, figuring out how to handle new situations. Sometimes they choose to cling to their mom or dad. Sometimes they try delaying tactics such as dragging their heels before a big day out. Sometimes they just freeze up and try to disappear. Sometimes they're interested in joining in the fun, but don't know how to make that leap.

Since all of these reactions are perfectly natural, the best approach for parents to take is to work *with* them, rather than *against* them. Further, they can work to strengthen what also comes naturally—the child's desire to play with other kids. After all, shy children like Jamie will tell you that they want to join in. They just need to take their time.

In this chapter, you'll learn the importance of play, the lessons it teaches your child, the types of play, and the skills that are required to make new friends by playing together. You'll discover that there are specific skills and strategies that can be used to help your child get involved with other kids—skills that can be coached and developed, even if your child has slow-to-warm-up tendencies. I'll also explain how active a role you, as a parent, should take in your child's friendships. Lastly, I'll touch on the hot topics of talking to strangers and bullying, and what should or should not concern you.

Before we begin, return to your Successfully Shy Journal for a few moments of reflection.

Successfully Shy Journal

In your journal, please answer the following questions:

- Who are your child's friends?
- How did these friendships develop?

(continued)

- In what ways do your child and her friends differ?

- What does your child like to do socially?

- What does your child like to do when he's alone?

- What are weak and strong aspects of your child's social behavior?

- What is your involvement in your child's expanding social circle?

Your answers indicate your child's basic style of play—a topic I'll discuss at length in this chapter. If your shy child is like most shy kids, he may play well with kids he's known for a long time, since the warm-up period has been worked through. He may also be at ease in small circles of kids, but not feel comfortable in crowds. He may also wait to be approached by new kids, because he needs to know that he's wanted by them and he may be too nervous or unskilled to make the approach himself.

Notice that nearly all of the attributes I listed are positive and indicate what your child does well. These skills, friends, and activities make up his comfort zone. Throughout this chapter, I'll show how you can use these comfort zone elements and help your child go one step beyond to make a friend.

Your role is critical. You won't have to take over and create those friendships yourself, nor will you force your child to make introductions alone. Instead, you'll discover the right level of involvement to help your child be successful in a sometimes difficult or awkward situation.

YOUR ROLE IN YOUR CHILD'S SOCIAL LIFE

Although your child must develop his play skills on his own with his friends and peers, there's much that you can do to set him up for success. Remember: Your child listens to and picks up on the cues you send about how to view the world, so don't underestimate the power you have in shaping his perception of the world around him. Here are some general guidelines to keep in mind.

Adjust your expectations of what is normal or acceptable social behavior. As the parent of a slowly warming child, you must understand that your child is stressed by going beyond your family's comfort zone. He experiences a healthy dose of nerves when faced with going to an after-school activity or confronted by a new group of kids on the playground, at the beach, or at an extended family gathering.

Prepare your child for the stressful event. Instead of fighting your child's natural warming-up process and creating more stress, you can use this warm-up period constructively and positively. The key is to prepare your child before the stressful event so that she doesn't become overwhelmed by stimulation and can acclimate naturally at her own pace.

For example, instead of struggling with Jamie before going to gymnastics, Diana could take Jamie to gymnastics early and go through a few moves with her as the other children arrive. This way, she won't be made tense by entering a room full of rowdy children who are already immersed in their activities. Plus, when class is ready to begin, Jamie will feel that she is adequately warmed up and has had some one-on-one time with her mom.

Encourage, but don't intervene in, your child's social activities. According to research summarized by University of Georgia developmental psychologist David Shaffer, Ph.D., parents who indirectly monitor their children's social activities by gently encouraging and loosely supervising them tend to aid their children's social success. In contrast, parents who directly intervene in their children's playtime and fully participate in it actually impede their children's social skills and peer acceptance. After all, if a child knows that her parent will take over, she won't develop her play skills, and her friends will resent the intrusion. In addition, parents who force their child to "say something" or play with a new group of strange kids will merely take all of the fun out of play, and the child will equate making conversation with something unpleasant.

A social worker wrote to me about her mother's negative influence during difficult social encounters when she was a child. "She always yelled at me and pushed me to 'talk' and not stand around awkwardly ('Say something, don't just stand there!')," the social worker wrote. "I used to feel like I didn't fit in with other kids when I was younger, and now I still feel that way with adults."

Help your child to approach social activities with optimism. Since your child's attitude toward social activities is influenced by how you view these events, you can help to lessen his fears by being encouraging and optimistic when you talk about these social situations. Use enthusiasm and reason instead of force, and allow your child to shine in his own interactions. For example, if he resists attending day camp, tell him, "You'll see the kids you met last year, and I'm sure they'll be excited to see you again," instead of telling him that he has no choice but to go to camp and make the best of it.

THE LESSONS OF PLAY ARE THE LESSONS OF LIFE

Despite what your shy child is signaling, shy children very much want to play with other kids. In fact, during early childhood, playing is the child's "job" or developmental task that must be mastered. Being able to "play well with others" is so important that some of the most noted names in psychology, such as Sigmund

Freud and Erik Erikson, have considered the lessons of play to be the lessons of life. According to these thinkers, playing is necessary for healthy emotional, cognitive, and psychological development, because children can try on roles and behaviors that they will use later in life, whether it's pretending he's a fireman or taking orders from a more dominant child. Additionally, it's how children make their first connections with their peers, almost like how an adult must first make small talk before developing more meaningful conversations with other adults.

In addition, through play, children learn to be socially flexible, to negotiate and share and take turns. Children also learn to take risks while they're playing. Not only are they outside of their familiar comfort zone when they're introduced to a new child, but they try new activities when they're with their friends. Friendships are also naturally fraught with risks, because other children can't be expected to provide unconditional love, like mom and dad do. Further, when kids play, they learn to be tolerant of diversity, because their playmates are "others"—they adhere to different rules, schedules, and beliefs; they present social challenges; and they're simply unique individuals who must be understood. Lastly, playing provides the child with early successful experiences that enable her to stretch her comfort zone, which will be ever shifting throughout her life. Meeting these challenges successfully early in life will provide a child with necessary experience they will draw on later in life.

THE PLAY SKILLS TIMELINE

Play becomes more complex as children develop emotionally and intellectually, and as they get older, their attention shifts from parents or caretakers to their peers, a shift that typically occurs around the age of four. Here's a general timeline of how play develops:

- Six months: Children first begin to play. They'll do similar activities near each other, but not with each other.

- One year old: By the end of their first year, kids are aware of other kids, but they don't interact all that much.

- Two years old: By this time, children are more engaged, especially with adults, and will share toys, talk and laugh, and get involved in social games such as peek-a-boo.

- Three years old: Children can play "pretend" by the age of three, but not in any formal or thought-out manner.

- Four years old: Children are now able to plan their pretend play by assigning roles to each other and creating a simple plot or narrative. Their focus shifts from their parents to their peers.

While playing with others and developing friendships are critical during early childhood, having a peer group, being accepted socially, and developing social skills become increasingly important as the child gets older. In middle childhood, between the ages of six and ten, kids socialize in peer groups that interact on a regular basis and give members a sense of belonging. In early adolescence, these peer groups turn into social cliques made up of same-sex members with shared values and sensibilities.

Be aware, however, that this play-skill timeline is just a general checkpoint. Kids—shy and non-shy—often vary from it for a number of reasons and become what's known as "off time," meaning that they lag just a little bit behind their peers, although they can do the same tasks just as well, albeit at their own pace. A child's play skills can be limited by many factors, such as not being encouraged by parents or peers, not being able to tolerate a lot of environmental or social stimulation, missing out on social opportunities because of a slow-to-warm-up tendency, or receiving the wrong kind of input from family and friends. In addition, a lack of playtime opportunities early in life can often cause a child to fall behind her peers later, as this shy twentysomething waitress explained:

"I grew up in a rural area with not a lot of friends to play with, so I played alone most of the time. I believe that as a result, I didn't develop certain social skills most kids develop early in childhood—pre-school age," she confessed. "I never went to day care or pre-school. I don't have any brothers or sisters. I still have difficulty making small talk with acquaintances. I think spending a lot of time growing up alone would make anyone shy."

PLAY SKILLS

While being able to play with others is incredibly important, it doesn't always happen naturally. Play is made up of a number of skills that are used in a variety of social situations. These skills begin developing in the safety of the family's comfort zone, and they're expanded and improved when kids play with other children outside of their comfort zone. Some of these play skills include:

- Problem-solving. Whether it's how to approach another child or how to maintain a difficult friendship, playing is full of problems that must be solved.

- Cooperation. Without a certain level of cooperation, no friendship can be struck or maintained at any age.

- Negotiation. "It's my way or else . . ." Or else what? Isolation and loneliness? Friends know how to give and take when it's appropriate.
- Initiation of interaction. Kids can develop their leadership qualities by extending invitations and seeking out the company of their peers.
- Communication. Kids must speak up and express themselves, whether they're happy, sad, tired, frustrated, excited, worried, or feeling shy.
- Expression of social interest. Even shy kids take an interest in other children; they just don't know how to build on it and act on it in an appropriate manner.
- Empathy. When your friend falls off her bike, you know how it feels, and you should let her know that her pain is halved when it's shared.
- Tolerance. No two children are alike, and no two kids are always in synch. Being tolerant of others' differences is a skill that should be nurtured and applauded.
- Planning. A child learns to anticipate the steps he'll have to take to play with friends, whether he's organizing a basketball game or asking your permission to do so.
- Fairness. Children must learn to abide by the rules of the game, even when they're on the losing side. Coaches may call this play skill good sportsmanship.
- Loyalty. Children need to learn that temporary spats shouldn't turn into long grudges and that sticking with a friend in need is a valuable asset.

If children lean these skills now, when they're young, they'll become the kind of kid that others will want to befriend. No matter how shy they may feel, they'll never be alone.

Successfully Shy Journal

In your Successfully Shy Journal, please jot down answers to the following questions:

- Where is your child in the play-development timeline?

- Is he on time, or a little bit behind the curve?

- Based on the timeline, are you expecting too much, too soon?

- How does your child play?

- Who does your child play with?

- Do you play with your child? If so, how? (For example, do you roughhouse? Do the two of you generally play a game with rules or do something more freeform?)

- Do you interact with your child when she's with her friends? How?

- List the play skills that your child already has. List the play skills your child needs to improve.

Finally, look at the level of your child's social skills and social development, and identify two or three ways in which your child could improve. For example, you may realize that your child mostly interacts with you when the two of you are out among other children, and that this is normal behavior for a young child, but not for a child your daughter's age.

Now that you have this information, think about how you could help your child play better with other kids and not cling to you so much. Then back up a step and begin practicing in your own home—your child's own comfort zone—and overtly coach your child to become more independent. For instance, if you find that your daughter clings to you when you're on the

(continued)

phone at home, as well as when you're with other kids, explain that while you love to be close to her, you cannot divide your attention between her and your phone call. Promise her that when you get off the phone, the two of you will spend time to-gether—and make good on your promise. Then, when you're out in public and she's clinging to you, remind her of this episode and promise to spend time with her once she has said hello to the other children who surround her. The success she experienced at home will help her earn success in public.

TYPES OF PLAY

"Play" encompasses a variety of social interactions and activities, but contrary to conventional wisdom, it doesn't always involve in-teracting with other children. Play can be divided between solitary play, which occurs when a child plays alone, and group play, when children interact together. Both types of play teach children im-portant lessons about themselves, their skills, and their relation-ship to other kids.

Time Alone: Solitary Play

Solitary play, which shy kids often prefer, can teach important lessons. According to some examinations of solitary play, parents shouldn't be overly worried about their child's preference for non-social play, as long as their child spends her time wisely.

Jamie, for example, has been going to the playground a few days a week this past summer, but Diana's concerned about her slowly developing interactions with the other kids. "She's starting to play with the kids on the playground," Diana told me. "She'll play around them, or do the same activity, but there's no real con-versation and it takes her a while to interact with them. She shows some confidence with them, but it's not immediate. I feel that she's missing out on a lot of fun, and that if she joined in early, she would have a better time."

According to solitary-play studies, Jamie's behavior is just one type of non-social play that has been analyzed and categorized. Some types of non-social play are perfectly harmless—beneficial, even—while others are a bit more troublesome if too much time is spent engaged in them.

Parallel Constructive Play. This type of play occurs when children are located near each other and are engaged in a constructive activity, such as building a sand castle or finger painting, but they don't interact. These kids are completely immersed in their activity and their project. Kids benefit from parallel constructive play by solving problems, meeting their goals, and being self-reliant. Parents should not be concerned about their child's tendency to play this way, and should provide indirect support and encouragement along the way so that they will join other children eventually.

Solitary Constructive Play. Children engage in this type of play when they're building a sand castle or finger painting alone, not near other children. This solo play is fine occasionally, but not all the time if the child wants to build friendships. Other children don't approach this independent child, thinking that he prefers to play alone, and so don't have the opportunity to get to know him. Alternatively, other shy children won't know how to break in, either. If your child always plays this way, present opportunities for him to engage in his favorite solo activity when he's with other children, and invite the others to join in.

Solitary Functional Play. Children who engage in solitary functional play, in contrast to the other types of play, are not playing with a purpose in mind, such as building a dream home for their dolls or finishing a jigsaw puzzle. They are not thinking about anything in particular, nor are they involved with other children. They play aimlessly, either with or without a toy. They often repeat their actions without trying other alternative actions. For example, they'll beat on a soup pot over and over and over again or they'll throw a ball against a wall endlessly.

Unlike the other types of solo play, solitary functional play does not benefit the child. Children who prefer this type of play are not building skills such as cooperation, negotiation, and communication, and they are not stretching their comfort zone or learning how to positively cope with new experiences.

If your child spends a lot of her time playing in this manner, encourage her to spend more time constructively. Ask her what she is doing, and why. Offer her more challenging toys, such as puzzles and games, and teach her how to play with them. Get her involved with other children, especially non-threatening younger children or slow-to-warm-up kids. Lastly, spend more time listening to and having uninterrupted conversations with your child, who may be experiencing feelings of frustration or anger about other aspects of her life, without being able to express them.

Fantasy Play. Playing "pretend" or dressing up in wild outfits and acting out fantastic scenarios is a part of childhood. But getting lost in fantasy play, alone, can be harmful to your child's development. Children who get too caught up in their solitary fantasies have a hard time navigating real-world social situations and relating to other children. They take a long time to solve interpersonal problems, interact poorly with their peers, and have a relatively low status within their classroom.

If your child gets lost in his fantasy world, try to break through his daydreams and keep him grounded. Encourage him to share his fantasy world with you, offer him opportunities to play constructively, and provide him with positive social events, especially

with younger or more shy children. Reinforce his pro-social behavior and provide encouragement and direction along the way.

Wait and Hover. This occurs when a child, faced with another
group of kids, watches the activity and waits—and waits and waits.
This type of behavior is preferred by almost all shy children, including young Jamie, and is actually a positive social signal. These
wait-and-hover kids are interested in joining other children but
hesitate before getting involved with them.

This type of play is positive and indicates that the child is willing
to join in. During the warm-up-period, she will observe the other
children and tends to mimic her peers' behavior. For example, if
the group is building a sand castle, the solo child will start digging
some sand herself. She's waiting for a sign that it's okay to come
into the group—either a direct invitation or an opening in the
group. Unfortunately, the group is often too caught up in the action to notice the waiting and hovering child, or moves on to another activity by the time the child on the fringes has gathered up
the courage to join in.

Later in this chapter, I'll show you how to guide your child
through this wait-and-hover period so that she can initiate contact
with other children. Building on her interest in other kids is the key
to helping your child become successfully shy.

TIME TOGETHER: SOCIAL PLAY

In contrast to solitary play, social play is what we typically envision
when we think of playtime—sharing toys in the sandbox, taking
turns on the jungle gym, participating in after-school activities,
being involved in extra classes or lessons, playing a game of pickup
at the basketball court, roaming around the mall, or simply
hanging out after school. But just as the types of solitary play are
not equal, neither are the types of social play.

Structured Social Play. The first kind of social play is structured or organized play, which occurs when kids are part of a formal program, such as extra-curricular activities or lessons, which have regular meetings and members, rules, and defined roles. Kids benefit by learning how to play by the rules and take on roles, developing technical skills, and feeling like they're part of something larger than themselves. For shy kids, the comfort of seeing the same kids week after week, or summer after summer, can help them expand their comfort zones.

However, this type of play often has a downside. As with direct monitoring—when parents insert themselves into their child's playtime—structured social play means that adults, not kids, dominate the activity. When a dispute arises on the baseball field, for example, the coach, parents, or the umpires settle it. And when this happens, the children learn to either mimic the adult and become more bossy or domineering, or they learn to depend on an authority figure to resolve their differences. Neither result will boost a child's social skills, and since shy children are often hesitant to approach a person in authority, shy kids may not thrive in this setting.

Further, structured social play is often competitive or goal-oriented, which may interfere with your shy child's social comfort and performance. Shy kids feel acutely self-conscious about their skills and abilities and believe that everyone is judging them negatively. Because of this hidden but intense anxiety, your shy child may be thrown off by the pressure of fielding a fly ball in front of dozens of spectators or executing a great karate chop in a room full of mirrors. She'll remember only her mistakes and fail to consider all of the times she has performed well. To lessen her anxiety, she may shrink back and hope that she isn't noticed or resist going to these activities in the first place.

Another hidden downside of organized play is that many parents may feel that if their child is involved in a number of organized lessons or sports, the child has a healthy social life. Unfortunately, this is the wrong assumption. After all, if your son has no time to develop friendships outside of the organized setting, he'll remain merely a teammate or classmate, and not turn into a friend. He may be busy, but he isn't socially engaged.

Unstructured Social Play. When adults see kids hanging out at the mall, they usually think that the kids are just wasting time or that they're up to no good. That assumption is often wrong. As seen through the eyes of a psychologist, these kids are involved in unstructured social play, a key element in building strong, healthy relationships.

Under the umbrella of unstructured social play I include all sorts of activities that have no purpose other than to simply be with someone else, and not alone. Although often overlooked, this purpose is significant. Without social interest, and without the bonds of friendship, we suffer. Without shared experiences, even the trivial or banal ones, we are isolated and have iron walls around our comfort zones. And without the ups and downs inherent in relationships, we can't understand our selves or our place in the social fabric.

Unstructured social play can be used to turn an acquaintance into a friend who's included in your shy child's comfort zone. The best place to start is with an acquaintance from one of your child's structured activities, and then slowly but consistently develop that connection. For example, if your son is in Boy Scouts, you can invite one of the other scouts to your home so that your son can build that relationship without the stimulation or rigidity of the group setting.

Successfully Shy Journal

The following questions will help you identify the gaps in your child's social experiences.

- Is your child socially involved with other children, or is she merely busy with commitments or obligations?

- Does your child prefer structured or unstructured forms of play?

- Does your child get a fair shake in social activities, or does he fly under the radar and hope that he isn't noticed?

- Is your child involved mostly in competitive activities?

- Does your child have the opportunity to turn acquaintances into friends?

- Do you treat your child's social activities as an obligation, or as something to be enjoyed?

- How do you support your child's social life?

What's most important is that your child has a wide variety of social experiences that reflect his interests, help him connect with other kids, and teach him how to become an individual within a group. He needs to spend some time in structured settings, such as swimming lessons or playing on a soccer team, because he needs to learn how to follow rules. He also needs to spend time doing unstructured activities, like flying kites, that enable him to learn how to cooperate and negotiate with other kids. Your child needs to spend some time with new kids, but he also needs to spend time with old friends, who can let him truly be himself. Make sure that you provide these opportunities for your child, no matter what his level of shyness.

FINDING HEALTHY SOCIAL ACTIVITIES

While you can't go out and make friends for your child, there is much you can do to expand his social options. Consider the following strategies.

Spice it up. Like life in general, a healthy social life demands variety and should be more fun than work. For example, if your child is involved in mostly structured play activities, work impromptu visits to the park or play dates with classmates into his schedule.

Let your child be the boss in some activities. Reconsider your child's involvement in parent- or adult-dominated activities, which often breed competitiveness and social passivity in the children.

Take a second look. Take care not to overlook your child's ability to handle ambiguous, loosely defined social groups. They may be more critical to your child's social savvy than you realize.

Question authority. How do your child's authority figures handle conflict, foster cooperation, and encourage your child? Make sure they're setting a good example.

Expose your child to different peer groups. Kids who have problems with peer groups at school can often find a new circle of friends outside of school and thrive.

Pick the right activities. Forget what's trendy or supposedly essential to your child's future. Instead, focus on your child's strengths and give him opportunities for creativity and self-expression.

Back off. It's tempting to intervene when a child falters, but it's important to let your child sort out conflicts and their consequences. You can give advice if he requests it, but don't make decisions for him.

Take a small step forward. Invite someone from your daughter's soccer team into your home, and get to know her parents. Your daughter will feel more comfortable when she isn't pressured to perform.

Stay in the picture. Create family activities so that your child isn't totally focused on his peers. As he gets older, your strong bond will last.

Watch out for burnout. Shy kids often cannot tolerate a lot of social stimulation, so make sure your shy child isn't burned out by her many activities.

Lighten up. Don't turn play into work by requiring your child to excel in all of the activities she tries. Shy kids rarely believe that they're as talented as their peers, so focus on the journey instead of the goal.

BREAKING THE ICE: APPROACHING OTHER KIDS

Diana related an interesting story about her concern for Jamie's social involvement, specifically, how she relates to kids she sees frequently but who are not yet considered to be friends.

"I don't want Jamie to miss out because she's too cautious to join in something fun," Diana told me. "She's watchful, but she's not ready to join in right away. For instance, I've been taking her to the playground a lot this summer, and she sees some of the same kids there. The last time we were there, one of the boys who was playing near the sprinkler waved to her and called out, 'Hi Jamie!' I could tell that she wanted to go over to him, but she wouldn't. I asked her why and she said that he was playing with other kids, and didn't really want to play with her, because if he did, he would have come over and invited her to join in directly. It seems that she needs that reassurance, or a direct signal or invitation from someone else before she'll join in."

Jamie's behavior on the playground perfectly illustrates how a shy child typically reacts to other children who are already immersed in play. These shy kids take note of the other children and show interest in joining them, but don't take matters into their own hands and break the ice.

Jamie's behavior also provides a clue to the answer to the question her mom posed earlier in this chapter: What can Diana do to make the warming-up period less stressful?

The answer lies in developing Jamie's interest in other children and coaching her on how to turn that interest into the ability to approach other children. Instead of waiting for a direct, overt invitation from another child, Diana can teach Jamie how to break the ice and become successfully shy.

Three Social Approaches

Let's take another look at Jamie's playground scene and see how she could handle the situation in a socially savvy manner. She arrives with Diana at 11 A.M. as they often do, loaded down with buckets and shovels, some snacks, a bright beach ball, and a doll or two thrown in for good measure. They set up camp on the bench near the medium-sized slide and notice a few other children playing near the sprinkler. It's a hot day, and Jamie's got her swimsuit on just in case she and her mother decide to take a dip. Jamie takes a look at the kids splashing and running and laughing and recognizes Colin, who often visits the playground on hot summer days.

"Hi Jamie!" Colin calls out to her.

Jamie responds with a weak wave and grabs on to her mother's leg.

"Jamie," Diana says, "why don't you go over to Colin and his pals?"

"I don't think he wants me to play with him," Jamie says. "He's playing with all of those other kids."

SHYNESS TRIGGERS

FAMILY REUNIONS

Many of us have relatives scattered around the country that we see only on special occasions—family reunions, holidays, or weddings. These are all big gatherings made up of people familiar to you but who may be complete strangers to your young child. Yet these people don't act like strangers—they rush in and almost smother your child with love. It's no surprise that shy kids often freeze up during these situations and stick close to their mom or dad, who is embarrassed by the child's bashfulness.

To ensure that your next family reunion will be a joyful one, follow these tips:

- Treat the situation as you would any unfamiliar situation. Before the big day, prepare your child for what to expect. Then give her time to warm up when you arrive, and support her throughout.

- Turn strangers into family. While you have a long history with your relatives, they're strangers to your child. Before the family event, tell stories, go through photo albums, and explain your family connections so that your child can recognize his distant relatives.

"But he waved to you and said hi," Diana explains.

"Yeah," Jamie agrees. "But he didn't tell me to come over."

At this point in the action, Jamie and Diana have three options if they want to play with Colin and the other kids. One approach is to disrupt the action and make a scene, the second is to wait for an invitation—the strategy that Jamie and most shy children prefer—and the third strategy is the socially savvy approach that brings social success and can be easily taught to your child.

- Get to the festivities early. Since your child needs more time to warm up, get there early, and greet people individually as they arrive.

- Be part of the action. Bring games and snacks and help serve other guests. Your child will feel useful and she'll get a lot of compliments.

- Don't label. When "She's so shy!" inevitably comes up, respond with "She just needs more time to get to know you."

- Break away from adults. Let your child cling to you while she adjusts, but then help your child approach the other kids using the strategies I discussed in this chapter.

- Create a dress rehearsal. If you're going to a wedding, let your child try on the clothes and shoes she'll wear prior to the big day. If you're going to a picnic, practice some of the games.

Lastly, let your child know that she's a part of a family that loves her very much and wants to be involved in her life. While it may seem like a lot to handle, all of this attention is how her grandparents and aunts and uncles show their interest and love. She can hold back from their embrace if she wants, but there is no reason why she should.

Disruption. If Jamie wanted attention, she could jump into the group of kids and disrupt their activity. She could run over to the sprinkler with a giant squirt gun, toss a beach ball into the middle of the action, or jump on top of the slide and scream "Look at me!"

Obviously, Jamie and other shy kids are unlikely to pursue this strategy. It puts them in the spotlight, which shy kids usually shun, and it simply requires too much energy from their already over-stimulated bodies. However, some shy kids—and shy adults—may learn to use this strategy, which is also known as "forced extroversion," because they don't know how to pleasantly approach other people.

This strategy works at times, because the disruptive child gets attention and can often persuade other children to join him. However, the attention is often negative, since most children don't tolerate disruptive kids because they interrupt activity that's already underway. Disruptive kids are often shunned and disliked. Overall, it's a strategy that should be avoided.

Wait and Hover. This is the option that Jamie prefers. She notices other kids, plays near them but not with them, and waits for a clear signal that she is invited into their circle of friends. Most shy children prefer this fairly passive strategy, because it gives them time to warm up to their new surroundings and figure out if the kids are friends or foes.

Meanwhile, parents like Diana become frustrated that their typically friendly, fun-loving child won't reveal that side of her personality to children who could become playmates. These parents feel that their shy child is missing out on a lot of fun and opportunities to meet other kids they see regularly. The warm-up period becomes a stressful tug of war that pits parents against their slowly warming children. It's especially difficult if the parent is like Diana and has a shorter warm-up period and is baffled by the child's slow-to-adjust tendencies.

Overall, waiting and hovering is a safe option, but a lonely one. After all, the other kids are calling the shots and deciding if the lone child is to be allowed to join in. And if the child on the sidelines is unfamiliar to them, chances are that the group will be reluctant to ask the child to join in. Plus, oftentimes the group is so involved in their play that they don't even notice that there's another child who would like to be included. And don't forget that many other kids may be shy and unwilling to approach your child, even though they'd be great playmates for him.

Socially Savvy Approach. The third option Jamie could take is to approach Colin and his friends in a socially savvy manner, which is how popular, well-liked kids join other kids. To do so, Jamie will have to watch for an opening and offer something to the new children to show that she'd be a good friend who could fit into the group.

Jamie has lots of resources she could use. She and Diana brought an assortment of toys to the playground, so she could offer up some of them to the kids. With or without her mother's help, Jamie could grab her beach ball and take it over to Colin, and with a simple "Hey Colin, want to catch it?" she could add more fun to the mix.

If she isn't feeling so bold, Jamie could also spend some time alone with Diana so she could warm up to the activity on the playground. Then, when the kids in the sprinkler start to get tired and the group breaks up a bit, Jamie could make her move by approaching Colin or another child with an offer to play with one of her toys or share some of her snacks. Or, if Jamie hadn't brought along any supplies, she could come up with an idea for a new game using the playground equipment and see if one of the children would be interested in joining her.

STRATEGIES FOR PARENTS OF KIDS WHO WAIT AND HOVER

While the socially savvy approach offers the best odds for your child to successfully meet other kids and join in their play, it's often difficult for a shy child used to "waiting and hovering" to work up to this more aggressive approach. If your child, like Jamie, seems to struggle with this transition, try the following tips.

Don't stress. Kids who wait and hover do so because they need extra time to warm up. If you add more stress by demanding that they join other kids, you're only extending the warm-up time and creating more stress.

Observe the action with intent. Instead of just watching and waiting, watch the other kids with an eye toward what they need— a new toy, some help, or just another friend.

Talk about it. Discuss your options with your child. Diana could tell Jamie, "Don't you think Colin is hungry after all of that running? I bet he'd like some of your cookies."

Look for an opening. Sometimes it's tough to join ongoing play, but if you look for an opening for your child, she'll be more likely to fit in. Jamie had the perfect opening when the kids tired of running through the sprinklers.

Promote sharing. If your child has something that others may enjoy, have her offer it up, whether it's a toy, some snacks, or a good joke.

Offer help when it's needed. If your child needs your help when approaching other kids, provide it, and don't stress out about it. In time, she'll be able to shine on her own.

Encourage your child to try again. Remember that other kids may need more time to warm up to your child. If her new friend doesn't want a cookie, she may appreciate playing with a squirt gun.

Be a good role model. When you approach other kids or adults, explain your actions to your child. Likewise, when you see good examples in books, on TV, or on the playground, point them out. Your child will benefit from these examples.

Praise your child. Friendship is its own reward, but your praise for a job well done is priceless and further encourages your child to continue building new friendships.

Successfully Shy Journal

Now that you have solid strategies for how your shy child can make new friends, take some time out to write in your Successfully Shy Journal. Please answer the following questions:

- How does your child typically approach encounters with new children?

- How does your child feel about these encounters? How do you react?

- What strategies do you currently suggest to your child for approaching other kids?

- What could you do in the future to coach your child to be socially savvy?

This journal exercise is an important one—in fact, it's one of the most important exercises in this book. I believe that it's critical to help your child learn how to take that first step in approaching an unfamiliar child. Unfortunately, this step is often misunderstood by parents who think that telling their child to "just go and play with those kids" is enough instruction for their shy child.

The next time that your child encounters another potential friend, remember what you wrote in this exercise and watch your child cope with the situation. Note her desire to approach and avoid at the same time, and allow her to warm up fully. When you think she has relaxed a bit, help her out. Tell her what to say. Walk her over to the other children. Include them in your games. Then take a step back and let your child become more comfortable. It'll happen. Just relax and be there for your child.

A STEP TOO FAR: SAFETY AND BULLYING

So far we've discussed how your child can approach other children who are friendly but unfamiliar. And, if this were a perfect world, all unfamiliar people would be friendly and good-hearted. However, as we all know, some people should be treated with caution. You, as a parent, must convey this information to your child in a measured but firm manner so that he's cautious but not overly fearful.

Some shy adults claim that their parents' insistence on safety helped to create their shyness by instilling in them a deep fear of strangers. In a letter, one high-school student told me, "My parents would strike fear into me by saying that strangers were 'bad.' I can remember being four years old and not going out in public, or gripping my mom's hand and screaming if she let go, even to reach over and get something, after she read me a book about strangers."

While I agree that parents should tell their child to avoid adults they don't know, they should be careful about exacerbating their shy child's fears about unfamiliar people. After all, shy people naturally tend to find unknown people to be threatening, so this extra safety precaution, while well meaning, can create more problems.

I think that Diana's directions to young Jamie are a good example of maintaining a healthy balance between staying safe and being open to meet new people: Don't talk to strange adults unless you, the parent, are there and have introduced the child. "I think the warm-up period is positive in some ways," Diana told me, "because Jamie is cautious and won't talk to strangers I haven't introduced her to."

I believe that parents should have the same level of involvement when dealing with bullies. Seen through the lens of our social strategies, bullies don't know how to play appropriately. They are those disruptive children who throw a bomb into ongoing play, whether it's an organized activity or merely a one-on-one conversation between friends. These disruptive children are often disliked, rejected, feared, and avoided. They are often raised by domineering parents. They also tend to pick on vulnerable children who they believe can't defend themselves, and so their targets are often shy kids.

If bullies are tormenting your child, shy or not, you have many options, both short term and long term. The first short-term option is to defuse the situation by helping the bully learn how to play appropriately. For example, if the bully is pushing children patiently waiting in line for the slide, you can step in and say, "If you wait your turn, everyone can have a chance to play." If the bully is teasing your child or another child, say, "My son won't want to play with you if you're hurting his feelings." If the bully refuses to listen to reason, tell him, "If you're going to play this way, we're going to leave."

Your child will learn these scripts from your example, but you can also help him develop his own strategies to defend himself. Try to role-play a typical encounter, and use that opportunity to coach your child on how to stand up for himself. In a real situation, you can stand in his vicinity while he tells the bully to change his behavior. When necessary, you can also help him avoid the bully by taking a new route home from school or changing his schedule. You might also try contacting a person in authority, such as a teacher or counselor, or the bully's parents, and discussing the matter adult-to-adult.

The best long-term strategy is to help your child develop friendships with friendly children. There is some truth to the old saying that there's safety in numbers, and if your child has a circle of friends, bullies will be less likely to zero in on her. In addition, studies show that children who are bullied at school are able to develop friends when they're in a new environment and with a new group of people. Remind your child that she's capable of building relationships and that not all kids are bullies. Many, in fact, smartly avoid bullies as well. Your child is not alone, especially if you can be turned to for advice and support.

Take It To the Next Level

Now that you and your shy child are exploring the edges of her social comfort zone by making more contact with unfamiliar kids, you're ready to take these skills to the next level—day care or school. In these more structured settings, your shy child will have to learn how to play well and learn well without the guidance you provide. Oftentimes this brings about a small crisis in your child's social development, but with your gentle involvement, your shy child will shine.

CHAPTER 8

ENTERING
SCHOOL

Lots of people look back on their early school years with lots of fondness, but I don't," Emma told me. "I still have the photo of me waving goodbye to my mom before my first day of the first grade. Everything looks fine on the surface. I look so happy and eager to go to school. I've got a new dress on, and my hair was fixed really cute, and I've got a huge smile.

"But despite my smile in that photo, I had the worst time. I hadn't experienced anything like it before, and my anxiety lasted for a while. I'd feel sick to my stomach in the morning and want to stay home with my mom, but I had to go to school and spend the day with the other kids and try to learn something.

"I wasn't labeled shy because I was really outgoing at home and with my neighborhood friends," Emma explained. "Sure, I was a bit of a clingy child, but that was seen as being cute and affectionate, and I'd handled pre-school and kindergarten well. But getting through the first months of the first grade was very difficult. So much was different, and I had to be in the classroom the entire

171

day, without any breaks. I didn't feel well physically, and I couldn't focus on learning or making friends.

"At the time, I didn't understand why I felt the way I did, and nobody talked to me about it, either. My parents told me that I had to go to school and I couldn't make any excuses. My mom tried to make it easier on me by promising to drive by the school and wave to me at lunchtime. That would get me out the door, but then I'd just wait for her and she wouldn't come and that would make me feel even worse. I wouldn't let myself cry in front of the other kids—all of whom seemed to be having a great time—but I certainly wanted to cry and go home.

"I eventually got used to going to school—and feeling terrible in the mornings, too—but I had some anxiety every year when I started a new school year. I knew I had to be there, but for whatever reason I didn't want to be there and I was miserable."

Emma's story is one that almost everyone can relate to. Some children—especially shy children—simply dread going to school and have a hard time getting comfortable once they're there. They've got "school jitters"—they are tense and anxious, have trouble concentrating and making friends, suffer with nightmares and lack of quality sleep, and generally take a longer time to transition into the school routine.

I believe that school jitters are a normal, healthy response to a challenging situation. In just one day, the child's whole world changes before his eyes. The teacher, the classroom, the other kids, the academic expectations, and even his clothing are new.

This can be too much newness for shy, slowly warming children, who typically feel more anxiously aroused when they're in new, unpredictable settings. To cope with their anxiety, they withdraw into silent stoicism. They focus on their discomfort, and therefore aren't engaged in the classroom. And because they can anticipate how difficult school will be for them, they get jittery during the summertime, long before the first bell rings. Further, they stay jittery far longer than their more quickly warming, outgoing peers.

Because the school jitters problem is so widespread among students of all ages and personality types, I've devoted this entire chapter to the topic. Although it's a terribly common phenomenon, it's easily explained using the concepts I've introduced in this book, and there's much that a parent can do to help a child navigate these uncharted waters. I'll provide plenty of tips that you can apply to your child's entry into school so that both of you will look forward to the start of every school year.

Successfully Shy Journal

Before examining your child's school jitters, please think about how you faced the grade that your child is now in. Then answer the following questions in your Successfully Shy Journal regarding your own experiences in school:

- How did you fare during your first few days of the grade that your child is in now?

- Did you dread going to school or were you eager to begin the new school year?

- What were your fears?

Next, write about your first day of school as if you were experiencing it in the present moment. Record everything you remember—your teacher's name, what the classroom looked like, how you felt waving goodbye to your parents. Then, write down your child's expectations about school.

As you look through your answers, you may realize that there's a disconnect between your expectations and experi-

(continued)

ences and your child's. From an adult perspective, the first day of school seems fun—almost thrilling—and you probably think your child looks so cute in his new outfit and loaded down with all of his new supplies. But as a young student, you may have experienced the situation differently. You may have felt scared, bewildered, tired from lack of sleep, or nervous. Your child may feel the same way, which is why he can't relate to your positive attitude and excitement about the first day of school.

As you read through this chapter, remember what those first few days of the school year felt like, and bring up the subject with your child. Acknowledging his feelings will make him feel supported and safe during this time of transition.

WHY GOING TO SCHOOL IS SO NERVE-WRACKING

Emma's snapshot of her first day of school went something like this:

"I remember waking up long before my mom came in to get me up, and I was too nervous to eat breakfast," she said. "I remember my first-day-of-school dress and feeling uncomfortable in it and my new shoes. I'm sure that my parents talked to me about how I was going to have a great time during my 'big day.' But all I could think of was how to get out of it or how to make time speed by. When I was dropped off at the school with my sister, I remember feeling kind of shocked to see so many kids. I knew only a few of them, and they were off doing their own thing. When I met my teacher, I thought she seemed nice enough, but I knew that a lot of teachers were mean. The first morning was long, and I trembled when I had to stand up and introduce myself to the classroom. I barely touched my lunch because I had no appetite and the lunchroom was so loud and crazy. I don't remember talking to any other kids. I breathed a sigh of relief when the final bell rang and I could grab my schoolbag and head home, where I could be myself and not have to deal with so much pressure to get things right. I remember thinking that it was going to be a very long year."

If you can identify with the above scenario, you're in good company. When I've asked kids—shy or not shy—about their feelings about the first day of school, they've told me the following:

- "I'm worried about my teacher. I used to know who she was, and now I won't."

- "The scariest thing is that your parents are gone."

- "I think I'll look around and go, 'Uh-oh—I don't know anybody here.'"

- "At my school, when you go to third grade, you get homework. I'm scared that I won't be able to do it."

- "I'm going to a bigger school, and I'm worried about being the smallest guy in the school and what I'm going to do with the bigger guys."

These concerns and the pre-school jitters they create are completely normal. In fact, I think they're a positive sign because they show that the child has helpful, positive anxiety that indicates he's excited and eager to start the new school year. This kind of temporary anxiety keeps him on his toes and allows him to rise to his new challenges. It would be a shame if he didn't feel a thing.

While most children should feel some sort of nervousness or anxiety in the first day or week of the new school year, some children feel these emotions to a more intense degree or for a longer period of time. This prolonged tension becomes problematic. Long after the other children have made their transition to the new school year, these shy children struggle with lingering jitters that indicate that the newness of the experience has not been over-come. Only after a long period of doubt, self-consciousness, and anxiety will the child grudgingly incorporate these new experiences into his comfort zone.

It's important to help your child make the transition into the new school year. If he is allowed to shrink away on the sidelines, his inhibitions and worries have the power to color his entire school experience. Shyness can eventually affect academic development, because the shyness-related jitters, anxiety, self-consciousness, or inhibitions can prevent him from staying focused on his lessons, participating in class, or getting more help from the teacher. Shyness can also affect social development because shy kids are less likely to learn the necessary social skills that their peers are learning, and kids who aren't battling jitters will have an easier time forming friendships. Lastly, shyness can affect how the shy student handles the material items involved in study—he may be so tense that his handwriting is shaky or he is uncomfortable working with unfamiliar objects. Like other shyness-related conflicts, dealing with the fear and inhibitions of school early on is far better than waiting for the child to grow out of it.

FOCUSING ON THE SOCIAL SIDE OF SCHOOL

If you look more closely at what is causing your child's school jitters, you'll find that his concerns are often more complicated that what he initially expresses, and they tend to involve the social side of school. For example, he may tell you, "I'm scared that I won't be able to keep up with my homework." But what he's really trying to say is "I'm going to be embarrassed in class because I won't be able to keep up with my homework. The teacher will pick on me if I don't know the right answer or can't turn things in on time. And the other kids will think I'm dumb."

These social worries are normal because children naturally want to do well in a competitive, evaluative environment while doing well socially, too. But parents often disregard these conflicts or misinterpret them because adults are focused on the academic challenges of school, and not the social challenges. However, the socialization process provided by schools—the "informal curriculum" that runs through each school day—is powerful, especially in the early school years. After all, school teaches the child how to interact with others properly, follow rules, speak up in public, cope with authority figures, and navigate peer relationships. Fitting in, speaking up, and keeping up with classmates are social lessons that must be learned, no matter what the child's grade level.

How Shyness Is Triggered at School

The social challenges of school can trigger shyness because they're new, unfamiliar, unpredictable, and sometimes threatening experiences. Young children entering the formal educational system are pushed out of the family's comfort zone whether they're ready or not. Not only must they cope with all of the changes presented to them, but they must do so alone, without the steady guidance of their parents or caretakers. This separation can seem harsh to some children, like the young Emma, and, in fact, this is when some children are first identified by parents and teachers as being shy.

Older children may have trouble adapting to the new school year as well for different reasons. They may be shy and inclined to avoid what's stressing them or lack the social skills to keep up with their peers. They may backslide after a summer spent away from school and away from their daily routine. If these older kids are placed in a new school, or face an unusually difficult teacher, their eagerness to attend school will plummet.

Whatever the child's age or general personality type, the new school year presents a range of experiences that can trigger the three overriding aspects of shyness:

- Students can get caught in the **approach/avoidance conflict**.

- They may be **slow to warm up** to their new experiences.

- Students may struggle to **expand their comfort zone**.

Emma's first-day-of-school photo perfectly illustrates the approach/avoidance conflict. On her way out the door she looks like she's ready for her big day—she's smiling and proud to be dressed up and waving goodbye to her mom. However, once the reality of the day sets in, her positive, approaching attitude changes, and the avoidance side of the cycle sets in as she frets, becomes silent, and suffers. Her frequent headaches and stomachaches are physical signs that she isn't making the transition smoothly.

But since Emma must go back to school every day, she must adapt to her new routine. She has no choice. However, she warms up to school slowly: It takes her longer to make the transition, and she is more stressed out by it, than her more outgoing, quickly warming peers. And because the other kids seem to make the transition seamlessly and without much fuss, slow-to-warm-up students like Emma feel left behind and even more isolated. As the school year progresses, it's hard for them to focus on making friendships and concentrating on their schoolwork because they're still battling the discomfort that bothered most of the other children only during the first week or so. And although their jitters may feel less bothersome with each new school year, shy children still make slower transitions than their more positively approaching peers.

Because of this more anxious, avoidant, and slowly warming orientation to school, shy kids have a harder time integrating their new challenges into their comfort zone made up of familiar behaviors, places, and people. The expanding comfort zone includes:

- New behaviors: Following new rules, being away from parents and siblings, eating in a lunchroom, learning new lessons, and adapting to a pre-set routine
- New places: The regular classroom, the various classrooms in the school, the playground, and the child's desk or locker
- New people: The teachers, the principal, the other adults in the school, the classmates, and other children in the school

In many ways, shy students are merely reacting to the school year in the same way they react to any unfamiliar social activity, whether it's encountering other children at a public swimming pool or being affectionate toward a relative they see infrequently. Shy children, who are slow to warm up to many new experiences that have a social component, will simply need to take a longer time to expand their comfort zones. This is understandable when you consider that their comfort zones are expanding beyond their own control and often against their wishes.

Typical Shy Reactions to School

To help you assess your child's level of discomfort surrounding school, please work through the following list and rate your child's reactions. For each reaction, note whether your child experiences it at a low level, medium level, or high level. Also note whether these reactions are temporary or persistent.

- Has trouble going to sleep, staying asleep, or getting up in the morning on weekdays, but sleeps normally on weekends

- Able to eat only a light breakfast or lunch

- Loses interest in his favorite foods

- Talks about his fears about school

- Says only negative things about school or doesn't talk about school at all

- Is more clingy or fussy than usual

- Has more behavior problems on Sunday nights or Monday mornings

- Complains of stomachaches, headaches, or other vague physical problems

- Expresses little interest in school before the school year begins

- Can interact socially outside of the school setting, but not within it

Most children will exhibit at least a few of these signs at the beginning of the school year, and they point to the child's nervous but positive excitement about his expanding comfort zone. However, if these signs persist, if your child shows them to an acute degree, or if they are totally out of character with how your child usually adapts to what's outside of his comfort zone, he may be having more serious problems transitioning into the new school year and becoming more comfortable with his new routine. If this is the case, your child will need more input and support from you. Throughout this chapter, I'll show you how to aid your child's transition into school.

Successfully Shy Journal

After working through the list of typical reactions to school, take a moment for more reflection in your Successfully Shy Journal. Please answer the following questions:

- What are your child's reactions to entering school? How long do they last? Have they changed from year to year, or do they change as the school year progresses? Is his transition into school different from how he adjusts to other new situations?

- What triggers her reactions? Are they caused by school or something else? What do you do to help?

Your answers should help you uncover how your child experiences the shy process in the school setting. In the first step of the process, he knows he must approach, but he's trying to avoid the situation. In the second step, his anxiety is lengthening the warm-up period of adjustment. And in the third step, he's resisting the expansion of his comfort zone. For example, you may have found that your child has school jitters because he has heard terrible things about his teacher, and he's terrified she'll be mean to him in front of the class. That's his shyness trigger. He's going to school (approaching) but remains silent and anxious (avoidance). Unlike his classmates, he isn't developing a relationship with the teacher (slow to warm up). And he's simply not comfortable in class (comfort zone).

Now, select one of your child's triggers and write down the ways in which you can help your child through the process so that his shy reactions don't get out of hand. For example, you can provide a reality check about his fears, or develop your own relationship with the teacher to show that she isn't to be feared. You can provide him with examples about how he could

(continued)

safely approach the teacher so that he bonds with her. You can also cite the teacher's many positive qualities so that he doesn't dwell on the rumors of her sternness. In time, he'll find that he can cope with this situation, which will make him better able to cope with other authority figures, such as his T-ball coach or piano teacher.

HELPING YOUR CHILD COPE

Helping your child transition into a new school year is critical to his enjoyment of the school experience. If you, as a parent, can understand and explain what he's going through, your shy student will be able to understand his feelings and respond in more successful ways. Instead of suffering silently, your child will be able to break free of his worries and anxiety and focus instead on learning, bonding, and mastering new skills. Two ways you can help your child cope with school are to select the right school for your child, and to begin the transition into school early.

Select the Best School for Your Child

Parental choice in selecting a school is a relatively new phenomenon; only recently have parents been able to choose from a variety of school environments and locations, from magnet schools to charter schools, parochial schools to home-school settings. What's new, too, is that children are entering school environments earlier, oftentimes years before they enter kindergarten. Children often begin taking courses, or going to day care, when they're still in diapers.

As a parent, you've got a lot to consider, from when your child enters school to how often he'll attend it, where he'll go, and when you should change schools. Given the variety of educational offerings available, it's now much easier to choose the right type of school for your child and provide what's called "goodness of fit" between your child and her school.

"Goodness of fit" occurs when a person encounters a compatible environment and expectations. When this happens, the individual can cope with demands and develop as a person. When an individual is in a situation that's a "poor fit" for her particular personality or abilities, she isn't able to function well. For example, someone who is allergic to cats would not be able to work well in a pet store, an environment that's a poor fit for her. But if you asked her to work in a jewelry shop, far away from any cats, she would be able to do her job well.

So it is with shy students. Some school environments provide a better fit for a shy student than others. In general, shy students tend to do well in calm, nurturing environments that provide only a light dose of stimulation. They also do well when they aren't pressured to perform tasks they aren't ready for and are free to ask questions and make mistakes. In contrast, they generally tend to do poorly in loud, chaotic, overcrowded classrooms that further stimulate their already overstimulated systems.

Goodness of fit changes as the child develops and copes with more difficult challenges. To provide goodness of fit at the day care or pre-school level, parents must consider the basics: how often and how long the child will attend the program. Many parents have no choice but to enroll their children in a full-day, every day program, but if you are able to modify your child's schedule, I encourage you to be flexible. Your shy preschooler may not be able to tolerate 30 to 40 hours of stimulation a week, at least at the beginning of the school year. You may want to start with one day a week and work up to more days, or start with more days—but short-

BEING THE NEW KID

Entering a new classroom is hard enough when everyone is new. But it's even harder if you're a new kid because of a transfer, whether it's at the beginning of the school year or during one already in progress. In a way, this makes the child "off time," whether he's shy or not, and self-consciousness, anxiety, and doubt are multiplied. Throw in some shyness and you've got a potential crisis. If your child is changing schools, here's how you can help.

- Anticipate the shy process. Prepare your child for all of the new elements he'll encounter in the classroom, and do your best to make them familiar.

- Meet the teacher. Your child's teacher can be his best ally, so introduce them before the child's first day, and develop your own relationship with the teacher, too.

- Acknowledge the difficulty. You may feel you should overlook the negative in order to encourage a positive attitude, but talking about your child's adjustment to school will help him understand you're there for support and to help him sort out his feelings.

- Highlight his strengths. Get your child involved in his favorite activities so he'll be known as more than the "new kid."

Overall, treat a transfer as you would a regular new school year—but a more intense one. You may want to discuss the issues and strategies presented in this chapter with your child for a more direct way of supporting him. Finally, be open to questions and discussion as he gradually feels more comfortable with his new classmates and school setting.

ened—and gradually lengthen the time that your child is in school each day. This extra transition period will give your child the extra time he needs to gradually warm up to his new environment.

In kindergarten and elementary school, you can't be so flexible about your child's attendance. However, this can benefit your child, because simply going to school becomes a new routine. The mere day-in-and-day-out repetition will help him become more comfortable in school. On the other hand, allowing your child to take frequent sick days will teach him to get out of his obligations when he can.

What's critical at this age is finding the right kind of school environment for your child, one that encourages your child to develop social skills. Studies have shown that schools that emphasize academic excellence in young students tend to breed anxiety, because children are pressured to perform at peak levels and aren't able to develop the other facets of their lives, such as their social skills or creativity. These students are treated like mini-adults, but they don't have the emotional maturity or cognitive ability to deal with the pressure that goes with it. If your child is shy and already having difficulty with her social skills or level of anxiety, this sort of intense, competitive academic focus will be a poor fit and make her feel even worse.

Sometimes children react so adversely to school that parents consider home schooling their children to lessen their anxiety. I believe that home schooling can be beneficial in some ways as the parent is closely involved in the child's academic development and often provides a superior education, or at least a better education if the area schools are sub-par.

However, I would caution parents to think twice about home schooling their shy child. Home schooling can keep your child within the family's comfort zone just when his comfort zone should be expanded in all ways. In fact, shy children, in particular, can benefit from the socialization process provided by school. Without the constant daily exposure to this informal curriculum, a shy child may have a more difficult time becoming comfortable with unfamiliar children and tasks. He may miss out on the important social lessons of childhood, from dealing with complex friendships to learning how to speak up when he has a question. If you are home schooling your child, help him expand his comfort zone by making sure that he has enough social opportunities to build lasting friendships and gain exposure to a wide variety of children and social settings.

Overall, I suggest that parents of shy or slow-to-warm-up students select a school—especially for young children in day care, pre-school, or early elementary school—that emphasizes the "informal curriculum" that teaches children how to become a happy, healthy, functioning part of a larger social universe. Because your child is more likely to be anxious about the social aspects of school, and not her intellectual abilities, she'll benefit from this more nurturing, pro-social environment. After all, if she's feeling tense and inhibited because of her social fears, she'll never feel relaxed enough to focus on her studies.

But don't just listen to my advice. Consider, too, the advice given by Diana, the mother of Jamie, whose story appeared in the previous chapter on making friends. Jamie was enrolled in a number of day care and pre-school settings before finding the right fit for her needs in the first grade. Once comfortable only on the sidelines, Jamie found that a nurturing, upbeat, varied setting made her feel upbeat and outgoing too.

"Parents should find a school where their kids get a wide variety of activities," Diana advises. "When kids do something that's just a part of their day, it's no big deal. They just do it, whether it's going to Spanish class or gym or music class. They're charged up and excited about learning, and they just do it." As a result, Jamie has become more outgoing and fearless about attending school and connecting with friends.

Successfully Shy Journal

To help you select a school for your child or assess the one he's currently attending, please answer the following questions in your Journal:

- What is the class size?
- What is the teacher's emphasis—academics or socialization?
- How long is the school day?
- Which activities or subjects are provided?
- Is the environment more competitive or more nurturing?
- What is the teacher's attitude toward shy children?
- How does the teacher evaluate or assess students?
- Does your child know any other students in the class or at the school?
- Have you spoken to other parents about the school? What have you learned?
- How does the school encourage parental involvement?
- What is part of your child's "informal curriculum"? How does your child deal with it?
- Does this informal curriculum clash with or mesh with the messages you provide at home?
- Is the school a "good fit" for your child? If not, what can you do about it?

(continued)

If your answers indicate that your child's school environment is not a good fit for your child, you may want to take steps to change that. For example, you could offer to coach a sport or lead an extracurricular activity that isn't currently being offered but that your child would enjoy. You could discuss certain issues, like class size, with your child's teacher or the principal, with the hope of making changes. Ultimately, if the environment cannot be altered, you may want to check out other schools for your child.

If you don't know the answers to these questions, seek them out. If your child is already attending the school, observe her activities, become more involved at the school, ask your child's teacher for more information, or seek out the parents of your child's classmates. After all, if your child spends close to 40 hours a week in school, shouldn't you know what she's experiencing there?

Begin the Transition into School Early

Another way you can help your child overcome school jitters is to help her get used to what's new. What's stressing your child is her fear of the unfamiliar. When she thinks about starting the new school year, her thoughts are tied up in these unfamiliar and unknown aspects: *Will I make friends with the other kids? What's the teacher like? Will she be mean to me in front of the class? Will I get lost in the hallways?*

Fortunately, the newness of school wears off eventually, and many kids adapt rather quickly once they realize that the new school year is just a fresh extension of their previous experiences. But as we discussed earlier, this transition is particularly tough for shy kids, and they continue to feel threatened and fearful of what's so new, so terrifying.

The key to easing your shy child through this transition period is to prepare her long before the school year starts, which begins the warming up process as well. Referring to the first day of school as the "big day" and building it up to be a totally new, completely unknown experience will only heighten your child's anxiety. But reminding your child of the familiar aspects of school will help her draw on her past experiences and remind her of her past successes. She will be able to anticipate what will happen and draw on past skills and experiences and realize that the school day is full of nothing more than friendly classmates, a helpful teacher, and challenging but not impossible tasks.

The key to helping your child prepare for the first day of the new school year and gain a healthy perspective about school is to break down the new school experience into manageable parts - the academic part, the social part, and the material part - and demystify them.

What's New: The Academic Aspect

We typically think of going to school as an academic experience; children are there to learn and develop their intellect and skills. However, the academic aspect of school is intertwined with a lot of loaded issues: social involvement, the pressure to perform well, being judged, dealing with authority, and developing skills and healthy self-esteem.

Some typical academic fears include:

- What if I don't know the answer when the teacher calls on me?

- What if I can't handle my homework load?

- What if the teacher is a harsh grader?

- What if I'm expected to talk a lot in class?

EASING SHYNESS IN THE NEW SCHOOL YEAR

No matter what grade you teach, a teacher can make the beginning of the year go smoothly for all students. Here's how you can help your shy students expand their comfort zone so that you—and your classroom—have a place in it.

- Notice individual variations in warming up. Some students will jump right in, but almost half will need a little more time getting used to you.

- Greet your students individually. Don't let them just file into your classroom without a word. Say hello, introduce yourself, and make them feel welcome.

- Proceed slowly with your shy students. In the beginning of the year, give them more time to open up and become a part of group activities and discussions.

- Encourage cooperation. Activities at the beginning of the year should allow kids to get to know you and their classmates. Competitive activities can wait.

- Don't overlook shy students. Since they generally don't create a lot of fuss, they can get lost in a crowd. Point out their successes and other positive attributes.

Lastly, remember that while shy students need an extended warm-up period, they should become comfortable within a reasonable amount of time. If they are still having a hard time adjusting long after their classmates have acclimated themselves, find out if there's more going on, such as family problems, tension with another classmate, or even a physical problem such as poor nutrition or bad eyesight. Then lean on the support you have within your school, such as a counselor, nurse, or fellow teacher.

- Will the other kids laugh at me if I ask a question?

- What will happen when I have to work in groups with kids I don't know?

These worries are normal but can spiral out of control if the child doesn't get a reality check. That reality check can come when they go to school and realize that they're ready for what's ahead, but it can also come from parents who support their child's ever increasing academic demands. Here's how you can help:

Teach your child that the past is prologue. Remind her of her past successes and how she can apply her previous lessons to her new lessons.

Offer to help. If he's worried about not being able to handle his workload, remind him that he has already coped with homework and that you'll help him out if he needs it.

Explain the purpose of school. Making mistakes and being confused are part of the learning process, so she shouldn't be afraid to take a risk and speak up in class.

Point out educational aspects of daily life. Tell your child that each of us is learning something new all the time, and that this process is healthy. For example, when you ask for directions while driving, explain to your child that asking questions is how you get information, not how you attract negative attention.

Practice at home. When you review your child's homework, try playing the role of teacher. And try playing the role of the student sometimes, too.

Remind him that he isn't alone. Let him know that everyone feels a little nervous about speaking in class or taking a test, but that the more he does it, the easier it will be.

Overall, if your child knows that you believe she can handle any academic challenges, she'll believe that she can. And if you remind her that she has had lots of successful experiences in school, she can apply those lessons to her future schoolwork.

Successfully Shy Journal

In your Successfully Shy Journal, reflect on the academic challenges your child faces in his upcoming school year. Then answer the following questions:

- Which new academic tasks will your child encounter this year?
- How can these tasks be seen as an extension of what he has already mastered?
- Has your child expressed any doubts about his ability to handle these tasks? If so, what has he indicated?
- How are his academic fears related to his social fears?
- How have you dispelled his fears?
- How can you remind him that he's well prepared for his new challenges?

Your answers will indicate where your child may need extra time and effort when incorporating these new academic tasks into his comfort zone. For example, if he's having difficulty with his teacher's informal spelling bees every week, you can help him out. Quiz him at home, and let him quiz you, too. Discuss the purpose of making mistakes—they merely show where the child and teacher need to work harder. And remind him of all of the words that he already knows how to spell. He can build on success when he feels that he's already proved himself in the past. Step by step, week by week, he'll master the task presented to him.

What's New: The Social Aspect

Learning is a unique social experience, as children do not learn in isolation. They learn with each other and from each other. They support each other and compete with each other. What's more, students must learn how to navigate the power structure of the school. Teachers can be demanding or nurturing, intimidating or reasonable. Other kids are friends or foes or oftentimes both at once.

In the early years, academic aims take a back seat to the socialization process. Many children already know how to do much of what is expected of them academically and enter the school year well prepared for those challenges. But they must cope with all of the unspoken social lessons that underlie their day—the "informal curriculum." Some of these lessons include:

- Learning in a group setting

- Speaking and performing new tasks in front of a group

- Taking turns

- Sharing information and objects

- Eating, going to the bathroom, and getting dressed in public

- Being surrounded by peers who are not always friendly or familiar

- Following directions

- Navigating the power structure of the classroom

- Creating a relationship with an authority figure

- Being evaluated both as an individual and a student

All of these social challenges have the ability to unnerve a shy child, or even a more outgoing child who feels unprepared for the year ahead. While some of these social tasks are mastered early on, some take longer to be absorbed and must be reinforced every year. For example, if your child had a patient, nurturing fifth grade teacher but faces a more intimidating sixth grade teacher, these social fears will become more pronounced before the school year begins. And if your child is entering a new school, it's only natural that he'll feel more apprehensive about fitting in and performing well.

Like every other social challenge, preparing your shy child for the social aspects of school is imperative. If you can incorporate some of the social lessons listed above into your child's day before the school year begins, her jitters will be less intense and much more fleeting. Try these strategies:

Meet the teacher before the school year begins. If you can make a connection in a safe, friendly way, your child won't fear her.

Get a head start. Go to school early on the first day so your son can meet the other kids one by one. That way, the warming up period will be worked through before the day's official beginning.

Maintain your child's friendships through the summer. Your child will need to see a few friendly faces on that first day.

Get involved in group activities. Whether it's day camp or playing at the playground, your child will benefit from knowing at least a few rules of the game.

Share your stories. Explain how you felt before school started and why it's important to feel at least a little bit nervous before going to school.

Reinforce your child's social skills. Brush up on your child's ability to make introductions, share, and follow rules.

Overall, remind your child that even if he feels a little bit nervous before the beginning of the year, this feeling is temporary. After all, doesn't he usually feel a little nervous before trying something new? And doesn't he always overcome his jitters once he's gotten used to his new environment or made a few friends? Going to school is no different. He'll eventually feel more confident.

Successfully Shy Journal

In your Successfully Shy Journal, jot down all of the new social aspects of your child's school day, from creating a relationship with her teacher to coping with some of the less friendly kids in her class. Now, write down how your child is coping with these encounters. Then answer the following questions.

- What can be improved?

- What are you doing to help?

Oftentimes, parents resign themselves to letting their shy child suffer through school with a less-than-stellar social life. Parents often don't know how to help without interfering, so they tell their child to rise above the problem or ignore it. One common difficulty is when a shy child has a troublemaker or chronic teaser in her class, and the shy student lives in fear of being singled out for ridicule. While you can't go to school with your child, you can help your child by providing indirect support. Provide a reality check and calm her fears about this classmate. Discuss how she could handle a confrontation, and then act one out. Strengthen her friendships with other children by giving them opportunities to hang out. If she has good relationships with other kids, she won't be a target for troublemakers.

What's New: The Material Aspect

Besides the academic and social aspects, school has a large material facet as well. Children arrive at school loaded down with a backpack and supplies, and they wear a uniform or school-appropriate clothing. Much of these material goods are new—after all, don't we typically buy our children new school shoes, clothes, and supplies during the back-to-school sales? Once at school, they must become acclimated to their new classroom—or multiple classrooms—and their desk and locker.

Being surrounded by all of these new items can make a child feel more uncomfortable and therefore more inhibited. After all, if your daughter is feeling constricted by her stiff new uniform, can't remember how to find her new classroom, or isn't used to eating cafeteria food, she's not going to be able to concentrate on the academic task at hand or be sociable and friendly.

Just as you are making the unfamiliar academic and social aspects more familiar, you can make the material aspects of your shy student's day more familiar before the school year begins. Here's how:

Establish a school-friendly sleep schedule. Adjust your child's sleep schedule at least two weeks before the beginning of the school year. If he's been staying up later and sleeping in all summer, he won't be awake and alert and focused when school starts.

Pull out her new clothes and school supplies early. So what if they're a little worn on the first day of school? Have a dress rehearsal during the summer so she is comfortable in her back-to-school clothes. And encourage your child to write in her notebooks and try out her new markers.

Mimic school lunches. If she will be brown-bagging it, prepare a few and go on picnics. If she will be eating in a cafeteria, go to some self-serve restaurants so she'll know what to do

Involve him in your purchases. Your son can help you decide which color folders to buy or sort out his supplies from the previous year.

Visit the school. Drive past the school or follow the route of the bus or carpool. If possible, take a tour of the school when nobody else is around so your child can find her classroom, bathrooms, cafeteria, and locker.

Discuss the changes. If your child knows you empathize with her experiences, she won't feel so isolated and self-conscious.

Overall, preparing your child for the material parts of school will help him integrate these objects into his day. Overlooking this aspect is overlooking a major part of his experience.

Successfully Shy Journal

Write down all of the material objects your child encounters during the day. Then answer the following questions.

- How many of them were new on the first day of school?

- How did your child feel when they were new?

- What can you do to make him more comfortable physically and with the supplies he uses every day?

You can make your child more comfortable physically if you work with at least some of these material objects before the school year begins. After all, wouldn't you feel a bit overwhelmed if you were surrounded by strangers, wearing new clothes, and working with pencils, notebooks, and books that are totally unfamiliar to you—and you were being evaluated on your performance?

SHAKING OFF THE JITTERS

Now that you understand why your child is so nervous about attending the first day of school, you'll be able to help him shake off his jitters and be more comfortable at school. And if he's more comfortable, he'll be able to concentrate fully and find more enjoyment with the other kids. In the next chapter, I'll explain how shyness affects your child in the classroom, and what you can do to help.

CHAPTER 9

THE SHY
STUDENT

September has passed. By now, your shy student's early-morning jitters and anxiety appear to be subsiding, and she is incorporating her new schedule and extracurricular activities into her comfort zone at her own pace. She has made some new friends and seems to be keeping up with her homework assignments. You're not terribly concerned with how her shyness is affecting her in the classroom anymore. Nothing's showing on the surface, so you can breathe a sigh of relief, knowing that the crisis has passed, right?

Perhaps. Although shy kids do eventually adjust to their new school routines, I've found that not all that goes on within the student's new comfort zone is comfortable.

Recently I spoke with Natalie, a smart, talented high school freshman. While she's always done well academically, she's had her rough times in school.

"I don't think of myself as being shy," Natalie explained. "Just quiet. But other people probably think I'm shy because I don't talk a lot around people I don't know very well. I don't feel comfortable around strangers. When I was younger, I was more outgoing. You know how kids are. I think I was actually one of the louder ones."

I asked her what had caused the change. "I started worrying about what the other students would think of me. I felt like they were always looking at me. I was about nine years old, in the third grade, when it started. I became very self-conscious and very quiet."

Natalie told me that her inhibition was triggered by a single, powerful event, one that affects her even now. "My teacher yelled at me in front of the class," she confided. "I was unintentionally making the class laugh. And the teacher noticed and said in front of everyone that I wasn't that funny. It was really embarrassing, and I didn't want to be embarrassed like that again. Before then, I was the class clown. I'm not a class clown anymore, but I'm still funny.

"Now, in classes where I feel comfortable and like the teacher, shyness doesn't really affect me. If I like the teacher, I'll talk more. But if I don't like the teacher, or if I'm put on the spot, I'll turn red. And not many people come up and talk to me because I don't talk. There are times when I'd like to get to know people, but I don't like the spotlight."

Natalie's mother told me that she believes shyness has a hold on her daughter, even if Natalie doesn't admit it. "I think shyness does affect her," she confided. "I'll get comments from her teachers on her report card saying that they wish Natalie would contribute more and participate in class discussions. Right now she's taking a debate class, which she doesn't like. She's doing it, but she tells me she feels shaky beforehand, like she's going to pass out."

As you can see, the classroom is full of challenges for shy students like Natalie—challenges as mundane as cracking a joke or volunteering to answer a question in class and challenges as profound as building healthy self-esteem. These challenges have the power to create doubt, tension, and anxiety. Though shy children may keep their feelings of inner turmoil well hidden, these emotions can affect them in subtle but often profound and long-lasting ways that shape their view of the world when they reach adulthood. The good news, though, is that if these challenges are dealt with early, during the school years, they will merely become temporary obstacles, not life-long setbacks. Once again, a thorough understanding of the shy student's viewpoint will help caring parents like you understand how best to help your child achieve social success.

In this chapter, we'll take a step back and view the classroom through a wide-angle lens. Once you have a glimpse of the big-picture issues within the classroom, you'll have a better understanding of how shyness affects your student's underlying academic, social, and emotional development. Then we'll look at the specific school-related issues and activities that commonly trigger shyness—such as being called on in class, making a presentation, dealing with an impatient teacher, and coping with a rowdy classroom—and I'll explain how they can be successfully dealt with using the concepts and skills I've already introduced. As always, the steady presence of a concerned parent is key, and, as always, your unique take on your child's school experience begins with a few questions for your Successfully Shy Journal.

Successfully Shy Journal

In your Journal, please answer the following questions:

- Does your child enjoy school? How can you tell?

- What doesn't he enjoy?

- How has your child's disposition changed during the school year?

- How has he progressed academically, socially, and emotionally?

- Is your child acting out of character?

- How do you support your child's desire to learn and achieve his goals?

After answering these questions, consider how shyness may be affecting your child's attitude toward school. If your child is normally slow to warm up to socially challenging environments such as the classroom, commit to helping ease him through the warm-up period. If your child has not progressed emotionally or socially since the beginning of the school year, or is resisting school more intensely than usual, you may need to consider that more than shyness is affecting his school experience. In either case, keep what you have written in mind as you read through the chapter. When you read relevant information, make a note in this Journal entry, and come back to it later.

THE BIG PICTURE

Let me just get this off my chest: Shy students are just as intelligent and competent as their more outgoing peers. There is no correlation between shyness and IQ or shyness and ability to master academic tasks. What often happens, though, is that our educational system often works against the slowly warming, self-conscious natures of shy students, because the classroom is a social setting, and because it's full of evaluations.

Yet as challenging as the classroom environment may be for shy students, it's precisely what they need. The challenges presented by school—elementary school, especially—dovetail perfectly with what a shy child requires in order to develop emotionally, intellectually, and socially.

At the mundane level, kids need to learn how to read, spell, add, subtract, and listen to and participate in discussions so that they can become well-rounded, functioning adults. But they also grow and develop at a deeper, more profound level when they're in the classroom. They build a sense of mastery and a sense of themselves as unique individuals, which is an integral part of forming their identity and self-esteem. Shy children also face these challenges, but they tend to experience them in a unique way that has the power to affect them for a very long time, and at a very deep level. Shyness tends to intensify the experience, making naturally occurring challenges more difficult, more fraught with risk. Let's take a look at the big picture—mastery and identity building—before moving on to specific obstacles in the classroom and how you can help.

Mastering the Classroom

According to the noted psychologist Erik Erikson, we develop along a timeline that includes various stages of progress. Each stage includes a "crisis" that must be resolved before moving on to the next stage. According to Erikson, when children are in the early years of school—roughly ages five to twelve—their "crisis" involves building a sense of mastery by solving problems, meeting goals, acquiring skills, and feeling good about their accomplishments.

School provides the perfect environment for developing mastery. Each day, kids are faced with ever more challenging tasks that must be worked through before moving on to the next. Their grades show how well they've accomplished their goals. They graduate from one grade level to the next and continue facing goals and meeting them.

At a deeper level, a child's rapidly developing skills and accomplishments help build his identity. For example, when a child consistently scores well on spelling tests, he's known as a "good speller." When he consistently hits the right notes during music class, he becomes known as a "good singer." And when he devours every book about boy wizards, he develops a reputation as a "bookworm." As the years pass, kids form groups based on these unique identities and shared interests and abilities. The good singers find each other and form a group; the bookworms find each other and swap books and discuss them. When they're adults, they become part of the larger social fabric based on the identities they began exploring and building when they were young. Many of those bookworms eventually become English majors in college, while the good singers find outlets in choirs or theater groups for their talent.

With each task a child takes on comes a goal, and with each goal comes effort, frustration, and persistence. The willingness to hang in there and struggle in order to achieve a goal is called "achievement motivation," and the level of this motivation varies from person to person.

Some people are willing to do the hard work that comes with success, and they set high standards for themselves. When they don't do well, they try harder, or they try different strategies to attain their goal. For example, if they get a barely passing grade on a math test, they'll increase the time and effort they put into their math homework so they'll get a better grade on the next test. They might even ask for help from the teacher or their parents, or consider getting a tutor to help them with their difficulties. Overall, they feel that success is within their control.

Others do not have a strong achievement motive. These people want success to come easily and give up when it gets too difficult; this is what's known as a "learned helplessness" attitude. Instead of thinking that they must try harder to succeed, they're convinced they are victims of fate when they encounter obstacles. They assume they will fail when they're challenged. ("The test was unfair!" they cry after getting a bad grade. "Why bother talking to those kids? They won't like me because I stutter!" they wail when they find themselves alone.) They believe that their problems stem from what they lack—ability, smarts, talent—and their effort isn't enough to overcome their deficits. They're robbed of the satisfaction that comes from a job that's well done and success that was earned.

Shy children, unfortunately, frequently adopt this learned helplessness orientation. Instead of striving to meet their goals—and, at the same time, stretching their comfort zones—they give up because they assume they'll fail. They internalize their perceived failures. They avoid challenges and withdraw into their rigid comfort zone of silence. Instead of volunteering to speak in class, they avoid eye contact and discussion. Instead of asking for help with their homework, they wallow in confusion. Instead of approaching a group of children more than once on the playground, they assume that they'll be rebuffed again and again.

A college student I spoke with learned this strategy well: "I found it easier not to draw attention to myself, but also found myself questioning my thoughts and behaviors as others would see me. Over the years, I would avoid going places and doing things so that I wouldn't make a fool of myself in the eyes of those around me."

This is why I often caution against labeling a child "shy." All too often, "I'm shy" becomes a perfect, socially acceptable excuse for holding back from approaching new challenges: "I can't try out for the play—I'm shy!" "I never talk in class—I'm shy!" Shyness and avoidance become both a burden and a crutch, but not a smart strategy in the long run.

How to Help Your Child Become a Master

Your role as the parent of a shy student may seem to diminish as your child gets older and coaches, teachers, and peers gradually take center stage. Your influence as a parent changes from being direct to indirect and supportive. Instead of making decisions for your child, you give the child opportunities and choices, guidance when requested, strategies for success, and reality checks.

Although you can't be by your child's side during the school day, you can greatly aid your child by helping to foster a love of learning and a love of achieving new goals by strengthening his "achievement motivation." In time, this will help expand your child's comfort zone and help focus his attention on his tasks, not his shyness or self-doubt. Here are some strategies:

Create a safe home base. If your child knows he's loved unconditionally, he won't be afraid to risk making mistakes.

Foster independence. It's okay to step in and help when your child requests it, but let your child work through her tasks on her own.

Set appropriately high standards. Children rise or sink to the level at which they're expected to perform. Bring out the best in your child.

Praise success without punishing failures. Make sure your reactions are consistent and fair. If your child is making progress, however slowly, show her you notice.

Reinforce social skills. Continue exposing your child to new social environments and new people, and prep him if he seems unsure of how to behave.

Develop a stimulating home environment. A home filled with puzzles, games, art supplies, and plenty of books helps develop your child's natural curiosity and eagerness to solve problems.

Build skills. If your child has the necessary skills to do well in school, occasional jitters won't throw her off or make her doubt herself.

Don't shelter your child. Kids need to be exposed to challenges. Allow your child to be exposed to a few unusually difficult challenges.

Set a good example. If you want your child to do well in school, read to him and read books on your own. Show him how you use math in everyday situations at the store or while paying the bills. And take him along to the library when you have a question you want to research.

Become a team. Involve your child in decisions and talk about how you come to the right one. It's more satisfying to have limited choices than none at all.

Overall, you'll need to strike a good balance between helping your child take risks and respecting her slowly stretching comfort zone. For example, if she is worried about what to take to school for show-and-tell, don't excuse her from it or make the decision for her. Brainstorm with her to come up with options. Discuss the pros and cons of each choice, and let her make the final decision. Then rehearse at home so she'll know what to say. With enough preparation and practice, she'll work through her anxieties at home so they'll be diminished in the classroom. And she'll be proud of her good performance because it was earned, not handed to her.

Successfully Shy Journal

List the skills or tasks that your child is currently mastering. Now answer the following questions about his progress.

- What is your child's attitude toward his challenges? Does he back away from struggles, or is he willing to work hard?

- How does he go about mastering his challenges: Does he ask questions, seek help, use the same approach again and again, procrastinate, or try different strategies until he finds one that works?

- How does your child respond to failure? With excuses? Anger? A sense of helplessness? Determination to do better the next time?

- Can you identify any connection between your child's performance in school and his shyness? Does he use shyness as an excuse?

- How do you help him?

Many children find a particular school subject or activity to be especially difficult, but are generally confident that they can handle what comes their way. But if you find that your child seriously doubts his ability to reach his goals or can come up with a million excuses for why he isn't doing well in class, you need to intervene so that his self-doubt doesn't turn into a self-defeating spiral. Identify the skills he's already acquired that can be used now. You might even want to go back to chapter 1 and review some of the life skills I discussed. The "Four I's" of problem solving, as well as frustration tolerance, will be especially relevant. Then, when you notice that your child is stymied by a particular assignment, try guiding him in a more positive direction.

Developing an Identity

Along with mastery, developing an identity completes the big picture goals of the classroom. As we discussed earlier, much of a person's identity is formed through mastery. If Stacy does well on her essays, she thinks of herself as a "good writer." But how, exactly, does Stacy figure out that she's a good writer? One way is to look at her grades. If she's getting high ones, she knows that she's at the top of her class. But Stacy can also look at the other kids' performances and rank herself accordingly. After all, in our society, children learn in a very public, very social environment—the classroom—and there are no secrets.

When Stacy evaluates herself based on others, she's using a psychological process known as "social comparison." If Stacy knows that Tom is good at long division, and she isn't, then that helps Stacy understand herself and Tom a little bit better.

Social comparison can be intensified by the environment, especially during times of uncertainty, when we're more self-conscious and unsure of what to do. And since shy children are acutely self-conscious in the classroom, they use social comparison frequently and believe that all others are focused on them as well. According to one high school student, self-consciousness and social comparison follow her everywhere: "When I'm walking down the hall at school, sometimes I feel like people are watching me and I begin to wonder what they think." This intense self-focus is usually critical, which creates even more doubt, tension, and avoidance.

Other factors bring out social comparison as well. If the classroom is unduly competitive, kids will naturally use social comparison more often as they rank themselves against their peers. If the teacher is unusually harsh, kids will compare themselves in anticipation of being judged by the teacher. Again, social comparison is normal, but intensified by shyness.

What Gets Noticed and How

What kids find to be important when they compare themselves changes with time. Already at age three, kids can evaluate their accomplishments and figure out if they're good or bad. Between ages three and five, they're aware of how their friends behave, which shows that they're developing social awareness, the first step toward making comparisons. When kids are in kindergarten, they know who is smart, dumb, or good at gym, and they choose their friends and partners accordingly.

During the next few years, kids' perceptions of their peers change. Instead of merely noticing their peers' behavior and comparing it to their own, they notice others' behavior and stamp a psychological trait onto it. Nice, mean, smart, dumb—and shy—are common psychological traits identified by kids during the elementary school years.

Shyness, in particular, begins to be noticed by fourth grade students, and, unfortunately, it's not a trait that's well liked. When peers notice that someone is shy, they evaluate that child negatively, which creates even more inhibition in the child. Further, when shy kids evaluate themselves, they tend to do so negatively and usually do not do anything to change how they feel about themselves. They see their shyness as something they can't change, and something that holds them back from being successful and popular. Their perceptions of what life is like for an outgoing person tend to be idealized and totally out of their reach, while their existence as a shy kid suffers in comparison. As this gardener explained, "I feel my shyness started in grade school and that I let the losers make me feel like a loser. I projected to others my insecure feelings about myself." Years later, his childhood self-doubt and pain are still close to the surface because nobody intervened and helped him.

The Development of Self-Esteem

Understanding mastery and social comparison is vitally important because they are two building blocks of self-esteem, which is how we think about our selves. When we believe that we've done a good job at a particular task, or when we feel that we're at least equal to our peers, we have a healthy level of self-esteem. On the other hand, when we believe we haven't mastered a skill or don't live up to the standards set by our peers, our self-esteem tends to fall.

While this is a natural process of self-evaluation, it can be particularly sticky for shy children. When they compare themselves to their peers, especially when they're feeling unsure of themselves, they tend to think that their peers are more accomplished or confident or popular than they are. After all, if a shy child feels nervous and tense when she speaks in class, but nobody else looks so jittery, she will think that she's not as smart or well spoken as her classmates. This in turn will affect her self-esteem and confidence.

But assessing self-esteem can get even more complicated. Many times, individuals compare themselves not to their peers, but to the "ideal self," which is how they feel they should behave. While this can help motivate someone to do better, it can also turn into a self-defeating trap since the individual will never live up to his ideal self.

Children who are constantly striving to achieve their ideal self may have a difficult time accepting themselves, their occasional failures, and their triumphs, which will often be seen as qualified successes. Shy kids may think that they must be incredibly smart or outgoing to be valued or liked. And deep down inside, they don't feel smart or sociable and fear being rejected by their peers, their teacher, or their parents.

Successfully Shy Journal

Please work through the following questions in your Journal:

- How does your child identify herself?

- How does she talk about her peers and classmates? What does she notice? Why do you think she finds these qualities or behaviors to be important?

- Do you think her comparisons are mostly favorable, or mostly unfavorable?

- Do you think she places too much emphasis on her peers' behavior or personal qualities?

- Do you think this affects her sense of self, or her identity?

The aim of these questions is to help you understand how your child views her social universe and her place in it. Are her peers friendly, or not? Does she dwell on what she lacks, or not? Does she analyze her friends' behavior too intensely, or is she uninterested in what they're doing? If you deem her answers to be mostly positive, she likely has a realistic view of herself and her crowd, and therefore probably has a healthy level of self-esteem. But if you think she's judging herself too harshly—or judging her peers unfairly—you may want to provide her with a reality check. After all, not everyone in her class is snobby, or smarter. She just perceives them to be so.

If you had difficulty answering these questions, that's a sign that it's time to begin a conversation on this topic with your child. Ask her what she thinks about other people in her world, and identify what she notices and why. Then provide any reality checks you think are needed. The conversation this stimulates will turn into more dialogue as she gets older.

THE SHY STUDENT

Now that you have a better idea of how shyness has the power to affect your child's desire to learn and challenge himself at a very basic, very deep level, let's turn to how shyness affects how your child approaches specific tasks at school.

The classroom is a perfect breeding ground for shyness and heightened self-consciousness because it's an evaluative social setting that's somewhat unpredictable. Even the most mundane, routine activities can trigger shyness—raising one's hand, waiting to be called on, eating in the lunchroom, finding playmates on the playground, walking alone through the hallways, making a presentation, or even being singled out for good behavior. All of these activities make the shy student feel self-conscious and bring out his inhibitions and doubts.

Here's how the shy process is triggered at school:

- The *approach/avoidance conflict* is activated, because children naturally want to learn, but shy children are unsure of their abilities to do so in a social setting in which their skills are being judged by the teacher and classmates.

- Shy kids are *slow to warm up* to new activities and social arrangements. They're more physically aroused and anxious due to the approach/avoidance conflict, which extends their warming up period. But they also tend to wait and hover when faced with new tasks or new partners. They may warm up too slowly and find that the class has moved on to a new task just when they've warmed up to the previous one.

- Shy students' *comfort zones are narrower* in the classroom than their classmates', so they may prefer to read or work solo and may have a hard time doing other activities, such as volunteering to wipe off the blackboard or participating in the school play. They're also less likely to take risks, whether they're academic or social, because of their "learned helplessness" orientation.

Here's an example of the shy process in action. Let's say that Carol's second grade class must break up into groups to create Halloween decorations for the classroom. Carol has been assigned to a group with four other children she doesn't know well, since her teacher thought this would be a good way for her to develop some new friendships. Carol's the last one to get settled while the other kids start tracing some ghosts, goblins, and cobwebs onto the long sheet of paper. She watches what they're doing and sees a perfect spot for a bunch of bats and a full moon, but she doesn't say anything. Carol looks around the room and sees everyone else working hard, while she's just standing there, immobile. She catches her teacher's eye and decides to join in or else she'll get a bad grade. She grabs a black marker and starts drawing on the edge of the paper. Her perfect spot has been used for a giant pumpkin, even though it doesn't look great there.

Carol's experience doesn't mean she lacks intelligence or artistry, just time. She needs time to work through her approach/avoidance conflict so that she can act on her good ideas and develop her sense of mastery. She needs time to warm up to the new kids in her work group and get used to her new activity. And she needs more time to add all of this to her classroom comfort zone. She'll probably function better the next time she's faced with this task, but for now she may feel left behind or left out. In addition, she's not developing leadership skills because she's following her group's lead, and not participating in the initial group decisions, like what to draw.

This entire situation can make Carol feel more self-conscious, and this in turn heightens her anxiety and self-doubt. Taken together, this discomfort may affect her performance. If her hand's shaking, she won't be able to draw well; if she's tense, she won't be able to warm up to the other children in her group. All of these experiences can create a negative mental loop—"I feel tense so I can't draw; I can't draw so I feel more tense." And when she dwells on her negative mental loop, she can't focus on what she's been assigned to do. All in all, it's an invisible but powerful mental trap that can ensnare any shy student.

Common Obstacles in the Classroom

Now that you understand how the shy process is triggered in the classroom, it's time to move on to more specific hurdles in the classroom and how you can help your child overcome them.

Being Called On in Class

It's a universal fear: being called on by the teacher when you don't know the answer. Everyone's experienced the embarrassment that's caused by having the spotlight shone on you when you weren't paying attention or simply don't know what to say, but shy children find this to be particularly traumatic. Shy kids also get jittery when they're volunteering to answer a question but must wait to be called on. They start second-guessing their response and regret that they've decided to participate.

Let's say that Robbie's teacher is discussing the class's history assignment and wants to know if everyone has read the chapter that's been assigned. She scans the class looking for someone who will answer her questions. Robbie's pretty certain that he can remember what he read yesterday, but isn't sure why his teacher is asking so many simple questions. There must be something he missed, he reasons, or maybe she's asking trick questions. Robbie sinks in his seat, avoids eye contact with the teacher, and drums his pencil against the palm of his hand. He doesn't fool the teacher.

"Robbie," the teacher asks, "which president was in office during the Civil War?"

Robbie's thunderstruck. All eyes are on him. He's almost sure that the answer is Lincoln, but doesn't everyone know that? He stares up at the teacher, blankly, and drums his pencil even harder. He fidgets in his seat, feels hot and flushed, and shuffles his feet. He can hear his heart thumping and is sure everyone else can, too. While he's squirming, another student pipes up with the right answer. Robbie's been rescued. He breathes a sigh of relief, but realizes that no one knows that he had the right answer.

Many shy students are like Robbie and try to hide from their teacher without leaving the room. When they're called on, they're blitzed with anxiety and have to do two things simultaneously: wrack their brains for the right answer and try to cover up their jitters. It's a difficult task, so it's no wonder that shy kids avoid being called on.

You can help your child cope with the anxiety of being called on by following these strategies:

Prepare at home. Make sure your child is keeping up with his assignments, and discuss the material with him so that he's prepared to talk about it in class.

Defuse the situation. Let him know that jitters are normal, even if he can't see that others in his class feel a little anxious, too. Tell him you feel nervous sometimes, too.

Point out that much of his anxiety is invisible to others. Remind him that although he may feel betrayed by his body, nobody else knows that his pulse is racing or his palms are sweaty. His jitters and fears aren't as obvious as he thinks.

Making a Presentation

Another problem area for shy students is making a presentation. This requires a lot of preparation: Not only must the child put together her speech, but she also has to figure out how she's going to cope with her mounting anxiety. Oftentimes kids become so overwhelmed by their upcoming presentation that they do their best to deny, procrastinate, and avoid working on it. This coping mechanism is ultimately self-defeating, though, as Sophie's case illustrates.

Sophie's science fair project is due on Friday, when she must turn in a report and present her project to the class. She's thought about it for the past month, but hasn't been able to put anything together. Science is a weak subject for her, and so is talking in front of the class. She always gets so nervous and can feel herself blush, tremble, and sweat. She dreads it and tries to avoid it as much as possible. In fact, she quit going to her scout meetings because there was simply too much public speaking.

On Wednesday, she knew she had to come up with something. She did a little research on the Internet and found some interesting articles about newly discovered asteroids. She quickly wrote up the paper and created a mural of the solar system, but stopped there and became immersed in TV. Thursday came and went and she couldn't work on her presentation. She couldn't sleep that night either.

Friday morning was horrible. The alarm rang just as she was falling asleep, and she outlined her presentation in a panic. She couldn't concentrate all day. When she was called on to present her asteroid findings, she felt horrible from head to toe. She looked at the class, looked down at her notes, and started talking in a low voice. The teacher asked her to speak up. She stiffened and blushed. Her outline didn't seem organized, and she repeated a few points a few times. She looked at her teacher, whose eyes seemed

SHYNESS TRIGGERS

PERFORMING IN PUBLIC

If you want to see cuteness in action, just go to a school play. But beneath the costumes, there are a lot of nervous, scared kids on that stage. Since you can't excuse your child from performing in a school play, dance recital, church choir, or karate meet, you need to help ease his anxiety. Here's how:

- Understand dread. Whether you're an adult or a child, feeling overwhelming dread or anxiety can prevent you from taking action. Shy kids will feel this more intensely and procrastinate or avoid preparing.

- Talk about anxiety and worries. Let your child know that his feelings are normal but not debilitating. In fact, they'll give him energy when he's out on stage.

- Discuss the reality behind the fantasy. While his favorite singer may look comfortable on stage, talk about all of the work and jitters that go into every performance.

- Break down the tasks for your child. Help him rehearse his lines for the play, work on the costume together, and discuss the progress of rehearsals.

- Increase the challenge. As time goes by, increase the amount of time you rehearse, have another student come over to work on the play together, and then try a dress rehearsal at home.

- Go. It's as simple as that. If your child doesn't see you in the crowd, he'll wonder why he went through all of that fuss if you're not there to see him shine.

Lastly, no matter how well he did, provide him with a lot of praise. Not only did he get through without tears, but he conquered a huge challenge that haunts many adults, too. Celebrate after the performance and let him know that you're proud of him.

to burn a hole through her. When she was safely in her seat, she remembered all of the great things she could have said, but forgot to include in her notes. Oh well—she was no good at public speaking and never would be, she reasoned.

Sophie chose to be traumatized by her assignment. But you can help your child become energized by upcoming speeches. Here's how:

Prepare, don't procrastinate. Don't let your child wait until the last minute. Help her develop a schedule for upcoming assignments.

Check in occasionally. You don't have to micromanage your child's projects, but be aware of his progress as the deadline approaches.

Create a dress rehearsal. If your child has rehearsed her piece before going public, she can sail through it in front of her class.

Relabel anxiety. Explain that jitters mean that your child is excited, not overwhelmed. And excitement is key to doing a good job.

If you want more tips on helping your child deal with presentation making, go back to chapter 3. Stephen's experience at the 4-H show is a great example to follow. Good experiences early in life will create even better experiences later.

Facing a Tough Teacher

Every child eventually faces a teacher with a reputation for being mean and unfair. Shy children seem to intensely dread this showdown, and retreat even further into their shell to avoid attracting the teacher's attention—negative attention, almost certainly. And even once-outgoing kids like Natalie, who shared her story at the beginning of this chapter, can become withdrawn and inhibited by a teacher's negative remarks.

Brian's fourth grade teacher was a mean one. He'd heard about

Miss Miller since the first grade, and dreaded the day when he entered her classroom. And now that he was there, he knew the other kids were right. Miss Miller had terribly high standards. When you made a mistake, you couldn't recover. What's more, you were humiliated and ridiculed.

When Brian received his latest test score, he couldn't believe it: a "D" on his reading test. Normally one of the best readers in the class, he couldn't believe that this was the right score. He sank into his chair and tried to figure out what happened, when he was almost positive that he answered the questions correctly.

Miss Miller spied his discomfort. "Are you confused about your grade, Brian?" she asked, and all eyes focused on him. "Can't you read my handwriting? When I couldn't read yours, I just marked an answer as incorrect. Maybe next time you'll be more careful so I can read your answers."

Brian blushed and trembled. She never had a problem with his handwriting before; why all the drama now? And why did she have to pick on him in front of everyone else? He couldn't focus on anything for the rest of the day, and didn't enjoy hanging out with his friends after school. All he could think about was his embarrassment and shame, and when another episode would happen again.

Poor Brian! It isn't enough to tell him that everyone has had a similar experience. What he needs is some help coping with his teacher. Here's how:

Be aware. If a teacher is notorious, understand that your child's behavior will be altered under stress. He may become more inhibited to avoid attention.

Provide a reality check. Does the teacher merely have high standards? Or is he being unfair? Sometimes the toughest teachers bring out our best.

Discuss the consequences of your child's behavior. If your child stops trying to achieve so she doesn't stick out, she'll feel safer, but she'll never taste success.

Find the right level of involvement. You can't do your child's homework, nor can you fight her battles. Listen, and give advice when your child requests it.

Get the teacher's perspective. Talk to the teacher when necessary, and let him know you're concerned about your child's progress. Humanizing the teacher can defuse the situation before it spirals out of control.

Talk to other parents about your child's teacher. If other children are suffering, then there's a pattern. But if your child is taking the situation too seriously, he may be the one judging himself and the teacher too harshly. A bad grade now and then, or a missed opportunity now and then, are isolated incidents, not a permanent condition.

Making Sense of Chaos

Rowdy classrooms can throw off even the most dedicated student. But shy students are intensely bothered by environmental noise, and this out-of-control feeling makes them even more closed and inhibited.

Daniel's classroom is chaotic. His teacher has a hard time controlling all of the talking, fidgeting, and goofing off, and the classroom is too crowded in the first place. Daniel's having a terrible year, but nobody notices. In fact, his teacher thinks he's a dream student, since he doesn't talk out of turn, get in fights, or distract other kids with his antics.

When Daniel was asked to solve a long division problem on the chalkboard, he reluctantly complied. A few kids hissed at him when he walked up to the board, and he thought he heard someone call him "teacher's pet." He turned his back to the room and tried to sort through the problem. But all he could think of was the group of guys in the back of the room who were making noises and talking. Daniel was sure they were talking about him, probably planning some new way to tease him. He stared at the problem again, and made a few marks on the board. His handwriting was inscrutable, since his hand was shaking. The teacher hushed the class, which made Daniel lose his concentration. He finished the problem, but it took him forever. He almost tripped when he walked back to his seat. He wasn't sure if it was just his nerves, or if someone deliberately tried to trip him. He was sure he was going to get teased when class let out.

Instead of allowing your child to suffer through a year of chaos, you can help him become less bothered by classroom distractions. Here's how:

Notice signs of trouble. Shy kids are often overlooked because they don't create a lot of overt problems. But that doesn't mean they don't have problems. Ask your child if he is troubled by anything at school.

Be aware of background noise. If your child can study only in complete silence, build his resistance to noise. Try turning on a radio or TV in another room or grab his books and go over his homework in a crowded library or a coffee shop. On the other hand, if he's too overstimulated at home, his sensitive system will be overloaded. In that case, turn down the volume and give him peace.

Re-evaluate the classroom "goodness of fit." If the environment is simply a poor fit for your child, perhaps he can take tests in a private room, schedule sessions with his teacher after class, wear earplugs, or switch classes altogether.

Talk to other parents. Do other kids complain about the chaos? Your child may be too aware of others' actions and at-

---

ENCOURAGING SHY STUDENTS' PARTICIPATION IN CLASS

As you know, shy kids are just as smart as outgoing ones, but they have special issues within the classroom. Their anxiety often gets in the way of their ability to concentrate and learn. But with your guidance, this can be overcome. Here's how:

- Understand the anxiety-performance link. If your students feel pressured to get things right every time, their heightened anxiety will interfere with their performance. This is especially true for the shy ones.

- Provide a wide variety of activities in the classroom. Have kids work solo and in small groups as well as with the entire group so that the social pressure is minimized.

- Mix up the classroom. Create groups that pair shy kids with outgoing ones, and let them change their desk arrangements frequently.

- Use lots of open-ended and follow-up questions. You'll get more information out of your students, and their conversational skills will improve.

- Be mindful of shy students' sensitivity. Don't call on them first, and allow them to participate fully during subjects in which they excel.

---

tention, and feel that all eyes are on him when they're not.

In addition, you can also help your child stand up to those who are distracting him. Rehearse a few things he can say to the troublemakers, such as "Please be quiet," "Bug someone else," or "Stop wasting my time." The more your child can do to develop his sense of control over his environment, the better.

- Provide students with strategies. If no one is volunteering to speak, provide your students with strategies such as jotting down an answer or scanning a book for clues, or ask them logical leading questions. Then restart the discussion.

- Be available for private questions. Shy kids may be more likely to approach you for help after class or after school, when they know that other kids won't tease them.

- Set ground rules for discussion. No laughing, no teasing, and no "stupid questions."

- Provide an orderly environment. Kids can't concentrate if they aren't comfortable. Minimize noise, goofing off, and rowdiness.

- Teach kids how to solve problems and set goals. If you hand out a long-term assignment, discuss the steps kids can take to complete it, and create short-term deadlines for their work.

Overall, you'll find that your shy students will become more comfortable with the social aspects of school as the year progresses as long as you make allowances—but not excuses—for their behavior. By helping them to participate in a classroom discussion or master an academic task, you're teaching them how to cope with obstacles that could otherwise shut them down. Excusing them allows them to avoid or delay acquiring these skills. In addition, building a good relationship with your shy students will help them create good relationships with other authority figures, too.

Doing What's Difficult

University students can pick and choose their classes, but schoolchildren can't. They must take a variety of subjects with the goal of becoming well-rounded, well-informed adults. Unfortunately, many kids dread going to their least favorite class, whether it's math, biology, gym, or music.

Shy kids feel even more dread than other kids, because they're more sensitive to evaluation and take their shortcomings to heart. In fact, studies show that shy boys who lack athletic ability feel this lack intensely, which ultimately affects their relationships with their friends and potential girlfriends. And since this effect can start in the early elementary school years, it's worth noting whether your shy son feels even more inhibited because he doesn't enjoy playing sports with the other kids.

Take Michelle and Ethan, two best friends. They're both on the quiet side, but through the years they've managed to build a strong bond. They're both interested in a TV program about a dysfunctional family, so they're in a lot of fan groups about the show, and have even built a web page about the cast and characters. They also share a strong dislike of gym class. No matter what the sport, they have the same fears—that they'll be picked last for a team, get laughed at for running funny or not being able to catch a toss, or generally just be mortified by their lack of athletic ability. They put in the least amount of effort and crack jokes about how silly the entire situation is.

Ethan is especially sensitive to the horrors of gym, and he feels left out. He doesn't hang out with a lot of other guys, since he can't relate to them or their sports obsession, and he doesn't get a lot of respect from them, either. Ethan remembers that this started off when he was really young and just grew with the years. He's grateful for Michelle's friendship, but that doesn't seem to be enough. He's not having much luck with making new friends, since his classmates seem to only want to hang out with jocks, and he certainly isn't one.

Instead of wallowing in their negative identities, Michelle and Ethan can take positive steps toward boosting their enjoyment of their feared activities. You and your child can try these strategies:

Keep it in check. Don't let one weak area turn into the belief that your child can't succeed at a variety of tasks. Everyone struggles with at least one subject and finds the courage to move past it.

Give it another try. If your child is horrible at volleyball, don't let him avoid it in the future. Find ways to try it—or a related activity—in a fun, non-judgmental setting.

Go to your child's strengths. If he's great at math, he may become the baseball team's statistician. If he's a terrific writer, get him involved in the school paper or yearbook.

Remind him of the meaning of failure. Failure is merely feed back. While it may hurt at times, it isn't fatal. It just shows him where he needs improvement.

All of these strategies will help your child change his dominant response and develop his desire to approach what he usually avoids. After all, if he hides from his challenges, his fears will grow and swallow him. But if he manages to take at least a few positive steps forward, he'll be able to slowly but surely incorporate the difficult task into his comfort zone.

Successfully Shy Journal

In your Successfully Shy Journal, write down which activities are difficult for your child. For each activity you write down, answer the following questions.

- Why do you think she's having a problem with this activity?

- How does she cope with it?

- Do you detect any learned helplessness?

- Does she internalize her perceived failure, or does she keep it in check?

(continued)

- Which strategies would help her take moderate risks that bring her closer to her goal?

- How could you best communicate this to her?

Finally, write down an example of a time when she successfully met a goal after struggling with it, and make a mental note to remind her of it when she's feeling overwhelmed.

Now, pick one of the activities you just wrote down and begin developing strategies to help your child cope with it. For example, many shy kids get good grades in every area except one—participating in class discussion. If this is the case, you can ask your child why he doesn't speak up. Most likely, he's afraid of saying the wrong answer and being laughed at by his classmates or embarrassed by his teacher.

First, give him a reality check: How many kids are actually mocked for their answers? Very few, I'm sure. And if he's getting good grades otherwise, he must know the answers to many questions presented in class. In addition, discuss the purpose of discussion, which is to find out what students know, and what they need to work on. This is an issue for the teacher, too, since she may find that she needs to review some material. Then provide him with some strategies for getting into a discussion. If he gets nervous while being called on, he can jot down his answer so he doesn't lose his concentration. If he doesn't know the answer, he could scan his book for clues.

Lastly, help him set a goal for participating in class. Start with what's in his comfort zone, and ask him to raise his hand at least once this week during a discussion of his favorite subject. Then up the ante next week, by asking him to raise his hand twice. When he's gotten some experience, ask him to raise his hand during a subject in which he isn't so strong. By providing him with some strategies and breaking up this overwhelming task into more manageable steps, you can help him change his behavior and increase his confidence.

FEELING PRIDE IN YOUR ACCOMPLISHMENTS

Now that you have a better understanding of how shyness affects your child's classroom experience, you can appreciate how solving problems and mastering new tasks underlies your child's view of himself. And if he's sheltered from difficult experiences, he won't have the chance to take pride in his abilities. But, with the support of a properly involved parent, he'll have enough guidance to face his fears and challenges. Don't rob him of this chance to develop himself in all ways—academically, emotionally, and socially.

CHAPTER 10

SHYNESS
IN MIDDLE
CHILDHOOD

O ne of my colleagues told me a story about her early experiences with shyness and the effect they had on her
when she reached junior high. While she had always
been a quiet young girl, her shyness was intensified by a terrifying
episode with a group of neighborhood bullies.

"When I was really young, we lived in a bad neighborhood,"
Robin explained. "One day, I was chased by a group of kids when
I was riding my bike along the river. They chased me—I was all
alone and really scared—and threatened to throw me over the
bridge. I didn't tell anyone, especially my parents, because I
thought the kids would actually do it if I told. But that incident
made me even more timid than I'd been before."

Robin spent the next few years in quiet solitude, reaching out
to few other kids. She had a few close friends in elementary school,
but those friendships withered as they moved on to junior high.
There, faced with more kids and feelings of isolation, Robin decided she'd had enough of shyness.

"When I went to junior high, I told myself that I had to break out of it. I was sick of not being able to talk to people. I had two friends from elementary school, and that was it. I just forced myself to talk. I couldn't go on like that anymore."

Eventually, Robin was able to strike up friendships and widen her social circle. But this type of forced extroversion was a shock to her system. "I was much happier when I was able to talk to kids. It got easier the more I did it, but it was always difficult for me. And it still is to some extent."

Robin's story is an example of the complexity and drama of the social world of an older child. During the later years of elementary school and then in junior high, or from ages 9 through 13, kids' relationships with each other take on a new importance. They pull away from their parents and turn to their peers—who are usually just as confused for guidance.

For shy kids, this new emphasis on relationships with their peers is especially tricky. What struck me when I reviewed comments by shy adults about this time in their lives is that they felt isolated from and unable to fit in with their peers, who they perceived as happy and well-adjusted. Ironically, what they didn't realize at the time is that shyness affects a healthy portion of all kids, so they were actually in good company. They just didn't know it.

In this chapter, we'll take a look at the changing social world of kids in middle childhood and find out what they're experiencing that they may not share with you. This pulling away doesn't mean that parents are no longer involved in their child's life. In fact, parental guidance is absolutely necessary, especially for shy kids. It's just that parents need to guide their child in a different manner—at times indirectly, at other times overtly—so that their son or daughter develops more self-awareness and independence. In addition, I'll explore how you and your shy child can cope with some of the more difficult social experiences during this period—experiences such as dealing with expanding networks of friends and recovering from social setbacks. Just because your child is slow to warm up to these new challenges doesn't mean that he is fated to sit on the sidelines.

Successfully Shy Journal

In your Journal, please answer the following questions:

- If your child is currently in the middle childhood phase, how you do think he's coping with it?

- Is his shyness intensified, or is he taking steps to become more sociable?

- How do you help him to be sociable?

- How is he helping himself?

- Who are his friends? What do they do when they're together?

As you think through your answers, try to remember what you were like at this age, who your friends were, how you coped, and how these experiences affect you in adulthood. Do you see any links between your experiences and your child's? Then consider how your child's world differs from your own and which changes are significant. Keep these thoughts in mind as you read through the rest of the chapter.

CHANGES IN THE SOCIAL NETWORK

Although your child is shy, she is still a social creature. And during middle childhood, she is forced to expand her social network while building a unique identity in a highly pressured, highly dynamic environment. That's a big task for a shy kid, but not an insurmountable one.

Beginning at about age eight or nine, our social network changes in a number of ways. At the basic level, where and how we meet friends change. We go from forming relationships in our early years in highly structured environments, such as home and school, and move toward forming relationships in less structured, more ambiguous settings, such as the mall, the playground, through existing friendships, or even on the Internet.

At the same time, our network continually expands in size and density as we move from the comfort zone of our families. As young children, we begin meeting others through day care, school, play dates, activities, and larger social events. As time goes on, our classrooms and schools get bigger and are filled with greater diversity. We gather experience from mingling with different kinds of people and become more comfortable with others.

The nature of our friendships changes as we age, too. When we're very young, we'll play with anyone who is nice to us and has interesting toys. But as we develop specific interests and unique personalities, we gradually become more discriminating in our relationships, notice more subtle characteristics in our peers, and overtly choose our friends. We naturally find a best friend or two, and these close same-sex friendships become more intimate and are relied upon for important social cues. We also develop a circle of acquaintances and try to fit in by conforming to the accepted standards of behavior, which tends to change from group to group.

How we interact with these friends differs along gender-based lines. Boys tend to tease each other and overtly try to become the dominant alpha-male within their group. Girls tend to share more of themselves and confide in each other; becoming an alpha-girl is more subtle and usually requires the top girl to bond with a number of other girls. These same-sex groups or cliques then begin interacting with groups of kids of the opposite sex, and the friends start forming closer relationships. At first, the kids hang out as a group, but eventually they find a partner within their opposite group. These couples start building intimate relationships that reflect their individual identity, and which are sort of practice relationships for the ones they'll create in adulthood.

PICKING UP THE PACE: DEVELOPMENTAL COMPRESSION

Everyone goes through the socialization process described above, but I think that the current generation of kids and teens is going through it more quickly thanks to what's known as developmental compression. This phenomenon pushes today's kids to mature quickly and forces them to cope with a host of issues that used to be reserved for adults only. As a result, younger children are now struggling with issues such as body-image problems, sexual activity, anxiety, and substance abuse. Their friends, who are cueing each other on how to behave, don't have coping skills either, and parents are oftentimes left out of the loop.

You only have to go to the mall or the newsstand to find evidence of developmental compression, because marketers know that if they can create anxiety or spending habits in children, they can offer products to satisfy them. Many magazines now have teen versions, and the content is similar to adult fare. Kids' clothes seem to be smaller versions of grown-up styles, and snack foods, movies, vacation destinations, and music are all targeted to kids. Because kids find all of this attention appealing, they naturally want to buy these products or listen to this music to seem older—but this doesn't mean that they're ready to handle the emotions or actions that accompany them.

THE SHY SOCIAL NETWORK

Shy kids are just like all kids who go through the socialization process of middle childhood, except that they tend to work their way through it in their own way and at a slower pace, what's known as being "off time." Compounding this "off-time" tendency, developmental compression also works against the shy ones' slowly warming personalities, leaving them even further behind bold peers. Just when shy kids want to be accepted, they often feel alone on the sidelines, alienated and misunderstood.

The reluctance to make on-time connections can affect a child's entire world, as is evidenced in the words of one high school student who wrote to me. "My shyness has hindered my social development in a major way," she confided. "It's difficult for me to interact with my peers; I am afraid they will think badly of me. I only started dating this year, my last year in high school. It bothers me that I cannot speak up when I have a question or defend myself if necessary. Some people take advantage of the fact that I don't object to things, and I have been likened to a doormat because I let people walk all over me. I feel bad that I have missed out on so many fun things and that I haven't had the chance to talk to many people because I'm afraid to open my mouth."

It would be a mistake to assume that shy kids like this one don't want to expand their social network. Although they may not show it, they share the universal desire to become more socially connected. They just find it difficult to act on their impulses when they're unsure of themselves. Shy kids tend to be fine one-on-one, or in structured settings like the classroom, but feel uncertain in more ambiguous, larger, and looser environments like parties and

SHYNESS TRIGGERS

THE SLUMBER PARTY NIGHTMARE

Kids start to build a bit of independence during middle childhood, and one natural extension is spending the night at a friend's house eating junk food, watching movies, playing games, and sleeping in a strange bed or sleeping bag. But many shy kids have trouble during slumber parties because they're "off time" and a bit behind their peers socially. If they don't want to be seen as babies, they try to hide their fear and discomfort during the long, dark, sleepless night. Sometimes, though, they call home to get some reassurance—or a ride home in the middle of the night. To help your shy child enjoy this rite of passage, try these tips:

- Prepare your child. Talk about what it's like to stay in a friend's home and how it can sometimes be awkward and uncomfortable. Discuss what will be familiar to her, such as her friends and some of the activities.

- Talk to the parent. Let him or her know that your child may have a little difficulty during the night and ask to have the parent check up on her.

- Let your child bring something from home. If she wants to take her favorite pillow or stuffed animal, let her hang on to this reminder of home.

acquaintances' homes. They tend to cling to their small circle of friends, the ones they've known forever, and are more reluctant to reach out to peers who aren't in that circle. As a result, shy kids become truly social creatures later than their "on-time" peers.

In addition, once new relationships are created, shy kids sometimes find them difficult to maintain. Shy kids often lack the social skills that are needed to work through friendships, which are naturally fraught with difficulty and complications at this age. To com-

- Take your child into the home. Instead of dropping her off at the door, take a tour of the house, greet the parents and kids, and wait until your child feels comfortable.

- Call for an update. Discuss your child's mood with her friend's parent, and if she's not doing well, talk to your child. If she's doing well, just ask to have your message relayed to your child.

- Let her know she can call at any time. If she calls because she's scared, talk about it, then ask her to call back in half an hour to let you know how she's doing. If she's still worried, offer to pick her up.

- Welcome her home. Ask about what transpired, and if she's too overtired to talk about it, let her know that you'll talk about it the following day.

If your child didn't enjoy herself, let her relax and decompress for a day before you tackle some of the tougher issues. Your next step may be to host a slumber party so that your child is on her own turf, doing activities of her own choosing, and with her closest friends. If she had a great time, continue encouraging her growing independence.

pensate for their uncertainty, they may succumb to the pressure to conform and lose sight of themselves and their own values, or cut themselves off from their true friends. As another high school student wrote about her strained relationships, "I always wonder if my friends are talking about me behind my back, and that makes me worry. I tend to walk off and withdraw from my circle of friends, and I become shy."

Lastly, other kids begin noticing shyness in their peers during the middle childhood years. Unfortunately, kids don't appreciate shy children and therefore do not invite them into their growing social circle. This undoubtedly affects shy children's self-esteem and confidence at precisely the time when they should be feeling more confident and connected. As a result, the shy ones often become loners because they aren't ready to make the first move, and more outgoing kids aren't willing to take the time to get to know them at their own slow-to-warm-up pace. As one student explained, "When I was in grade school, junior high, and even the beginning of high school, many people rejected me. I didn't fit in with the cliques at school and because of that felt awkward and that I didn't belong. This caused me to be shy and hesitant to express my thoughts and opinions."

After looking at all of the complications created by a shyness-influenced social life, it's no wonder that, like Robin, many shy kids force themselves to become extroverted when they want to develop more relationships. The world won't wait for them, so they assume they have to break through and make things happen on their own, in an instant. Unfortunately, this coping mechanism will work against them in the long run, when they'll want to be themselves, totally, and not cling to a fake, uncomfortable public image.

BACK TO BASICS: MASTERING SOCIAL SKILLS

As kids expand their social network, they use basic social skills and acquire new ones that will enable them to deal with the challenging social situations they face. In a way, it is the "job" of children at this age to master new social skills, just as they are mastering the skills needed for math, science, and reading. And as their social lives become more important and complicated, kids will rely more and more on their ever-growing collection of social skills.

Unfortunately, some kids may not be adding social skills as they grow older. Some parents may not have guided their children during social encounters, and the children may not have a whole lot of social experience upon which to draw. Other children, especially shy children, may actually know a lot about social behavior, but are too reticent to act on that knowledge. And because they don't act, the behavior doesn't become routine and easy. Withdrawal and silence become the dominant responses.

If your child has a social skills deficit during this critical phase of life, it's not too late to help him master the basics, which I covered in chapter 7 on making friends. You'll need to help your child act on his innate interest in other people, and work on acting politely and properly when in their company. Simply being able—and willing—to introduce himself and feel comfortable is a step in the right direction. Sharing, feeling empathy, tolerating differences, cooperating, and communicating are other basic skills required for a successfully shy social life.

DEVELOPING SOPHISTICATED SKILLS

The basic social skills are essential for building an active social life, but kids in middle childhood must develop more mature social skills for their more complicated relationships. These new skills include:

- Balancing needs. Kids must learn how to balance their needs against others' so that their relationships are healthy, fair, and honest.

- Putting others at ease. Kids must learn how to finesse awkward situations. For example, instead of merely being able to introduce themselves, they must learn to make introductions on others' behalf.

- Disclosing personal information. Along with sharing toys and other possessions, they must now share themselves on a more intimate level and confide in friends without fear of betrayal or rejection.

- Being flexible. Kids must expand their comfort zones by sometimes following others and sometimes leading them into new territory.

- Reading and responding to unspoken cues. Older kids must be able to read unspoken cues put out by their friends and be able to act on them without causing more conflict. These cues include the hidden message within a conversation or an unspoken change in the dynamics of a relationship.

- Acting with integrity. Kids must learn how to be true to themselves while being honest in their relationships. They will often pay the price for breaking promises or acting out of character.

Eventually, all older kids and adults develop these skills to some degree. Shy kids, who are typically behind the curve in the socialization process, tend to develop these sophisticated skills later, or aren't as fluent in them. Sadly, if kids don't develop these skills, they'll find themselves stuck in lopsided relationships that favor a more socially savvy child. These relationships tend to be fraught with risk and dependency, since the shy or socially lacking child can be easily dominated or outmaneuvered in tricky situations. With the balance of power constantly tilting toward the other child, the passive or shy child won't get his needs met and won't get enough positive attention that's rooted in respect. What's more, the shy child will feel that he has no other option but to be overlooked and will settle for coasting along in unsatisfying relationships.

Successfully Shy Journal

I'd like you to consider the current state of your child's social skills by thinking about your child's recent social encounters. In your Journal, please respond to the following questions:

- How often do you see your child interact with good friends and acquaintances?

- In what context?

- Which social skills were involved?

- Did your child introduce you to her friends?

- Did she make the other kids comfortable?

- Did any conflicts arise, and how were they resolved?

- Who was the dominant child?

- How did they end their time together? Did they make plans to get together again?

After working through these questions, pick out one or two issues that you'd like to discuss with your child. Think about what she did well, and how she may improve her social skills. When you have quiet time with her, talk about your observations, ask her why she acted the way she did, and give her a few constructive hints.

If you had a difficult time answering these questions, create an opportunity for your child to interact with friends while you're around, whether it's inviting a friend over for dinner or taking a group of kids to the movies. Watch how the group interacts, and then discuss your observations with your child.

Making Social Comparisons

During middle childhood, kids turn to other kids—and not their parents—for clues on how to behave. "Everybody's doing it," no matter what "it" is, means far more to them than "my mom told me to do *that*." And because this is such a confusing time, kids are intensely interested in determining what's normal behavior among their friends so that they can fit in and avoid becoming ostracized for being "weird" or "uncool."

Just as kids use social comparison—the process of noticing others and making comparisons to their own selves—in the classroom to see how they measure up academically to their peers, they also use it as a gauge of their social standing. In fact, I'm sure that social comparison is used more frequently, and more intensely, in these new and unstructured social situations. Everything from what to wear, which music to listen to, and what to do when parents or teachers aren't around seems to be dictated and reinforced by the child's group of friends. This sense of conformity or uniformity helps ease uncertainty when kids feel vulnerable and unprepared for current challenges.

Shy kids seem to make social comparisons frequently because they're intensely interested in reading rules of behavior so that they can ease their own feelings of self-consciousness. But this experience doesn't necessarily translate into social success or helpful assessments. I believe that shy kids make comparisons that follow distinct patterns that serve to keep them away from other kids.

I've found that shy kids tend to compare themselves to the wrong peers and do so from a distance. They compare themselves to people they don't know well—including celebrities—who are bold because they stand out. They don't compare themselves in a realistic manner to friends they know very well or other quieter kids who are more like them. They're hung up on the socially successful exteriors of outgoing kids and, in contrast, the frustrated, anxious inner reality of their own world.

In addition, when shy kids judge themselves against their peers, they usually arrive at one of two unrealistic conclusions. Either they feel inferior to the extroverts, because the outgoing kids look like they're socially successful and comfortable in their skin, or, interestingly, the shy kids feel far superior, because they assume that the outgoing ones are fake, dumb, or ruthlessly popular. Either one of these conclusions will prevent shy children from feeling good about themselves in a realistic, healthy way.

Shy kids also take social comparison one step further and often fall victim to peer pressure by copying the looks and behavior of the outgoing or cool kids. While almost all kids do this to some extent, shy kids will do it more often, or to a greater degree, because they're more frequently or more intensely self-conscious and uncertain. Conformity gives them a sense of security when they're feeling vulnerable. They believe they won't stick out—and therefore become even more self-conscious—if they look and behave just like everyone else. And it's also terribly easy, because shy kids won't have to defend actions that are out of sync with other kids'. Conformity will mask their insecurities and shyness, but it will do little to help them be true to themselves and become self-aware.

Being Compared

Shy kids aren't the only ones who make social comparisons. As we discussed earlier, other kids notice the shy ones' behavior and pick up on their signals. Unfortunately, these comparisons are often negative. It seems that sometime around the fourth grade, the "free pass" shy kids used to have expires, and their peers start to notice their reticence, awkwardness, and vulnerability. These qualities make other children uncomfortable, so they stay away from the shy kids.

While they may not have shown it at the time, many shy adults tell me that their discomfort around their peers at this critical time had an indelible impact on their feelings of self-worth, self-esteem, and general happiness. This discomfort is especially rough on shy boys, who feel pressured by our culture to be assertive, outgoing, and brave. It's generally believed in our society that a key way to develop these qualities is athletic ability and involvement, and so those boys who opt out of sports activities tend to feel like outcasts. As a cameraman explained, "I was never picked to be on a Little League team in elementary school or even after-school clubs in high school. I was not accepted or desired—I still feel that way as an adult."

It's also crucial that you're aware of your own evaluations of your shy child. It's only natural that you compare your child's behavior against his peers—or perhaps his brothers and sisters—since this will give you an indication of what's normal, and what's not, as well as how you're faring as a parent. But if you're consistently making unfair comparisons and finding that your child doesn't measure up to his peers, that message is being sent loudly and clearly, no matter how well you think you're hiding your feelings or how sensitive you think you're being. Think twice about enrolling your child in too many activities just because her peers are enrolled in them. Think twice about telling him that you wish he could be more like the outgoing kids in his class. And think twice about making him feel inferior or defective when he's simply acting like himself.

Successfully Shy Journal

In your Journal, please answer the following questions:

- Do you compare your shy child to her friends, other kids in her class, or her siblings? Which ones?

- Do you notice a pattern?

- Do you encourage your child to be more like the social butterflies and class clowns?

- Do you ever compare your child favorably against her friends and peers? Do you let her know?

- Do you compare yourself to other parents? How do you rate?

Since it's normal to make social comparisons, I'm not going to ask you to stop. But now that you're more aware of your comparisons, I will ask you to be fairer when making them. If your child is shy, she may never become a complete extrovert, so why bother holding her to that standard? With your caring guidance, she can become a healthy, self-accepting, loving, successfully shy individual. Be kind and don't place conditions on your love.

THE NEXT STEP: BECOMING A LEADER

As you can see, a child develops his individuality within a highly pressured social context. He must be able to withstand negative peer pressure and act on his own internal values while maintaining healthy friendships. Developing "soft leadership" skills such as leading by example, negotiating, and allowing discussion and debate will enable him to make decisions that are right for him. Eventually, as he gains confidence in his judgment, he will be able to influence others instead of being compromised by them.

Shy kids are, in my mind, well able to become social leaders and withstand peer pressure. I've found that shy kids' natural cautiousness is an asset when bolder kids come up with wild and risky schemes that will undoubtedly get them into trouble. In fact, friends who want to have fun but not get into dangerous situations should value the shy ones' level-headedness. Their "off-time" qualities may compel them to resist pressure to mess with adults-only situations such as drinking, dressing provocatively, and becoming sexually active long before they're ready to do so.

As a parent, you can't directly intervene in your child's social life, especially since you're not always around. But you can give your child the tools to help him stand up for himself and lead the situation in a positive direction. What's critical is that you discuss some of these situations with your child before he encounters them, and help him come up with good responses and decisions. This forewarning will provide him with alternatives and increase his resistance to peer pressure.

A friend told me about a situation that her stepson encountered recently. Michael was at his friend's house and had the opportunity to watch an R-rated movie on cable. Michael knows that he isn't allowed to watch this type of movie. But his friends Patrick, Ray, and Henry were curious about this film and willing to risk getting in trouble just to see it. Michael found himself in a predicament: He could go along with the group, which would be the easy choice since his friends' opinions mean more to him than his parents', and potentially face punishment if his parents found out. Or he could leave or tell the guys that he doesn't want to watch the movie and risk being teased by them. To figure out his next step, Michael had to draw upon some soft leadership skills, skills that can be nurtured in children. He was able to convince the other kids to watch something else on TV that they could all agree on, and nobody complained.

Here's how a parent can help a child like Michael become a leader among his peers:

Discuss difficult issues. Talking about sensitive topics in a sensitive manner helps your child become comfortable with tough subjects. In Michael's case, you could discuss which media content is appropriate for someone his age.

Explain why your rules are valid. In Michael's case, you could explain that he isn't ready to witness what will happen in the movie until he's ready to handle it in real life. Also, be consistent in presenting your standards to your child. If your standards shift often, your child won't know what's expected of him and why.

Give your child more responsibility. If you're reluctant to let go of your child, she'll be unprepared for difficult situations. If Michael had experienced only kiddie films, his curiosity could have easily overruled his natural cautiousness.

Provide opportunities and alternatives. If your child doesn't have positive goals and activities, off-limit activities will seem even more appealing. For example, if Michael and his friends were also curious about baseball, riding their bikes, or watching age-appropriate TV shows, they would have alternatives to their adult-oriented movie.

Create a script. Your child can't speak out if he doesn't know what he should say. Michael could have been prompted to say, "I just don't feel like watching that movie. Let's check out what else is on TV now."

Teach your child to trust his instincts. If his gut is telling him that he's in dangerous territory, then he probably is. Encourage him to do a reality check before making any decisions. If Michael thinks that the drawbacks to watching the movie outweigh his desire to watch it, he'll be more likely to make an appropriate decision.

Help your son or daughter to look for signs of cooperation. If Michael is hesitant to watch an off-limits movie, chances are that some of his friends feel the same way. Michael could turn to someone who agrees with him and then try to sway the other kids in the group.

Keep the lines of communication open. It may seem that your child has no interest in being close to you or following your rules, but appearances aren't what they seem. I've found that when kids are feeling vulnerable and confused, they'll turn to someone who can understand their insecurities and difficulties. And if you make it clear that you will always love them, even when they make mistakes, they'll turn to you for support when they most need it.

SPECIFIC SOCIAL ISSUES IN MIDDLE CHILDHOOD

Now that you have some background information about the social world of older kids, I'd like to bring into focus some specific issues that trigger shyness, such as the challenges of developing a healthy social identity or recovering from a setback in a relationship. Once again, these challenging social situations can be navigated by working through the shy process of identifying the approach/avoidance conflict, taking time to warm up, and slowly expanding one's comfort zone. When you as a parent discuss these steps with your child, she'll be better able to understand what she's feeling, and how common her feelings are.

Feeling All Alone

Feeling alone and isolated is a big issue during middle childhood. Many shy adults tell me that they felt like they just didn't fit in when they were kids, and they attribute these feelings to something that was beyond their control that made them stick out. A divorce, a stutter, or a weight problem made them feel self-conscious, lonely, and unlovable when they desperately wanted to fit in.

This childhood pain is still apparent in their adult lives. A computer programmer wrote: "I got my inferiority complex and shyness because of my parents' divorce, when I was in elementary school. I was teased by other kids because my mom had a nervous breakdown and was called crazy by their moms and dads. Plus, I was never praised by my dad and never received the approval I wanted from him."

A secretary explained: "When I was six and a half, I developed a stutter which has never gone away. It was also the time that my parents got divorced. Before these events, I was a very outgoing child with other children."

A plumber confided: "Both my parents are alcoholics, being active as far back as I can recall. I alienated certain people and situations because of it, and isolated myself to avoid unnecessary pain, shame, embarrassment, and loss of possible or potential friends."

You can't just snap your fingers and make your child's pain disappear. But you can lessen it by being compassionate about his troubles. A few good strategies include:

Talk about social comparison. Your child's pain is all too real, but his peers' is invisible. Instead of letting him compare himself to glossy surfaces, remind him that even if his peers look brave and confident, everyone has feelings of doubt or embarrassment.

Acknowledge her problems, but don't dwell on them. If she stutters, don't make her even more self-conscious about it. Just listen to her with your full attention, and you'll come to understand her unique challenges.

Go to his strengths. If he loves to do a certain activity, let him shine. He will be proud of his accomplishments and will be less troubled by his perceived shortcomings.

Find good role models. Read biographies or watch issue-oriented TV shows targeted to youth that profile people who have overcome obstacles. Then discuss how some of these lessons can be incorporated into your child's daily life.

Lastly, remind your child that her perceived faults are perceptions, and nothing more. As Eleanor Roosevelt famously said, "No one can make you feel inferior without your consent." I hope you pass on this message to your children.

Coping with Social Change at School

Kids' classrooms and schools become larger and more complex as they get older. Older students are forced to mix with unfamiliar kids, join activities, switch classrooms, pick their seats in the lunchroom, and create relationships with new teachers. This can be overwhelming for a slowly warming child who can—and may even want to—get lost in the shuffle.

Faced with more options and responsibility, shy kids are left to fend for themselves in school, usually without the assistance of a teacher who knows them well. "All I have to do is walk into the lunchroom and I can pretty much tell what's happening in the kids' social lives," claimed one seventh grade teacher who spoke with me. "I think some of the shy kids, the really shy ones, are left out of the crowd. They're so quiet, you don't really know what's going on with them. There's not much a teacher can do."

Although you can't spend the school day with your child, you can help her become more socially connected at school. Here's how:

Make her friends welcome. Allow her to invite friends into your home and offer to help out when they need to be driven to the mall or other activities.

Prepare your child for what's ahead. If he can anticipate what may happen, he can develop strategies for coping with his more demanding day.

Point out good examples. Talk about examples of friendship and overcoming adversity in your lives and the media. Then discuss why they should be emulated.

Maintain old ties. If your child has switched schools, make sure she's still connected to her old friends. She'll need these familiar faces while she creates new relationships.

Be there. If your child can't confide in you, he may not confide in anyone. Encourage him to talk about his experiences, and don't dismiss his concerns.

Overall, remind your child that she typically warms up slowly to new situations and people, but that hasn't prevented her from finding good friends who stick with her. Let her feel her way through her new network and provide guidance when she needs it.

Developing a Positive Social Identity

Because they're quiet and tend to be well-behaved, many shy kids are either overlooked or ignored by their peers, who may never realize that a shy peer may be a talented artist, great babysitter, budding astronaut, natural comedian, or generally interesting person once you get to know her.

Because other kids never get past the shy child's quiet exterior, the shy kid lacks a positive social identity. Without this healthy identity, some shy kids are actively shunned or bullied by kids who think the quiet ones are passive targets. The damage caused by these bullies is intense and can be long lasting. One college student explained her experiences with bullying this way: "I was the subject of ridicule when I was a kid. I didn't stand up for myself. I was always kind of meek. Part of it was that I was the new kid and the easy target, but I think the kids knew that they could get away with it because I wouldn't fight back. Plus, I wasn't encouraged by my parents to do anything like getting into sports or other activities."

You can help your shy child build a healthy social identity so that shyness will be seen as just one facet of her unique personality. Here's what you can do:

Encourage her interests. Even if she shines in activities that may be off-beat or solitary, encourage her. If she knows that she's good at something, she'll be more passionate and confident as a whole, and her specialty can serve as a bridge to further social interaction.

Find an alternative activity or setting. Research shows that shunned or neglected kids can be socially successful when they're able to create relationships in a totally new environment with totally new kids. A sport, time at camp, or extra lessons or activities are options.

Go over the basics. Your child may suffer from a social skills deficit, so work through the core skills she'll need for making friendships. Then help her if she needs you.

Reward his approaches, not his avoidance. Don't allow him to skip school because he doesn't want to face some kids. Treat him to something special if he's coping with a difficult social environment.

Provide a reality check. Not all kids are ganging up on your child, nor can or should one bully have the power to affect your child's life. Teach her how to separate the good kids from the bad ones, and she'll develop a more realistic attitude toward her peers.

Be aware of your child's social life. Don't insist that your child become the most popular kid at school, but be aware of his place in the social universe. If he's suffering, reach out to him. But if he has at least a few good friends, help him nurture those rela-tionships.

In addition, remind your child to offer something positive to other kids, even if it's something as simple as a smile. If she acts friendly, then she'll soon be known as a nice kid, even if she is a bit quiet. And that assessment can go a long way toward building a friendship and raising your child's level of social confidence.

Having Lots of Activities, but Few Friends

On the face of it, it may seem as if your child has a lot of friends since you've gotten her involved in activities and she seems to have conquered her shyness. Besides going to school, she's on the soccer team and the swim team, studies the viola, is taking cooking lessons, goes to summer camp, and participates in church activi-ties. But look again: Has she created friendships with the kids she meets, or does she just zoom from activity to activity without having the chance to get to know anyone well? If your shy child has a busy social calendar, but few good friends, here's how you can help:

Give her more free time. Your child can't be herself if she isn't relaxed and at ease. Cut down on her obligations if she's showing signs of stress.

Allow him to participate in decisions. Offer options for his activities and let him choose which ones are right for him.

Develop potential relationships. If your child sees the same kids at her lessons and practices, they can become better friends if they have time to hang out and get to know each other in an in-formal setting.

Be alert to signs of unhealthy competition. Many activities are competitive in nature, which can create more stress. Let your

THE FIRST DAY OF PRACTICE

Just about every kid has something going on outside of school, whether it's dance or music lessons, soccer practice, or religious studies. Even shy kids can have a heavy load of social activities that stretch their reserves. As they will during most times of transition, they'll spend a longer time than their peers do warming up to their new coach, teammates, or physical challenge. If your child isn't acclimating to his new activity, try these strategies:

- Find a good fit for your child. If your child shows no interest in music, don't bother with piano lessons. Instead, choose activities that your child will like and want to do outside of lessons or team practices.

- Survey the social landscape. Meet the coach, teacher, or teammates before the first day so that your child's warm-up period begins early.

- Discuss the importance of being connected. If your child loves to kick around a ball in the backyard but not with his teammates, discuss the benefits of being part of an organization.

- Turn teammates into friends. Carpool or invite teammates over to the house. Spending more time with his teammates will help your child to build relationships with them.

- Minimize competition. If all of his activities are competitive,

child do fun things that pique his curiosity, not threaten him with failure and embarrassment.

Explore your true motives. Are you signing up your child for all of these activities for her benefit, or yours? While you want the best for your child, make sure what you're doing is right for her.

Finally, don't forget about the importance of sleep for your you're sending him a powerful message. Give him some variety and let up on the pressure.

- Encourage good sportsmanship. Your child doesn't need to be a star. Let him know that even pros sit on the bench at times, and work on skill development instead of games won or goals scored.

- Find a healthy level of involvement. You don't want to second-guess the coach or antagonize the referee or parents of the opposing team, but you do want to attend games and show your support in a positive manner. You might even want to volunteer to sell refreshments at games.

- Look for signs of resistance or backsliding. If your child isn't transitioning into the new season after a normal period of adjustment, ask him why. Perhaps he fears being ridiculed by the coach, is playing the wrong position for his talents, or is worried about being perfect. Then work on solving that problem.

When the season's over, talk about what transpired. If he enjoyed himself, find ways that you can extend the experience—perhaps by going to a soccer camp or attending professional soccer games as a family. If he didn't enjoy it, find out why. Perhaps he needs to play on another team or try a new activity altogether. Let him know that you are proud that he stuck out the season and at least gave it a try.

child, even if he is too old for a daily nap. Kids need more sleep than adults, and lack of sleep affects almost all areas of their lives, including friendships. After all, would you want to be friends with someone who was always cranky, irritable—and too busy to have fun? Cutting down on busyness allows your child to be well-rested and ready for each day.

Recovering from a Social Setback

Kids' friendships are inherently unreliable because children are going through so many changes that they don't fully understand. And just about everyone has had a friendship break off suddenly or has found an instant best friend who later turns into a major enemy. Shy kids, though, seem to have a harder time coping with sudden reversals in friendships, because they often have a small circle of friends, or one very close best friend, and are overly dependent on that relationship. When the friendship is severed, shy kids tend to feel abandoned, distance themselves from new relationships, and distrust other kids.

As this illustrator explained, "When I was in grade school, my best friend turned against me, most likely due to jealousy, as I did very well in school and she didn't. Her cruel behavior and her successful campaign to turn other friends in our circle against me made a painful impact on me early on. Although I hate to give her that much credit, I think that's when I learned to distrust people, at least initially—and to become fearful of group situations because of the potential for people to 'gang up' on me."

Although you can't fight your child's battles, you can help her weather the strain of changing friendships. Here's how:

Know her friends. If she's hanging out with kids who you think are inappropriate and you worry that she's headed for a fall, let her know. She may feel the same way but not trust her judgment.

Look for signs of dependency. Many shy kids have one best friend and very weak links to other kids. While the intimacy can be comforting, make sure this friendship isn't imbalanced, with your child being dominated.

Give her time and space to recover. She may not bounce back as quickly as other kids, but she will bounce back. Remind her that her troubles are temporary, even if they seem permanent right now.

Watch for signs of more serious trouble. Kids can develop depression, eating disorders, and anxiety when they're struggling to find a healthy way to deal with a setback. Don't allow one setback to turn into a general downward spiral.

In addition, remember that conflict in relationships is normal and can even be a positive thing. Use a situation like this to teach your child how to resolve conflicts. Does he need to apologize? Give it a rest? Speak up for himself? Choose more reliable friends? Identify some of the problem areas so he can use this information to turn around the situation.

Managing Virtual Friendships

Technology has totally invaded our lives, and our kids can't even imagine a time when a typical home didn't have a microwave, computer, cell phone, and video games. While many of these devices can help us stay connected to our friends, they can also distance us by creating "virtual" friends when we spend more time e-mailing our buddies than hanging out with them. We can also use technology to serve as conversational substitutes when we'd rather go to a movie than talk, or play computer games with our friends instead of get to know them. And how many kids simply tune out the conversation around them by being immersed in their gadgets and games?

While there's little data on the subject of technology use and shy kids, I suspect that shy kids may often gravitate to technology to help them overcome their inhibitions with other kids. Unfortunately, while they may be instantly connected to their friends via their computers, they may not have any real conversational skills. Or they may prefer to e-mail friends rather than see them face to

face and potentially have awkward moments and less than perfectly composed sentences. They may also prefer to go to "technology arcades" when they're with friends, one bonus being that
they don't have to make conversation while they're there.

To help your child be less reliant on technology, follow these tips:

Limit her time on the computer or phone. Set time limits for
e-mail sessions, video games, and phone calls so that your child is
aware of the time she's spending.

Create a balance between virtual friends and real ones. E-
mails are no substitute for conversations, and a shy kid who resists
seeing friends in person is developing bad social habits.

Monitor your child's computer use. Like it or not, children
are probably exploring everything possible on the Internet when
we're not looking. Make sure that your child isn't getting into dangerous territory and connecting with inappropriate strangers.

Insist that your child meets his virtual friends in person. If
they've created friendships online, make sure that they go offline—
safely. Arrange a meeting in a public place, and accompany your
child for safety's sake.

Lastly, make sure that the benefits of technology outweigh the
problems created by it. Your child must develop real-world social
skills because her life will be lived in the real world. Don't allow her
to use technology as a crutch when she wants to reach out to other
people.

Just Fine Just the Way They Are

Lots of adults tell me that they simply prefer being by themselves,
and don't feel any sort of anxiety or self-consciousness about
their preference for solitary activities. These successfully shy
adults probably came to this realization earlier in their lives,
when they gravitated toward quiet activities that they do alone,

whether it's writing, drawing, reading, or running. I'm not bothered by a shy individual's preference for solitude as long as she is actively engaged in something positive and not tuning out and zoning out.

On the other hand, I've found that many parents seem to be concerned with their children's quiet nature and preference for solitude. After all, we live in an age of activity, and we're culturally biased against those who are reflective, thoughtful, and quiet. It's almost as if we trust only those who crave the spotlight, since they're easy to spot, assess, and value, while we can't figure out those who have a lot going on under the surface that takes time to reveal. Raising a child who is happy alone can make a parent feel that there's something wrong with their child, who seems to be so different from so many other kids.

If your child is one of these quiet but comfortable people, there's no need to change his behavior, unless, of course, your child indicates that he wants to change and become more socially connected. But if your child is polite, has friends, is developing his interests, and has faith in himself, then relax. He's fine just the way he is.

Successfully Shy Journal

In your Journal, I'd like you to assess the meaning of solitude in our age of activity. Please answer the following questions:

- What does your child do when she's alone, and how much of her spare time is devoted to it? Is it balanced by social time?

- How comfortable is she with her solitary time?

(continued)

- How comfortable are you with the amount of time she spends alone?

- How much time do you spend in solitude? Are you comfortable with it, or do you need constant stimulation and companionship?

After you answer these questions, I'd like you to consciously take note of your child's daily need for quiet time, as well as your own need for it, and how you each spend this downtime. If your child is doing something constructive with his time, praise him. But if he's spending his time zoning out in front of the TV or computer, it's time to intervene. I'd also like you to start a conversation with your child about the meaning of solitude and its many positive aspects.

MOVING TOWARD ADOLESCENCE

As kids make their way through childhood, they begin building experiences and friendships that will help them become healthy, satisfied adults. But when they reach adolescence, they encounter a new series of challenges. While many shy teens do just as well as other teens, adolescence can make a shy kid feel even more awkward, misunderstood, and self-conscious. In the next chapter, I'll explain more about the world of shy teens and what you can do to help ease your child's transition into adulthood.

Becoming
Successfully Shy

PART THREE

If you've read this far, you and your child are no doubt already creating a shyness breakthrough. I hope that the strategies I've provided are helping your child take calculated risks that widen his comfort zone.

But while you're coaching your child through his current challenges, be aware that adolescence is a particularly intense and crucial time filled with shyness triggers. Whether your child is currently a teenager or will be one in a few years, it's helpful to know what to expect as your child gets older. In chapter 11, you'll gain valuable insight into the complicated subject of shyness in adolescence. This period can be so confusing and seemingly without rules that many once-outgoing kids become shy during their teen years, while many shy kids sink further into their isolation. What's more, a teen's relationship with his parents is often strained by the teen's inner turbulence and withdrawal. But parents don't need to withdraw as well. I'll provide a blueprint for a discussion you can have with your teen son or daughter, which is the first step toward working together to break out of adolescent shyness.

In chapter 12, "The Successfully Shy Life," we'll look beyond adolescence into what the future holds for your shy child or teen. I'll explain how the seeds of a shyness breakthrough planted in childhood can have powerful, positive results later in life. And I'll reveal how, as your child builds on the successes he has earned by confronting his shyness triggers, he will gain self-confidence that will overshadow and help him manage any lingering feelings of shyness. It is this Successfully Shy Life that I wish for all shy children.

CHAPTER 11

SHYNESS IN ADOLESCENCE

There's a huge growth spurt during adolescence that makes the middle childhood years look calm and peaceful. A teen's comfort zone changes at almost every level—social, emotional, intellectual, physical, sexual, and existential. As a result, adolescents typically experience turmoil, transition, and transformation as their world expands.

Many teens go through a shy or slow-to-warm-up phase as a way of coping with their new challenges, whether or not they had been shy previously. It seems that adolescence intensifies shyness while shyness intensifies adolescence. Like most teens, adolescents who had been shy as children feel acutely self-conscious and think in a self-centered manner. The difference is that they may try to disappear through shyness so that they won't be noticed.

"You will sometimes see students at lunch surrounded by others, or on the 'edge' of a group, but not interacting," Margaret, a high school math teacher, explained. "They choose to remain basically alone. You will see students who simply wander around at lunch or sit alone in one spot while others are socializing and running from one activity to another. We have had students who walk down the hall 'hugging' the lockers; their heads are down, and they watch the floor to avoid meeting and having to greet or somehow interact with someone else, be it peer or teacher. Sometimes they exhibit openly rude, unfriendly behavior that tells others that they want to be left alone.

"I have no problem with shy students who do not behave in an openly offensive manner," Margaret continued. "I do think that they miss out on a lot of the fun of being a kid, but what *I* consider fun may not be fun for them. There are many wonderful opportunities for involvement in a wide variety of activities at this high school, and those students who do not take part miss out on opportunities to make friends and to become a part of something valuable.

"My fear is that those who are extremely shy and fearful of contact are basically unhappy and find school an uncomfortable place to be. This can lead only to continuing discomfort and discontent in the adult world, where they *have* to learn to deal successfully with others to survive."

Margaret's observations confirm what I've discovered through my own research: Shyness during adolescence is a common and critical issue; it is often masked by stereotypically non-shy behavior such as rebellion or aggression; and it has the potential to affect the individual's experience as an adult. Shyness in adolescence is powerful and, more importantly, can be hazardous to a teen's general well-being.

After all, adolescence is supposed to be a fun, carefree time, a period to be spent expanding one's universe—hanging out with friends, being involved in extra-curricular activities, dating, experimenting with new behavior and feelings—before life gets serious after high school. All of these supposedly fun, lighthearted activities are a little more difficult for shy teens, who tell me that they're often stumped by typical teen challenges and rites of passage.

Throughout this chapter, I'll explore how shyness impacts adolescents, as well as the surprising, often contradictory ways in which shyness appears during this time. I'll also detail the types of shy teens I've identified, and what a parent can do to provide their shy teen with the tools they'll need to successfully cope with their social, emotional, and academic challenges. Finally, I'll provide empowering strategies for parents and their shy teens so that they can work through this chapter together and gain insights into shyness. As teens learn how to apply targeted coping strategies to their current challenges, they'll feel less shy and more confident in their larger, more adult comfort zone.

Successfully Shy Journal

Before we begin discussing adolescence in greater detail, pause for a moment and reflect on this life phase. In your Journal, please answer the following questions:

- If you are the parent of a teenager, how is he changing emotionally, intellectually, socially, and physically?

- How do you think these changes are connected to his shyness or social skills development?

- What do you and your teen talk about?

- When you were a teenager, did you have a shy phase?

- Which issues were especially difficult for you? Which issues didn't seem to bother you as much?

(continued)

- How did you cope with difficult issues as a teenager?

- How do your adolescent issues continue to crop up in your adult life?

- How much of your teen self do you see in your adult self?

As you read through this chapter, continue reflecting on your own adolescence. Perhaps you'd rather forget all of the mistakes you made, but try to remember what your world was like. For example, if you were a shy teen, you can empathize with your child's current plight. This chapter will help you and your teen develop strategies to widen his comfort zone. If you did not experience shyness during adolescence, you may not understand your teen's discomfort and awkwardness. In turn, you may have expectations for his social behavior that he can't meet without guidance. For example, you may expect him to take a date to the prom because you did, yet he's never gone out on a date before and isn't quite sure how to ask out a girl for a regular Friday night date, let alone a big event like the prom. This chapter will help you get in touch with your shy teen's world and how you can play a positive role in it.

THE ROLE OF ADOLESCENCE

When we think of the growth spurt that teenagers experience, what comes to mind is often the physical changes that occur. But the truth is that this growth spurt affects an adolescent's entire being—body, mind, and self. In fact, the purpose of adolescence is to give the teen an opportunity to try on new roles and behaviors, sort of a "dress rehearsal" for adulthood. The backdrop for this rehearsal is intensely social, and teens are acutely attuned to their social status, social identity, and public image.

Because of the enormous changes that are a part of the adolescent growth spurt, teens must expand their comfort zones quickly, even while they are thrust into more complicated situations involving friends, responsibility, individuality, sexuality, and career interests. To cope with these situations, teens experiment with new behavior and more-complex thought patterns, both of which serve as rehearsals for adulthood. In our culture, they can find safe ways to deal with their curiosity by doing such things as volunteering, holding down a part-time job, babysitting, dressing differently, joining extra-curricular activities, questioning authority, going out on dates, and thinking about career prospects. It's okay for them to have short-term interests because the consequences of moving on to something new or making a mistake are not serious.

Experimentation is a good sign. It indicates that the teen wants to expand her comfort zone by taking a few risks and creating a unique identity. Experimentation leads the teenager into the future armed with more knowledge about herself and how the world operates. So when a teenager indicates an interest in new activities, I think her parents should encourage her to find safe outlets to pursue them. On the other hand, when a teenager—typically a shy, slow-to-warm-up teenager—doesn't want to try new things and resists change, she is merely delaying the inevitable, perhaps out of fear of moving into a new phase of life. Or, as one high school sophomore explained, "If a person is shy, and they make a decision based on their shyness, they're missing out on what that opportunity might have brought them. You only get one life, you might as well live it."

ADOLESCENT DEVELOPMENT

The adolescent growth spurt fuels the desire to experiment and colors all areas of the teen's life. This accelerated development affects the teen's entire self in the following ways:

- Physical changes are rapid. Perhaps the most obvious change is physical and hormonal, but the growth doesn't happen all at once or in proportion. It begins at the extremities—hands, feet, legs, and arms begin growing before a teen's voice deepens or he fills out all over. Awkwardness, self-consciousness, and bewilderment often result, and comments about a teen's appearance, no matter how well-meaning, are taken to heart.

- Gender differences become specific. Boys and girls become truly distinct creatures, which affects them physically, emotionally, socially, and behaviorally. Girls tend to go through these changes about 2 years before boys. Socially, boys feel that they need to fit the macho masculine stereotype, so they try to out-do other boys and impress girls. Girls place more importance on fitting in and developing intimate bonds with a few friends and a boyfriend. Looks play a major role in their sense of self-worth and belonging. Boys tend to feel worse about their shyness than girls because of the social expectations for them to be socially assertive.

- Emotions are constantly in flux. Teens' emotions don't always match up with their intellectual abilities or desires, so they often can't cope with escalating challenges in a healthy manner. Sometimes they retreat and regress until they feel safer, and then turn around and show a sign of surprising maturity.

- Intellectual and cognitive changes are self-focused. While their academic challenges are getting harder, high school students are also pressured to make decisions about college enrollment and career direction. Plus, because of all of the other changes taking place, teens tend to use self-centered thinking and have trouble shifting perspective to gain insight into another's viewpoint. Self-consciousness is the norm.

• Social lives become even more complex. Teenagers' relationships become more intense and complicated, and they place greater importance on them. They start to develop more intimate and physical relationships that prepare them for adult relationships. Their public image is important to them because they feel completely self-conscious, like they're always looking into a mirror, even when they're with others.

• Identity issues are being sorted out. Teens develop their interests more seriously than they did in the past and build their unique identity. Cliques, social status, and popularity issues help them figure out who they are and how they rate. They try new activities and play around with their personas until they have a better grip on their identity and where they fit in the universe.

While all of these changes are occurring, the teen is a pressure cooker of conflicting emotions, feelings, and sensations. Feeling unprepared or ill equipped for these changes can harm a teen's fragile sense of self. If he sees that other kids aren't bothered by the pressure to grow up, while he himself is more than happy to hang on to his old world, he's not going to feel as confident or mature as his peers. And without any insight into others' feelings, he's not going to know that every teen is unnerved by and uncertain about the changes he faces now and in the future.

The heartache this insecurity can cause in a shy, sensitive teen is tremendous. "My shyness affects my relationships," a high school junior confided. "I can't control my shyness. I have always been quiet. People don't ignore me, but they notice other people first. My shyness limits the things I can do, my relationships, school clubs, sports, and extracurricular activities. Crowded halls make me feel like I can't breathe normally. Everyone else seems to be outgoing and normal except me. It's not my fault, and I can't control it."

TODAY'S GENERATION

Every adult will claim that they had the worst adolescence in history and that today's teens have much more freedom to be themselves. But I think that no matter how difficult it was for previous generations, the current generation of teens is facing some extra-tough issues.

As I explained in the previous chapter, developmental compression is speeding up a pre-teen and teen's growth process. Today's kids are forced at a younger age to cope with a host of adult issues that they're simply not prepared to handle, and they're paying the price with unhealthy sexual activity, body image problems, aggression, anxiety, and depression. If an adolescent is already a little resistant to change, as many shy people are, developmental compression will push her even further behind the curve.

In addition, I think that our accelerated society has lost some of the structure that helped to guide previous generations, while our willingness to tolerate violence, sexual explicitness, cynicism, and lack of civility exposes teens to a harsher, crueler world. What used to be considered healthy teenage rebellion can, with access to a weapon, the Internet, or illegal drugs, turn dangerous quickly and frequently. When you add to this all of the expanded personal and career options that a teenager is offered, it's no wonder that many teens feel temporarily withdrawn, anxious, and shy. They're simply overwhelmed by all of the choices available to them and find themselves unable to make positive, healthy decisions in this age of anxiety.

However, despite the increasingly negative influence of our culture on today's teens, especially the shy ones, I still have reason for hope. Although our society has generally dissolved many of the forces that provided structure for past generations, parents can still provide them for their kids. No matter how much your teen claims that she wants to be treated as an adult and be allowed to do everything imaginable, she still wants to have limits, guidance, and your approval and attention. Make sure you're there to provide your teen with a reality check, some desperately needed predictability, and unconditional love.

ADOLESCENCE AS A SHYNESS TRIGGER

Shyness is such a common response to the dramatic, chaotic changes of adolescence that I think of this entire life stage as one big shyness trigger that jumpstarts the shy process. After all, adolescence fits all of the characteristics of known shyness triggers: It is new, unpredictable, and seemingly threatening—and getting even newer, more unpredictable, and more threatening with each day, thanks to our accelerated culture. Withdrawal, acute self-consciousness, and social anxiety seem to be rather normal responses when you consider that a teenager's life is being turned upside down.

The social demands alone can serve as a shyness trigger. As

with any challenge, there are two general coping strategies available—to approach them or to avoid them. When adolescents approach their social challenges, they become more connected with other kids, join cliques, exert peer pressure, date, act out, or become the class clown. When teenagers avoid their social challenges, they withdraw from their relationships, physically isolate themselves, become more likely to mask their feelings with drugs and alcohol, and refuse to confide in a trusted friend or parent.

Sometimes teens try to approach and avoid at the same time, which typically manifests in starting and stopping new friendships, playing games within relationships, developing mad crushes on someone they won't talk to, feeling lonely and anxious, and blending in with the crowd. When teens do these things, they're getting caught in the approach/avoidance conflict, the first step in the shy process. If they've been shy all of their lives, this pattern will likely become cemented during adolescence. But teens can also become temporarily or situationally shy during this period. If they continue to be stuck in this conflict, they'll become shy, period.

Besides their social challenges, teens are also coping with developmental demands that complicate their ability to approach or avoid others. Their natural self-centered thinking makes them unusually self-conscious and intensifies their focus on their mistakes, uncertainty, and insecurities. Anxiety is the natural result. Their physical changes make them want to hide, especially if they're generating unwanted attention thanks to an "off-time" growth spurt, which happens to early-blooming girls and late-blooming boys. Lacking the ability to blend in, they shut down to deflect even more attention.

Successfully Shy Journal

Now that you have more background information about adolescence, please answer these questions in your Journal:

- How is your teen expanding her identity and interests via activities, relationships, and personal exploration?

- Is your child developing on time or off time? Has this always been the case, or has she just become off time during adolescence?

- Do you see signs of approach, avoidance, or the approach/avoidance conflict?

- Do you agree that there are differences between the generations? What's better? What's worse?

After you've finished answering these questions, think about ways in which you can ease your teen's transition into adulthood, or what would have helped you during this time. Perhaps you could be more sensitive about your teen's insecurities or give him more time to warm up to difficult social activities. Perhaps you could explain to him the many developmental challenges of adolescence so that he'll feel less isolated in his confusion.

GENERAL STRATEGIES FOR PARENTS OF TEENS

As your child enters adolescence, it's normal for your relationship with him to change and perhaps become more strained and detached. You may even come to feel that as a parent, you don't have much influence on your teen's behavior. I can assure you, however,

GETTING A JOB OR VOLUNTEER POSITION

One of the rites of passage during adolescence is landing a part-time job or volunteer position. Actually, it's one of the best ways your teen can spend her free time, because not only will she earn money, but she'll learn responsibility, how to organize her time, and gain some skills. Shy teens will especially benefit from working or volunteering, since they'll come in contact with lots of different people on a regular basis. Unfortunately, many are stymied by just filling out an application and interviewing for a job. Here's how you can help:

- Work through the steps together. Go through the want ads, discuss who your teen's personal references will be, and run through a mock interview.

- Select a slightly socially challenging job. It may be tempting for a shy teen to take a position that provides little contact with others, but he will benefit more from working with people in a semi-structured environment. Fast-food restaurants, shops, and offices are good choices.

- Build on current skills. If she's confident about her abilities, she'll have an easier time taking direction and talking to people. If she's a great gardener, she may try working at a florist's shop. If she loves computers, an office job is best.

that you do. Your attention, guidance, and love are desperately needed. When you think about what could happen without your guidance, you'll realize how much power you have.

The important thing to remember is that while adolescence is a passing phase, what occurs during this period can have lingering effects on your son's or daughter's adult life. Coping with these changes in a positive manner can teach a teen that challenges are

- Don't get stuck in a rut. If she's been babysitting for a few years, it may be time for a change. She could work or volunteer in a day care center and continue building her skills.

- Assist in the process. If he's filling out applications at the mall, go with him and shop while he goes about his business. He can check in with you if he has questions, but he should do the bulk of the work on his own.

- Don't overlook volunteer opportunities. Your teen may want to earn money, but she may have a more valuable time volunteering. Plus, she may get a better reception as a volunteer, since her colleagues will be so grateful that she's there.

Lastly, be aware of your child's vulnerabilities. You may have filled out dozens of applications and held a number of jobs, but your child hasn't. Remember how intimidating it can be to merely ask for an application when you don't have an employment history and you're not so sure about your skills. Help your teen along the way, and she'll have an easier time landing her first job.

not to be resisted or feared. On the other hand, denying or burying fears and insecurities can teach an adolescent to give in to the dark or difficult feelings that accompany change.

The goal is to build a strong foundation on which your teen can build as he explores the challenges of adolescence. To do this, try the following strategies.

Be in her life. You may need to be in your teen's life in a different way, but don't let yourself be cast aside just because she is developing a life and a mind of her own.

Encourage independence. Give your teen more say in decisions that affect him, and let him take responsibility for everyday obligations such as making appointments, paying cashiers, and inquiring about colleges and part-time jobs.

Value small talk. Not every conversation can be a deep heart-to-heart talk. Recognize the value and importance of small talk, which shows that you're interested in your teen and want to find common ground.

Let him work or volunteer. Part-time jobs or volunteer positions can help your teen build job skills and social skills, manage his time, and become more comfortable with people from different walks of life—all of which add up to a larger comfort zone.

Maintain a solid home life. If your teen finds a solid foundation at home, he'll feel less stressed by the changes in his world. Create as much predictability and routine as possible.

Clarify your decisions. Your teen can't make good decisions if she doesn't know how. Talk through your own decision-making process and walk her through a few of her own situations.

Curb your criticisms. Shy teens are especially self-conscious and sensitive, and drawing attention to their insecurities only makes things worse. Find other ways to make your point.

Include your teen. If you start including your teen in your own activities, he'll learn how to be more at ease around adults who are already part of your comfort zone.

Talk to other parents. If your teen is uncommunicative, you can learn a lot by talking to the parents of her friends and classmates. Plus, you'll find a support system for yourself during this turbulent time.

Lastly, remember to be persistent and patient. Your teen is in a constant state of flux and, to put it mildly, won't always be pleasant or talkative. As the adult, you have the benefit of hindsight and maturity. Keep trying to build and maintain a positive relationship despite your differences. Your teen will learn how to create healthy relationships if he knows that the two of you can make your relationship work.

TYPES OF SHY TEENS

However common teen shyness is, adolescent shyness doesn't always look like stereotypical shyness. Teens find new ways to disappear and go undercover, most likely because shyness is stigmatized during this intensely socially active phase. I've found that teens tend to mask their shyness behind other personas—any persona that doesn't reveal their true feelings and insecurities. While each individual is unique, I've found that most shy adolescents fit into a few general categories, and identifying and understanding these types of teens reveals how they can be helped.

The Shy Absentee

This type of shy teenager literally disappears. The challenges of her adolescent world prove to be too much, and she retreats into her shell, refusing to come out of her room or attend school on a regular basis. This type of shy teen builds up walls around her and sticks to the safety of her private comfort zone.

A high school senior wrote to me about why she skipped school. She had always been shy, but became the target of abuse when she got older. "When I was in junior high, the girls would call me a snob because I wouldn't talk, and one girl said I was 'too pretty, but snobby,' and if she ever saw my face again, she would shave off all my hair and poke out my eyeballs with an eraser," she wrote. "I refused to go to school for weeks."

I have no problem with allowing a teen to retreat temporarily so she can feel safe and secure on her own terms. But I caution parents to keep these retreats as short as possible. Otherwise, your teen will not only fall behind her peers and allow her relationships to fade, but she'll also allow avoidance and isolation to become her dominant response to challenges. She won't learn other coping mechanisms when she desperately needs them, and she'll continue to reward herself for avoiding tough but necessary situations. The entire outside world will stay firmly beyond her comfort zone, and she'll have a harder time wearing down her walls as time goes on.

If your teen is a shy absentee, try the following strategies:

Send the right message. Don't reinforce her avoidance by letting her stay home from school or buying her more gadgets and toys for her bedroom.

Reward her approaches. Set some attendance goals and stick to your promises when she meets your expectations.

Go to her strengths. Help her find an activity she loves and figure out ways to make that activity social. She'll find new friends who will respect her, and her confidence will rise.

Investigate and strategize. Find out exactly why she's avoiding school or a certain crowd of kids and discuss ways in which she can confront the issue head on.

Overall, make sure that you know how your reclusive teen is spending her time. If she's skipping school without your knowledge or engaging in forbidden activities within the safe confines of her room, she needs your help. She just doesn't want you to know that she does.

The Shy Conformist

Shy teens also disappear by blending in and hiding in plain sight. They look just like their friends, talk like their friends, and do the same things. But appearances are deceiving. What looks like a sociable, well-liked teenager is often a confused, vulnerable teen who's the victim of intense pressure to conform.

While all teenagers' thoughts tend to be self-focused, these teens are so self-conscious and so aware of social mores and appearances that they force themselves to conform, utterly. They feel safe and secure only when they look just like everyone else. They don't stick out, so they don't get unwanted attention. Their self-esteem depends on what others think of them. Lacking confidence, social skills, or a healthy outside perspective, these kids rely on social comparison to guide their behavior.

Boys and girls tend to conform in different ways. Girls tend to focus on their appearance, feel that there's a constant spotlight on them, and take criticism to heart. I found the following comments from a female student at a Big 10 university to be particularly revealing: "Whenever I don't think I 'look' good, I become even more shy. I don't know what to say in conversation. I forget what to say next. I'm always thinking, 'Does he like me? Do I look good?' I get very depressed when I don't think I look good and in turn do not want to talk or be seen."

Oftentimes, these girls become passive in relationships and are sexually active merely to maintain the relationship. There's some evidence that shy girls have more body-image problems than their more outgoing peers. Early-blooming girls may also have a more intensely shy adolescence.

Boys, on the other hand, try to conform with their behavior, and they're held to a different standard—the macho standard. To be popular, they have to act tough, be athletic or aggressive, refuse to reveal their insecurities, and take unnecessary risks. If a teenaged boy doesn't fit into this stereotype, he risks losing the respect of his peers and, in turn, the chance to have a relationship with a girl. Late-blooming boys and shy boys find this period to be especially tough, and their sense of self can suffer.

Self-esteem issues are at the heart of the shy conformist's dilemma. She desperately wants to be liked, but is afraid of being herself and then being rejected. I believe, however, that if you help her find her internal compass and strengthen her decision-making ability, you'll help her successfully cope with her shyness and lessen her need to conform. Try these strategies:

Question her behavior. If she's following the crowd, ask her why she isn't making her own decisions. Forcing her to defend her actions forces her to think about them.

Talk about integrity. You don't have to preach, but you can find interesting ways to talk about values, choices, and integrity. Discuss times in your life when you didn't follow the crowd, or point out examples in the news or during TV shows or movies in which individuals refused to compromise.

Divert his attention. If your teenager is actively involved in a positive activity, he won't be overly concerned about his appearance or being accepted. He'll be himself without the debilitating self-consciousness.

Finally, remember that your teen is a terribly sensitive creature. He wants to be loved and accepted for who he is, but doubts his self-worth and attractiveness. Keep your personal criticism to a minimum, and help him be aware of his strengths and uniqueness.

The Shy Scholar

The shy scholar most closely resembles the stereotypical image of a shy teen—a straight A student who follows all of the rules and is too quiet and timid to get into much trouble. In many cases, this stereotype is true. One study by Gary S. Traub, Ph.D., of Florida State University, concluded that shy college students tend to have higher grade point averages than their more outgoing peers. Further, even other teenagers tend to agree with this stereotype, as indicated in this comment by a high school senior: "Shy kids perform excellently because they have no distractions, whether it be a boyfriend or girlfriend. They miss out on fun, friends, and temptations (good and bad)."

Despite the "good kid" stereotype, however, many shy scholars have a lot of troubles, but their quiet demeanor or success in school conceals them. These kids may dive into their schoolwork as a way to avoid socializing, or they may think that if they play by the rules and perform perfectly, they won't receive any negative attention. Parents, teachers, and friends are fooled by their perfect behavior and don't look for signs of more serious trouble, such as depression, anxiety, and loneliness.

Further, since shy scholars don't allow themselves to experiment with new actions or people, they don't fully experience adolescence. Their very rigid comfort zone is not a perfect defense against adolescent turmoil.

If your teen is a shy scholar, you may feel that you shouldn't mess with success. But if you believe that your teen is using schoolwork to keep larger, more threatening issues at bay, I urge you to try these strategies:

Give a kid a break. If your teenager is holding herself to impossible standards, let her know that life will go on even if she gets a B now and then.

Facilitate friendships. Be willing to let your teen spend more time with her friends, and introduce her to kids who share her interests.

Help her find her balance. Make sure that she's spending enough time with friends or on fun activities, and not spending all of her free time on homework.

GOING OUT ON A DATE

Many shy teens—especially the boys—are terrified of asking someone out for a date. As a result, many teens fall behind their peers and don't start dating until they're out of high school. But the best time to start dating is during adolescence, when teens are not expected to be experienced or sophisticated daters. To help your shy teen learn how to go out on a date, explain the following strategies to him:

- Start slowly. He doesn't have to take a girl out to an elegant dinner and the movies. He can start with phone calls, hanging out after school, and going on group dates so that he gets to know the object of his affection in a low-key way.

- Don't assume rejection. Many shy people assume the worst and then never take a risk. Instead, she should develop a friendly relationship with someone she likes, and she'll have a better chance of dating that person.

- Accept all social invitations. Even if he's not dating, he'll feel more comfortable around his peers, some of whom could become potential dates.

Ask. If you suspect that your teen is hiding from shyness triggers when she's between the pages of her book, gently encourage her to share her fears with you so that you can work out some potential solutions together.

You, too, must consider your own expectations for your child. If you value your shy scholar because she doesn't cause you much trouble, or if you are more focused on another child who has more obvious—and seemingly more pressing—issues, make sure that you give equal time to your quieter, more timid child. She may feel

- Go out on practice dates. If she's only kind of interested in someone, she should go out on a practice date just so she can experience what it would be like to be dating someone she truly likes.

- Don't wait for the prom or homecoming. These special occasions are loaded with anxiety. If he's attracted to someone, he should start building a relationship now, before the pressure is on.

Lastly, make sure that your teen doesn't live in his head. It's easy to get caught up in all of the things he could have said or the rejection he may face if he asks someone out. These thoughts can spiral out of control if he doesn't take a small risk and actually take some action. The worst thing that can happen is that someone says no. This small word should be seen as information, not rejection or failure. Once the hurt has healed, he'll learn how to move beyond it and on to another date.

that she can't show her vulnerabilities to anyone, including a parent who's counting on her to behave.

The Shy Rebel

The flip side of the shy scholar is the shy rebel, the teenager with wild behavior, a strange wardrobe, and a defiant attitude. Shy rebels cover up their insecurities and fears so that others won't realize that they're uncertain about their actions. These kids often force themselves to be extroverted as a way to break through their shyness. They seem to blast their way through adolescence, too cool for extra-curricular activities or other mainstream stuff.

Rebellion is healthy, especially in a teenager. But rebellion can also include lots of risky behavior, such as underage drinking, drug use, or sexual activity. In fact, I've found that shy teenage boys, more often than shy girls and shy adults, often turn to drugs or alcohol to turn on their extroverted personalities and gather up courage in public. They're also more likely to smoke cigarettes than their non-shy peers, perhaps to alleviate their anxiety and awkwardness.

If you have a shy rebel in the house, keep the following tips in mind:

Be aware of your rebel's shyness. His behavior may be concealing the fact that he's uncomfortable with new people and doesn't know how to behave and fit in.

Refresh his social skills. While he may not want to be polite and introduce you to his friends, insist that he behave properly when he's with you.

Keep things positive. If he isn't willing to follow the crowd, make sure that he has other positive outlets, whether that's being in a band, drawing, or working in a stimulating environment.

Acknowledge his talents. He may be rebelling because he doesn't feel appreciated or wanted. Let him know that you notice his strengths.

Lastly, keep in mind that shyness and rebellion can be passing phases. If your teen finds acceptance and security while expanding his comfort zone, he'll eventually tone down his rebellion. But if he remains a rebel because he can't figure out how to behave otherwise, you'll need to step in to prevent him from getting himself in trouble in the adult world.

The Shy Cynic

This is the type of shy teen that we hear of all too often. The cynically shy teenager experiences a potent blend of shyness, aggression, loneliness, and hatred. Eventually, after bottling up these emotions for too long, the shy cynic explodes—often exploding in the headlines as well, as another violent teenage loner who finally vented his rage.

The shy cynic has usually been bullied and oftentimes becomes a bully. In the words of Margaret, the teacher whose views opened this chapter, "It almost seems that shyness and bullying are opposite sides of the same coin. Those who bully may actually be shy, but they equate shyness with weakness, and the only way they can combat that image is to find others who are physically weaker and put them down the way they have been put down by those who are stronger. Often they lack social and intellectual skills to deal effectively with their environment and resort to physical abuse of others as a means of making themselves 'important' to those around them."

High school kids have their own views on these cynically shy bullies. "People who are shy could often be bullied because people may not know much about them and may assume that they are stuck up or snobby," one sophomore wrote. "Bullying might lead a shy person to do something like Columbine." Another student explained, "Shyness is like a fear of something. Bullying and violence are ways to overcome shyness."

A cynically shy teen is a complicated teen. But if you don't get involved now, you may regret not trying to unravel your child's complex personality. Try these strategies:

Surround your child with better influences. If he's hanging out with friends who are reinforcing his cynicism, help him find alternative activities.

Know what's going on. Get involved at school, meet his friends, set a curfew, and keep tabs on what he does when he's out of your sight. You may feel like you're being too strict, but you need to be aware.

Be persistent. If he rejects your interest, keep trying. It may take a while to break through his cynicism, but it's what he wants you to do to show that you care.

Build a positive identity. If the kids at school are bringing him down, help him find an interesting job or volunteer position, which will allow him to build positive skills—and self-esteem.

Get help. If you think that your child has emotional issues you aren't equipped to handle, find someone who can help, whether it's a counselor, mentor, pastor, or trusted friend.

Lastly, remember that anger is also a sign that your child wants you to get closer. That strong reaction shows that he has strong feelings about your relationship, whether they're good or bad. Ignoring him, or giving up on him, sends the false message that you just don't care. Although it may be difficult at first, you can transform your relationship—and your child's behavior—if you refuse to be pushed out of his life.

COMBINING FORCES

No matter what type of shy teen you're living with, it's crucial that you help him understand his shyness and teach him how to work through the shy process. Now that your child is a bit older and must take on more responsibility, your role as a parent will change to a more indirect, behind-the-scenes one. Gone are the days when you can overtly take him over to another child at the park and teach him how to offer up his shovel and pail. Now you have to teach him how to help himself, whether that means scheduling an orthodontist appointment on his own or filling out a job application. You can do so by having some conversations with your child about the nature of his shyness and how he can meet his everyday challenges.

You're definitely still in the picture, but now you will combine forces with your child so that he will learn how to take control of his social life—and his shyness. By doing so, your teen will learn to expand his comfort zone while knowing that he has you as a safety net. That way, he won't be taking a huge risk that he's not prepared for. He'll also learn that you recognize that he's feeling awkward in social situations and that you have strategies that will help him out—strategies that are tailored to his specific needs.

To help you get started, I've created a blueprint that you can follow during some heart-to-heart discussions with your teenager. First, read through the remainder of the chapter so that you have an overview of how your discussions will progress. Over the course of a few days (or in one long session if your teen opens up and expresses interest in continuing), you will be explaining the shy process to your child. It's ideal if you follow your teen's cues and wait for him to bring up a shyness-related problem he's been having, but if your teen is uncommunicative, you may need to start the conversation yourself.

The first step is to explain what shyness triggers are and help your child to identify the shyness triggers in his life. After each discussion, ask your teen to take some time in private to answer the questions posed in the Successfully Shy Journal exercises. (Or, if he prefers, you can fill in the answers as the two of you talk.) Then use your teen's answers as a springboard for further discussion and brainstorming for possible solutions. If you feel comfortable sharing your Journal, you can even show it to him as a way to open the discussion. Explain what you've been learning and, if you wish, invite him to write his answers in your journal.

Step One: Understanding
What Triggers Shyness

The best way to start the conversation is by discussing what typically makes your teen feel shy, and what the shy process or shy experience feels like for her. If your teenager is like the ones I've surveyed, she most likely has trouble with talking to authority figures, approaching members of the opposite sex, striking up friendships with new kids, and dancing in public. I'm sure that she'll have a few other sensitive spots, but most of her difficulties will fall into one or more of these categories.

Select one situation that makes her feel shy and apply what you've learned about the shy process to that experience. For example, let's say that she's having a hard time in her history class, but she won't ask her teacher questions or get help with her research from the school librarian. When she mentions that she's struggling in this class and rebuffs your suggestion to discuss it with her teacher, you have a perfect opening to discuss shyness.

First, explain how this event qualifies as a shyness trigger: It is new, unpredictable, and threatening. Point out that having one-on-one conversations with authority figures is a relatively new experience for her, and so it's natural that she doesn't know what to expect. Also, talking to her teacher lets the teacher know that she's struggling, which your teenager may believe could change how the teacher views her and perhaps affect her grade. Your teen definitely does not want this negative attention. Point out that she's assuming the worst (that the teacher will think poorly of her) and that she must develop a better relationship with her teacher if she's going to do well in the class. Remind her that it's normal to feel a bit apprehensive about approaching her teacher, but that she doesn't have to be completely intimidated by it.

Successfully Shy Journal for Teens

Write out your answers to the following questions, which will help you identify the situations that are shyness triggers for you.

- Which situations make you feel shy? How do you feel when you're shy?

- In each situation, what is new, unpredictable, or threatening?

- Which situations used to make you feel shy but don't anymore?

- How did that happen?

It may feel strange to reflect on your shyness since many people don't ask you about what it's like to be shy. But shy people like you have a lot to say. And there are a lot of you, too. Almost half of us say we're shy. So, take comfort in knowing that you're in good company.

Step Two: Deciphering the Shy Process

The next step is to introduce your child to the phases in the shy process. Begin by explaining the approach/avoidance conflict. (You can turn back to chapter 3 to refresh yourself on the basics of the shy process, if necessary.) Quite simply, she's creating more anxiety by stalling. Explain the benefits of approaching and the drawbacks that come from avoiding this challenge.

Next, discuss the slow-to-warm-up period, which explains why she's hesitating about approaching her teacher or the librarian for help. Point out that while it usually takes her a longer time to get used to someone new, especially someone who's an authority figure, she usually does warm up to people if she's given enough time. Remind her of past experiences that prove this to be true.

Finally, talk about the comfort zone, and explain that while asking this particular teacher for help isn't part of her comfort zone now, that's only a temporary situation. She can make this shift by developing a smart coping strategy, which is something you'll help her to devise.

Overall, remind her that what she's feeling is normal but not insurmountable. While many people hesitate to try something new, they eventually find that their fears are worse than the supposedly terrifying event. And, in time, they find fewer things to fear and therefore feel more confident within their larger comfort zone.

Successfully Shy Journal for Teens

In this exercise, you'll explore how the shy process plays out in your life. Turn back to your answers in the first exercise. For each of the shy situations that you wrote down, list some examples of how you wanted to approach it but also wanted to avoid it, too. Now answer the following questions.

- How did being caught between wanting to approach the situation and wanting to avoid it make you feel?
- Can you think of any other situations in which you took a while to become comfortable?

After you write down your answers, keep them handy. They're the situations that you'll focus on when you develop your shyness breakthrough strategies.

Step Three: A Closer Examination

If you look closely at how your child currently responds to his shyness triggers, you will likely find that he has a lot of ways he can cope with shyness that he has always overlooked. These are elements of his comfort zone. When he takes an inventory of it, he'll be able to find ways to make his comfort zone larger, and at the same time feel more confident and less shy in situations that used to make him feel uncomfortable.

Your teen's comfort zone is made up of familiar people, places, and activities. When he's in his comfort zone, he feels confident and at ease, and he can be himself without any anxiety or worries. When he's outside of it, he is in foreign territory. Shyness is triggered. To make himself feel better, he crawls back into his comfort zone and hides.

Successfully Shy Journal for Teens

In this exercise, you're going to take an inventory of your comfort zone.

- First, write down the names of the people with whom you feel comfortable.

- Next, write down the things you like to do, the activities that make you happy.

- Finally, write down the physical places in which you're comfortable.

After you've taken your inventory, write down the people, places, and activities that are currently outside of your comfort zone but that you'd like to have included within it. Write down the names of people you'd like to know better, the activities

(continued)

you'd like to experience without fear, and the places you'd like to go to and feel that you're on home turf.

Don't worry if the list is long. You're not going to have to conquer everything outside of your comfort zone all at once. But this inventory will help you think about where you want to go and how you can get there.

Step Four: Taking Smart Risks by Expanding the Comfort Zone

One of the worst ways your teenager can expand her comfort zone is to break right through it—to simultaneously force herself to talk to a stranger, do a completely new activity without preparation, and be in a place she's never been in before. One of the best ways to expand her comfort zone is to do it gradually, on her own terms, and with some strategies in mind.

To help her do this, get out your teen's comfort zone inventory list so that the two of you can develop an effective strategy to expand it. You're going to pick out two pieces of the comfort zone and one piece that's outside of it. When you combine these three pieces, you'll find a system for expanding your teen's comfort zone.

Start by having your teen select a person in her comfort zone. Perhaps she'll pick out one of her best friends. Let's say her name is Sara. Then have her pick out an activity that she loves to do. Let's say that it's listening to music. Now that you have two elements that are within her comfort zone, you're ready to add one element that's outside of it—the place. With this strategy, your daughter will take a safe risk while holding on to a few familiar things.

Let's say that the place your daughter selects that's outside of her comfort zone is the mall. Now, combine all three elements— your daughter feels comfortable with Sara, loves listening to music, and wants to feel more comfortable at the mall. Can she try to put this into practice and invite Sara to the music shop at the mall? Sara's support, and your daughter's love of music, will help her come to terms with her unease at the mall. She may not feel completely comfortable at first, because she tends to warm up slowly to new social situations, but eventually she will feel at ease.

Likewise, let's try incorporating a new person into your teen's comfort zone, which is another issue that shy teens struggle with. Let's say this new person is Jay, and he's in your daughter's class and lives on your street, but your daughter doesn't know him all that well. Now have her choose an activity she loves to do—play tennis, perhaps? And she feels comfortable playing tennis on your driveway, right? And she has seen Jay walk around with a tennis racket, too—another bonus. Why not encourage your daughter to ask Jay to play tennis with her in your driveway? If she concentrates on what's already in her comfort zone, she'll be more at ease with the elements that aren't quite in her comfort zone just yet. In this case, it's getting through an afternoon with Jay, but if she focuses on her tennis game at first, she'll find that conversation will get a little bit easier. And if she plays tennis with Jay a few more times, she'll find that he'll become a part of her comfort zone without a lot of stress.

Now let's figure out how to incorporate a new activity into her comfort zone, while the people and place are part of her old comfort zone. She has a group of friends and she loves to hang out at the park. Why not try a new activity with her friends when they're at the park, like biking or exploring some of the nature trails? Or asking about volunteer opportunities there? She'll expand her comfort zone at her own pace, on her own terms, and she won't feel like she's forcing herself to be someone she's not. She's in charge, not her shyness.

Successfully Shy Journal for Teens

To make sure you understand how to gradually expand your comfort zone, go back through your comfort zone inventory list and write down more ways that you can move the pieces around. Remember to choose two elements that are currently within your comfort zone and combine them with one element that is currently out of your range of comfort. Next, pick out one combination that you'd really love to try. Write down a few ways you could put that into action. Then, go for it!

A Few More Tips

After you and your teen have moved around the elements of her comfort zone, it's time to start developing strategies that will help her get started. As always, preparation is key. Perhaps the two of you can rehearse what she can say to the new person she wants to meet, someone like Jay. The two of you could also be more specific about identifying what she wants to accomplish, which will increase her chances for success. For example, instead of trying to meet new kids, your daughter may try to meet new kids who share her interest in animals. This targeted approach will help her come up with effective strategies.

These comfort zone-stretching steps can also be used to figure out why your teen feels shy in certain situations. If she's at a dance with a bunch of kids she doesn't know, she's outside of her comfort zone and is forced to warm up too quickly. She can feel more at ease if she gives herself a moment to figure out if there's anything at the dance that's within her comfort zone, whether it's a person, place, or activity. Does she see a friendly face? Are they playing her favorite song? Do they need some help with refreshments? She can focus on that familiar element and hang on to it until she warms up a little bit more. Then, at her own pace, she can try to get closer to what's new. Her nervousness and self-consciousness and shyness will melt away as she gets pulled into the action—I promise.

Being more aware of her comfort zone boundaries can also help your teen make bigger decisions about her life direction. After all, how can she decide on a college major if she isn't aware of the types of activities she loves to do? And how would she know that she loves to do something if she's too timid to try it? (Safely, and at her own pace, of course.) Expanding and exploring her comfort zone will also help her make decisions about potential friends and boyfriends. If they don't have enough elements in common, your teen will have a harder time feeling comfortable, communicative, and confident with them.

While adolescence can be difficult, it doesn't have to stop your teen in her tracks. She can warm up to adolescence slowly, as long as she continues expanding her comfort zone and her awareness of her needs, fears, and strengths. Keep the lines of communication open and extend your support, and you'll find that she'll live up to her true potential—a confident, capable adult.

CHAPTER 12

THE
SUCCESSFULLY
SHY LIFE

H elping your child work through the shy process when he's young will help him lead a successfully shy life— a life that's free of the debilitating self-doubt and anxiety that comes from living in shyness' grip. Teaching him the shyness-busting strategies and life skills that are a part of The Shyness Breakthrough Plan will help him expand his comfort zone and provide him with tools that will serve him for the rest of his life.

Each task builds on the next, from learning how to share toys at the playground, to getting through the first few weeks of kindergarten, to learning how to cope with a large junior high school, to seeking out stimulating jobs, career options, and rewarding friendships. Completing each task successfully will help your child build a sense of mastery and greater confidence. In addition, he can also apply what he has learned about the phases of the "shy process" to situations that aren't especially social in nature, such as making decisions about his life direction, because the pull to approach and avoid new challenges is strong no matter what the context.

Learning these skills and tools early will help your child avoid getting bogged down in anxiety, fear, and ambivalence. In time, he'll become less self-conscious and more self-aware, and that's probably the greatest gift you can give your child. A self-aware individual can make healthy choices and take smart risks, and will determine his own fate. His shy, slowly warming nature will be only one component of his fascinating, unique identity. His rapidly growing repertoire of skills will help him be in control of his shyness, not controlled by it.

THE POWER OF TIME

When we're in the thick of raising our children—jetting from one activity to the next, rushing to get dinner on the table, and all the while worrying about our child's or teenager's shyness—it's easy to get caught up in the moment. But I'd like to remind you that just as shyness is powerful, so is time. Time, in fact, is so powerful that it can be your ally in healing shyness wounds. I'm not talking about allowing your child to "just grow out of it" while you sit back and allow her to warm up on her own. But knowing that time is on your child's side, that she will have countless opportunities to develop strategies to overcome her shyness and build on her budding confidence, will give you an advantage.

I'm reminded of Diana, whose daughter Jamie was too shy to play with the boy who waved to her at the park. After relating that story, which I described in chapter 7, Diana went on to explain that with time, Jamie was able to conquer some of her fears and become more open with people she didn't know well. Jamie had her own bashful breakthrough while developing her love of ballet. Even though Jamie resisted at first, Diana made sure that she attended every class, knowing that time and persistence would wear down her daughter's slow-to-warm-up hesitancy. Diana knew that eventually, Jamie's desire to dance would overshadow her fear of dancing with other kids.

Diana went on to explain that ballet was the sort of activity that got Jamie excited and made her feel confident. "Ballet is different because it's so structured and kind of strict. In class, she has to jump right in. She can't hang back and do her own thing. It takes away a certain freedom of choice," she said. "Also, ballet gives a child an air of confidence. She holds her head up a little higher now.

"In every class, the kids gather around in a circle and everyone has to dance a solo, and the other kids have to watch and clap and appreciate that performance. This has had a significant impact on Jamie and has given her some confidence. Before, she wouldn't have danced for relatives. Now, she'll do a little number on the sidewalk while we're waiting for the train! I can't tell you what a change that is. But she's used to it. It's no big deal for her.

"In her ballet recital, she was such a natural. She had her little fairy outfit on, and a little halo. When it came time to dance, the halo started coming off, but she adjusted it and went on. It kind of slipped again, but she took it in stride and kept dancing. That was something that would have upset her previously. That's a big change in only about six months."

Imagine what would have happened if Diana had backed off and let Jamie give in to her distress! At a young age, Jamie would have allowed shyness to control her life and her decisions. She wouldn't have developed her love of ballet, achieved a sense of mastery, and gained some confidence. Instead, she would have spent those 6 months fretting about her fears and anxiety. Her comfort zone would have decreased and solidified.

Jamie can use this lesson in other areas of her life. After all, if she can overcome her resistance to taking a ballet class and performing in public, then she'll find it much easier to overcome other instances of the approach/avoidance conflict, such as getting involved in another activity, talking in class, or finding the courage to work through other situations that create anxiety.

A Ripple Effect

As you can see, one shyness breakthrough can have a ripple effect throughout an individual's lifespan. As a shy child learns how to identify his strengths, desires, and unique needs, he can take smart risks that expand his comfort zone. In time, he will become so comfortable in his social network that he will have a positive effect on the people in his life and be a source of inspiration for others who are not so bold.

Another story about Jamie shows how this ripple effect happens, even in a young child's life. As Diana explained, the confidence Jamie gained in ballet class affected how she approached other challenges, too.

"At the Parents' Night at her school, the kids had to run an obstacle course," Diana said. "Jamie volunteered to go first. I was shocked! She did it, but she had a little difficulty and kind of wiped out. Everyone chuckled. You could just see the terror on her face when she realized what happened. And I thought, oh no, this one is really going to hurt her. But later, other kids also fell over and stumbled, and it wasn't that big of a deal that she fell.

"But Jamie didn't forget that she wiped out, and that she was the first one to go and therefore everyone was looking at her. Afterwards, the other parents came up and told her she did a great job. Still, you could see that she was embarrassed. Later, she told me that she was upset and that everyone laughed at her. And I said no, that she was just so cute and that's why everyone chuckled. But the point is that I was shocked that she volunteered. And also very proud of her."

I love this story. When I think of Jamie adjusting her halo in her ballet recital or volunteering to run the obstacle course first on Parents' Night, I see a little girl who's making a lot of progress. I can imagine her in high school, brave enough to be her own person despite tremendous peer pressure. I can imagine her in college, when she'll find the courage to ask a question during a lecture and provide her classmates with more insights. As a classroom lecturer for 25 years, I can't tell you what a gift that is to me and to the more reticent students in the class.

I also have other visions of Jamie's future. I'm sure that when Jamie's boss will ask her to take on a tough but necessary assignment, Jamie will react with enthusiasm. Her friends and colleagues will be shocked when they find out that Jamie considers herself to be shy, and because she's so generous, she'll share her insights and experiences with her shy friends. I'm also sure that when Jamie becomes a mother herself, she'll be a compassionate guide to her children when they're feeling shy, vulnerable, or afraid.

Overall, Jamie will be respected and admired for her social adeptness, bravery, and willingness to get involved in the lives of those she loves. Jamie will be an example to those who are not so brave or quick to warm up to challenges. She's already sharing herself with the world, and will continue to do so. That's a great gift that Jamie will give, and one that Diana is encouraging every day.

As you help your child understand his many layers of shyness, keep Jamie's story in mind. Bashful breakthroughs don't have to be earth-shattering events. They can be as simple as helping someone in a store, remembering to call an old friend, or extending an invitation to an acquaintance. Any of these gestures will help your child become more comfortable and confident, fulfilled and happy. They'll produce a ripple effect that can have only positive consequences.

Discussing What Matters

Another reason why I love Jamie's story is that she and Diana discussed Jamie's reaction to her performance during Parents' Night. If they hadn't, Jamie's embarrassment would have lingered and become more intense. Instead, Diana let Jamie know that she was proud of her and that her stumble didn't detract from her otherwise incredible feat. The message that Diana sent was that what mattered is that Jamie volunteered to get involved in the action. Her actual performance wasn't so important.

Talking with your child, as Diana does, is absolutely necessary. Your conversations help your child learn, put experiences in perspective, and provide him with strategies to use in the future. They demonstrate that you care about your child's life and you're willing to help, without pushing or criticizing. They also show that you can be trusted with his secrets, even when he's hiding something especially sensitive.

Talking to your child about shyness is even more necessary. Your explanation of the many facets of shyness lets him know that he's not the only one who feels apprehensive before a big challenge, nor is he the only one who gets hung up on his mistakes, and not his many successes. Your strategies for developing friendships and working through conflicts will help him address these issues directly. Your compassion—not your criticism—helps him become more accepting of the facets of himself that he doesn't always appreciate. Taken together, your conversations will enable your child to create a bashful breakthrough that will lead to a successfully shy life.

As with all good parenting strategies, creating this pattern of involvement and communication should start early. When you're able to talk about daily crises with your young child, she'll be more likely to come to you when she's older and has more serious concerns. While you may not have such a direct impact on your teenager's decisions, she'll see you as a source of information, and not a source of criticism or rejection. I'm always gratified when my adult daughter asks me what I think about her various dilemmas. She doesn't always take my advice, but she is interested in my opinion, since she knows that I have her best interests at heart.

In addition to acting as your child's sounding board, your willingness to engage in conversations also influences her other relationships. By demonstrating your care and concern during your discussions, you're providing her with an example of what a healthy, bonded relationship can be, and she can use this example when creating other lasting, intimate relationships. Your child will learn that discussing what matters is beneficial, not something to be feared or avoided.

DEVELOPING YOUR CHILD'S STRENGTHS

Throughout this book, I've encouraged you to go to your child's strengths. Take the time to acknowledge your child's talents and help him develop them. As your child becomes more sure of himself while he's happily immersed in his favorite activities, he will earn a healthy level of self-esteem and gain a sense of satisfaction from spending his time so wisely, happily, and productively.

These lessons are especially important for shy children. Shy children—and adults—tend to discount what they do well and instead focus on what is a struggle for them. Most specifically, they dwell on their social shortcomings and overlook their many other wonderful attributes. I think that they focus on their mistakes not because they're so terrible, but because they're so infrequent they stand out. This bias then affects their decisions and self-regard, and their shyness intensifies.

However, when shy kids learn to take a more robust view of

themselves, they find that shyness is only one part of them, and that this part appears only in certain situations. When they spend their time doing what they love, their shyness disappears. What's more, they gain confidence, feel they can master a task that's important to them, and can develop relationships that involve their favorite activity. That's why when you talk to a shy person about their favorite topic, they're rarely shy. They're so happy to talk about what they love that they cease focusing on their self-consciousness and anxiety.

Going to your child's strengths will also help her create a healthy perspective on life. If she finds that she loves something early on, she'll be able to develop that talent and make better decisions about how she spends her time and how she wants to lead her life. She can learn how to make that activity more sociable, whether it's attending classes, finding other kids who like to do the same thing, or introducing other friends to the activity. On the other hand, if she is never encouraged to develop her interests, she'll enter adulthood with little self-awareness and a lot of self-defeating behavior. She'll fall further behind her peers—become "off time"—and will have to play catch-up until she is finally able to discover her life's calling, form solid adult relationships, and become comfortable with her whole self.

THE SOLUTION IS IN THE HEART

As your child focuses on what she loves and becomes more self-expressive, she'll begin to understand that the solution to shyness is in her heart. When she loves what she does, whom she's with, and who she is, she'll be living a successfully shy life. When she goes beyond simply making contact with people and develops tight connections with others, she'll experience breakthroughs so frequently that she won't feel that her life is at all limited by shyness.

When she shares her unique gifts with others, she will become a true global citizen and friend to many.

This solution is not a "cure" for shyness. Shyness isn't a disease, so it doesn't need a cure. Rather, the solution to shyness is a life-long process that intensifies and fades with every new challenge that's positively approached, and not avoided or denied. Each experience creates a database of positive memories and an urge to continue exploring her world and sharing herself with others.

Although this book is now ending, your understanding of shyness will continue. As you and your child work through the shy process in your lives, remember to continue recording your experiences in your Journal and developing strategies that target the shyness triggers in your child's life. Think about what you've learned from this book, how you've implemented these ideas, and how your appreciation of your child has increased.

Then let me know how you're doing. I'd love to hear your stories, which, like Jamie and Diana's, can serve as a source of inspiration for other parents and shy children. Your willingness to share your experiences can provide a ripple effect that will help other children who want to break through their shyness. You can e-mail me at shydoc@carducci.com or send a letter to me at:

The Shyness Enrichment Institute
PO Box 8064
New Albany, IN 47151-8064

SELECTED REFERENCES

Adamec, R. E. 1990. Role of the amygdala and medial hypothalamus in spontaneous feline aggression and defense. *Aggressive Behavior,* 16:207–222.

Allen, O., R. M. Page, L. Moore, and C. Hewitt. 1994. Gender differences in selected psychosocial characteristics of adolescent smokers and nonsmokers. *Health Values: The Journal of Health Behavior, Education, and Promotion,* 18:34–39.

American Psychiatric Assocation. 2000. *DSM-IV-TR: Diagnostic and statistical manual of mental disorders* (4th ed., Text Revision). Washington, D.C.: American Psychiatric Association.

Arcus, D. M. 1991. The experimental modification of temperamental bias in inhibited and uninhibited children. Unpublished doctoral dissertation, Harvard University.

Arcus, D., and K. McCartney. 1989. "When baby makes four: Family influences in the stability of behavior inhibition." In J. Steven Reznick (Ed.), *Perspectives on behavior inhibition* (197–218). Chicago: University of Chicago Press.

Asendorpf, J. 1986. "Shyness in middle and late childhood." In W. H. Jones, J. M. Cheek, & S. R. Briggs (Eds.), *Shyness: Perspectives on research and treatment* (91–103). New York: Plenum.

———. 1990. Development of inhibition in childhood: Evidence for situational specificity and a two-factor model. *Developmental Psychology,* 26:721–730.

———. 1991. Development of inhibited children's coping with unfamiliarity. *Child Development,* 62:1460–1474.

Barenboim, C. 1981. The development of person perception in childhood and adolescence: From behavioral comparisons to psychological constructs to psychological comparisons. *Child Development,* 52:129–144.

Beidel, D. C., and S. M. Turner. 1998. *Shy children, phobic adults.* Washington, D.C.: American Psychological Association.

Beutler, L. E., P. P. P. Machado, and S. A. Neufeldt. 1994. "Therapist variables." In A. E. Bergin & S. L. Garfield (Eds.), *Handbook on psychotherapy and behavior* (4th ed., 229–269). New York: Wiley.

Burhans, K. K., and C. S. Dweck. 1995. Helplessness in early childhood: The role of contingent worth. *Child Development,* 66:1719–1738.

Carducci, B. J. 1998. *The psychology of personality: Viewpoints, research, and applications.* Pacific Grove, CA: Brooks/Cole Publishing Company.

———. 1999. *Shyness: A bold new approach.* New York: HarperCollins.

———. 2000a, Feb. Shyness: The new solution. *Psychology Today,* 33, 38–40, 42–45, and 78.

———. 2000b. "What shy individuals do to cope with their shyness: A content analysis." In W. R. Crozier (Ed.), *Shyness: Development, consolidation and change* (171–185). New York: Routledge.

Carducci, B. J., A. Fuchs, M. G. Wagner, and M. Carmickle. 2003, August. How shy teens deal with their shyness: Strategic and gender differences. Poster presentation at the annual meeting of the American Psychological Association, Toronto.

Carducci, B. J., D. Henderson, M. Henderson, A. M. Walisser, A. Brown, and D. Mayfield, D. 2000, August. Why Shy?: A content analysis of self-perceived causes of shyness. Poster presentation at the annual meeting of the American Psychological Association, Washington, D.C.

Carducci, B. J., and K. D. Ragains. 2002, August. The personal and situational pervasiveness of shyness in adolescents. Poster presentation at the Annual Conference of the American Psychological Association, Chicago.

Carducci, B. J., and P. G. Zimbardo. 1995, Nov./Dec. Are you shy? *Psychology Today,* 28, 34–41, 64, 66, 68, 70, 78, and 82.

Carson, J. L., and R. D. Parke. 1996. Reciprocal negative affect on parent-child interactions and children's peer competency. *Child Development,* 67:2217–2226.

Caspi, A., G. H. Elder, and D. J. Bem. 1988. Moving away from the world: Life-course pattern of shy children. *Developmental Psychology,* 24:824–831.

Cheek, J. M. 1994. Shyness. In S. Parker & B. Zuckerman (Eds.), *Behavior and developmental pediatrics: A handbook for primary care* (285–288). Boston: Little, Brown.

Cheek, J. M., and E. N. Krasnoperova. 1999. "Varieties of shyness in adolescence and adulthood." In L. A. Schmidt & J. Schulkin (Eds.), *Extreme fear, shyness, and social phobia: Origins, biological mechanisms, and clinical outcomes* (224–250). New York: Oxford University Press.

Chess, S., and A. Thomas. 1986. *Temperament in clinical practice.* New York: The Guilford Press.

———. 1999. *Goodness of fit: Clinical applications from infancy through adult life.* Philadelphia: Brunner/Mazel.

Coie, J. D., and K. A. Dodge. 1983. Continuation and changes in children's social status: A five-year longitudinal study. *Merrill-Palmer Quarterly,* 19:261–282.

Coie, J. D., and J. B. Kupersmidt. 1983. A behavior analysis of emerging social status in boys' groups. *Child Development,* 54:1400–1416.

Dekovic, M., and J. M. A. M. Janssens. 1992. Parent's child-rearing style and children's sociometric status. *Developmental Psychology,* 28:925–932.

Dodge, K. A., D. C. Schlundt, I. Schocken, and J. D. Delugach. 1983. Sociometric status: The role of peer group entry strategies. *Merrill-Palmer Quarterly,* 29:309–336.

Droege, K. L., and D. J. Stipek. 1993. Children's use of dispositions to predict classmates' behavior. *Developmental Psychology,* 29:646–654.

Eastburg, M., and W. B. Johnson. 1990. Shyness and perceptions of parental behavior. *Psychological Reports,* 66:915–921.

Eder, R. A. 1989. The emergent personalogist: The structure and content of 3½-, 5½-, and 7½-year olds' concepts of themselves and other persons. *Child Development,* 60:1218–1228.

Erikson, E. H. 1963. *Childhood and society* (2nd ed.). New York: Norton.

Glasgow, K. L., S. M. Dornbusch, L. Troyer, L. Steinberg, and P. L. Ritter. 1997. Parenting style, adolescents' attributions, and educational outcomes in nine heterogeneous high schools. *Child Development,* 68:507–529.

Grolnick, W. S., and R. M. Ryan. 1989. Parents' styles associated with children's self-regulation and competence in school. *Journal of Educational Psychology,* 81:143–154.

Harper, L. V., and K. S. Huie. 1985. The effects of prior group experience, age, and familiarity on the quality and organization of preschoolers' social relationships. *Child Development,* 56:704–717.

Hart, C. H., D. C. Burts, M. A. Durland, R. Charlesworth, M. De-Wolf, and P. O. Fleege. 1998. Stress behaviors and activity type participation of preschoolers in more or less developmentally appropriate classrooms: SES and sex differences. *Journal of Research in Childhood Education,* 12:176–196.

Hart, C. H., D. Nelson, C. C. Robinson, S. F. Olsen, and M. K. McNeilly-Choque. 1998. Overt and relational aggression on Russian nursery-school-age children: Parenting style and marital linkages. *Developmental Psychology,* 34:687–697.

Hartup, W. W. 1983. "Peer relations." In P. H. Mussen (Ed.), *Handbook of child psychology: Vol. 4. Socialization, personality, and social development* (103–196). New York: Wiley.

Hyson, M. C., K. Hirsh-Pasek, and L. Rescorla. 1989. Academic environments in early childhood: Challenge or pressure? Summary report to the Spencer Foundation.

Kagan, J. 1994. *Galen's prophecy: Temperament in human nature.* New York: Westview Press.

Kaplan, P. S. 2000. *A child's odyssey* (3rd ed.). Belmont, CA: Wadsworth/Thompson Learning.

Kochanska, G. 1991. Socialization and temperament in the development of guilt and conscience. *Child Development,* 62:1379–1392.

———. 1992. Children's interpersonal influence with mothers and peers. *Developmental Psychology,* 28:491–499.

Kruska, D. 1988. "Mammalian domestication and its effect on brain structure and behavior." In H. J. Jerison & I. Jerison (Eds.), *Intelligence and evolutionary biology: NATO Series Vol. 17.* (211–250). New York: Springer-Verlag.

Lamborn, S. D., N. S. Mounts, L. Steinberg, and S. M. Dornbusch. 1991. Patterns of competence and adjustment among adolescents from authoritative, authoritarian, indulgent, and neglectful families. *Child Development,* 62:1049–1065.

Maccoby, E. 1990. Gender and relationships: A developmental account. *American Psychologist,* 45:513–520.

MacKinnon-Lewis, C., B. L. Volling, M. E. Lamb, K. Dechman, D. Rabiner, and M. E. Curtner. 1994. A cross-contextual analysis of boy's social competence: From family to school. *Developmental Psychology,* 30:325–333.

Page, R. M. 1990. Shyness and sociability: A dangerous combination for illicit substance use in adolescence males? *Adolescence,* 25:803–806.

———. 1991. Indicators of psychosocial distress among adolescent females who perceive themselves as fat. *Child Study Journal,* 21:203–212.

Pennebaker, J. W. 1997. *Opening up: The healing power of expressing emotions.* New York: The Guilford Press.

Pomerantz, E. M., and D. N. Ruble. 1997. Distinguishing multiple dimensions and concepts of ability: Implications for self-evaluation. *Child Development,* 68:1165–1180.

Rhudy, J. L., and M. W. Meagher. 2001. Noise stress and human pain thresholds: Divergent effects in men and women. *The Journal of Pain,* 2:57–64.

Richard, B. A., and K. A. Dodge. 1982. Social maladjustment and problem solving in school-aged children. *Journal of Consulting and Clinical Psychology,* 50:226–223.

Rogers, C. R. 1957. The necessary and sufficient conditions of therapeutic personality change. *Journal of Consulting Psychology,* 21:95–103.

Rosen, B. C., and R. D'Andrade. 1959. The psychosocial origins of achievement motivation. *Sociometry,* 22:185–218.

Rubin, K. H. 1982. Nonsocial play in preschoolers: Necessarily evil? *Child Development,* 53:651–657.

———. 1993. "The Waterloo Longitudinal Project: Correlates and consequences withdrawal from childhood to adolescence." In K. H. Rubin & J. B. Asendorpf (Eds.), *Social withdrawal, inhibition, and shyness in childhood* (291–314). Hillsdale, NJ: Lawrence Erlbaum Associates, Publishers.

Rubin, K. H., and J. B. Asendorpf. 1993. "Social, withdrawal, inhibition, and shyness in childhood: Conceptual and definitional issues." In K. H. Rubin & J. B. Asendorpf (Eds.), *Social withdrawal, inhibition, and shyness in childhood* (1–17). Hillsdale, NJ: Lawrence Erlbaum Associates, Publishers.

Rubin, K. H., X. Chen, and F. Hymel. 1993. Socio-emotional characteristics of withdrawn and aggressive children. *Merrill-Palmer Quarterly,* 39:518–534.

Rubin, K. H., T. Daniels-Beirnes, and L. Bream. 1984. Social isolation and social problem-solving: A longitudinal study. *Journal of Consulting and Clinical Psychology,* 52:17–25.

Russell, A., and V. Finnie. 1990. Preschool children's social status and maternal instructions to assist group entry. *Developmental Psychology,* 26:600–611.

Shaffer, D. R. 1999. *Developmental psychology* (5th ed.). Pacific Grove, CA: Brooks/Cole Publishing.

Shoda, Y., W. Mischel, and P. K. Peake. 1990. Predicting adolescent cognitive and self-regulatory competencies from preschool delay of gratification: Identifying diagnostic conditions. *Developmental Psychology,* 26:978–986.

Sternberg, L., J. D. Elmen, and N. S. Mounts. 1989. Authoritative parenting, psychosocial, maturity, and academic success among adolescents. *Child Development,* 60:1424–1436.

Stipek, D., R. Feiler, D. Daniels, S. Milbern. 1995. Effects of different instructional approaches on young children's achievement and motivation. *Child Development,* 66:209–233.

Stipek, D., S. Recchia, and S. McClintic. 1992. Self-evaluation in young children. *Monographs of the Society for Research in Child Development,* 57, Serial No. 226.

Teevan, R. C., and P. E. McGhree. 1972. Childhood development of fear of failure motivation. *Journal of Personality and Social Psychology,* 21:345–348.

Traub, G. S. 1983. Correlates of shyness with depression, anxiety, and academic performance. *Psychological Reports,* 52:849–850.

Trull, T. J., and E. J. Phares. 2001. *Clinical psychology: Concepts, methods, and profession* (6th ed.). Belmont, CA: Wadsworth/ Thomson Learning.

Winterbottom, M. 1958. "The relation of need for achievement to learning experiences in independence and mastery." In J. Atkinson (Ed.), *Motives in fantasy, action, and society.* Princeton, NJ: Van Nostrand.

Younger, A., C. Gentile, and K. Burgess. 1993. "Children's perceptions of social withdrawal: Changes across age." In K. H. Rubin & J. B. Asendorpf (Eds.), *Social withdrawal, inhibition, and shyness in childhood* (215–235). Hillsdale, NJ: Lawrence Erlbaum Associates, Publishers.

Younger, A. J., and A. M. Piccinin. 1989. Children's recall of aggressive and withdrawn behaviors: Recognition memory and likeability judgments. *Child Development,* 60:580–590.

Zimbardo, P. G. 1990. *Shyness: What it is, what to do about it* (reissucd edition). Reading, MA: Addison-Wesley.

Zimbardo, P. G., and S. L. Radl. 1999. *The shy child: A parent's guide to preventing and overcoming shyness in infancy to adulthood* (2nd ed.). Cambridge, MA: Malor Books.

INDEX

Underscored page references indicate boxed text.

313